QUANTUM AND WOODY

KISS KISS,
**KLANG
KLANG**

DANIEL KIBBLESMITH | KANO | FRANCIS PORTELA | ANDREW DALHOUSE

CONTENTS

Quantum & Woody created by MD Bright & Priest

Collection Cover Art: Julian Totino Tedesc

Assistant Editors: Benjamin Peterson (#1) and
David Menchel (#2-5)
Editors: Danny Khazem (#1-5),
Charlotte Greenbaum (#2-4), Karl Bollers (#5), and
Warren Simons

Quantum and Woody!®: Kiss Kiss, Klang Klang. Published by
Valiant Entertainment LLC. Office of Publication: 350 Seventh
Avenue, New York, NY 10001. Compilation copyright © 2018 Valiant
Entertainment LLC. All rights reserved. Contains materials originally
published in single magazine form as Quantum and Woody
(2017) #1-5. Copyright © 2017 and 2018 Valiant Entertainment
LLC. All rights reserved. All characters, their distinctive likeness
and related indicia featured in this publication are trademarks
of Valiant Entertainment LLC. The stories, characters, and
incidents featured in this publication are entirely fictional. Valiant
Entertainment does not read or accept unsolicited submissions of
ideas, stories, or artwork. Printed in the U.S.A.
First Printing. ISBN: 9781682152690.

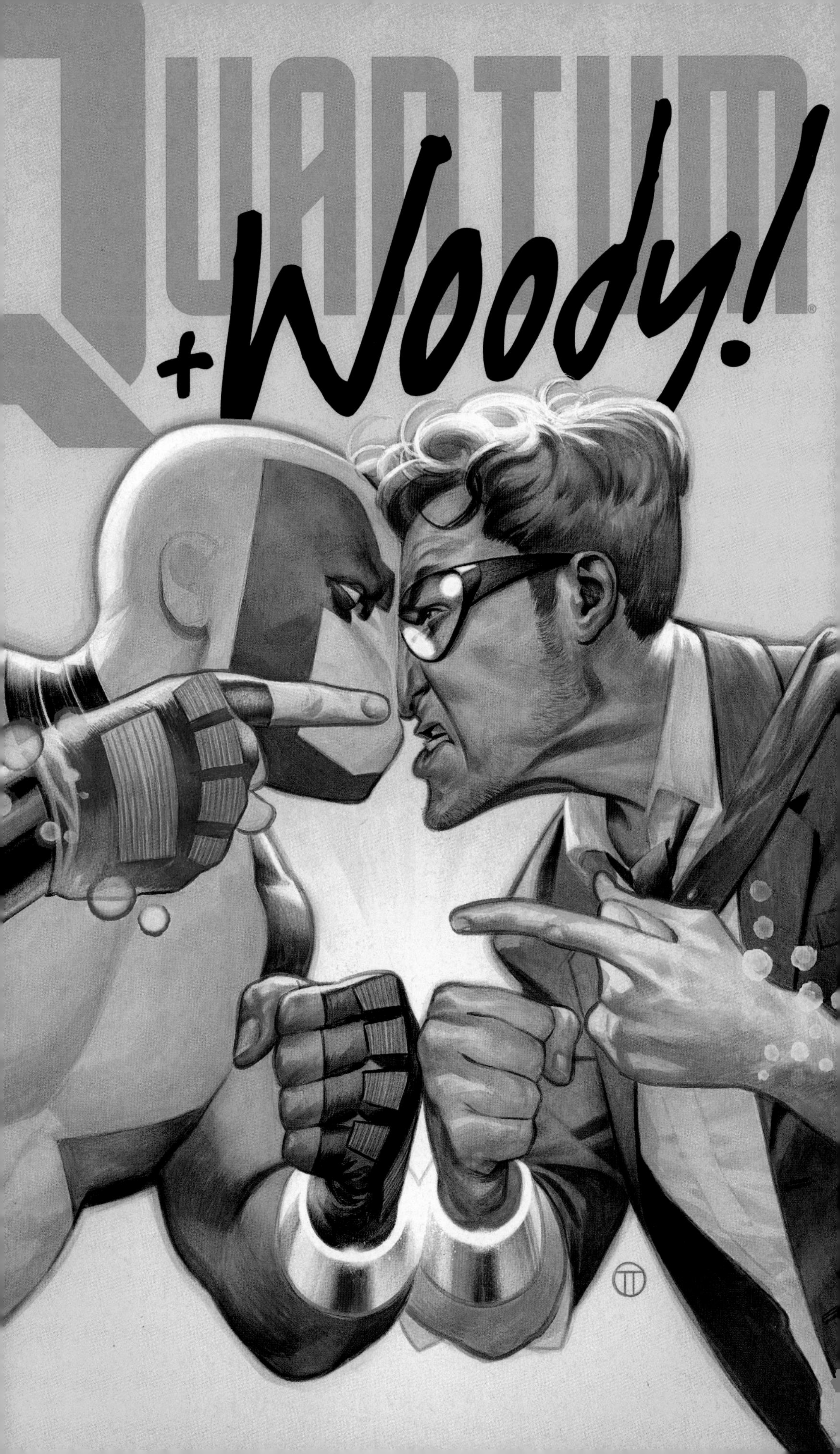
QUANTUM®
+ Woody!

Adoptive brothers Eric and Woody Henderson,
while investigating their father's murder, fall victim
to a scientific accident gone wrong. Now, they
must KLANG their wristbands together every
24 hours, or else they'll be pulled apart by
the quantum forces that empower them.
Together, they fight crime...when they're
not fighting each other.

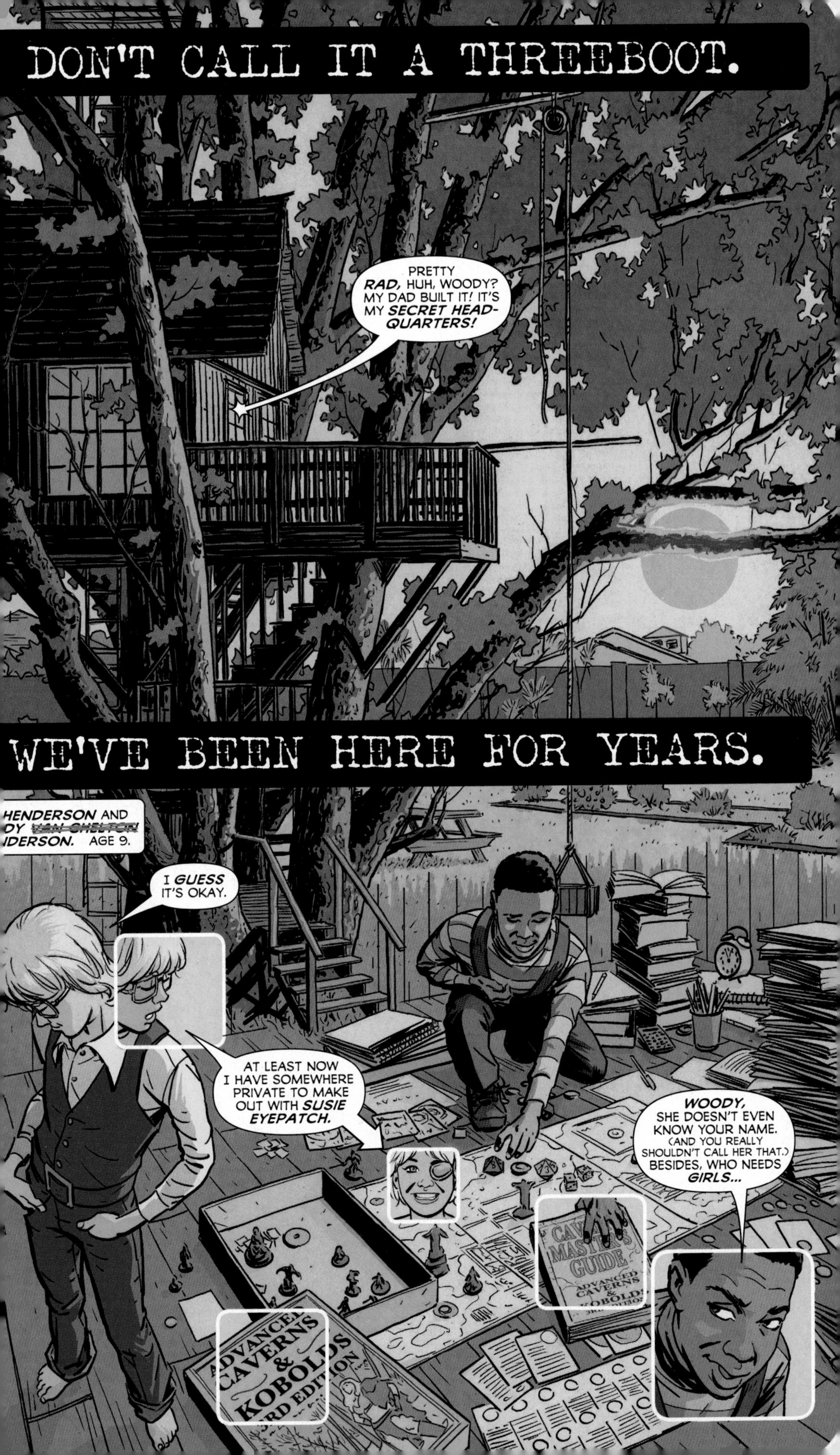
DON'T CALL IT A THREEBOOT.
PRETTY RAD, HUH, WOODY? MY DAD BUILT IT! IT'S MY SECRET HEAD-QUARTERS!
WE'VE BEEN HERE FOR YEARS.
HENDERSON AND DY ~~VAN SHELTON~~ IDERSON. AGE 9.
I GUESS IT'S OKAY.
AT LEAST NOW I HAVE SOMEWHERE PRIVATE TO MAKE OUT WITH SUSIE EYEPATCH.
WOODY, SHE DOESN'T EVEN KNOW YOUR NAME. (AND YOU REALLY SHOULDN'T CALL HER THAT.) BESIDES, WHO NEEDS GIRLS...
CAVERNS MASTER'S GUIDE
ADVANCED CAVERNS & KOBOLDS
ADVANCED CAVERNS & KOBOLDS 3RD EDITION

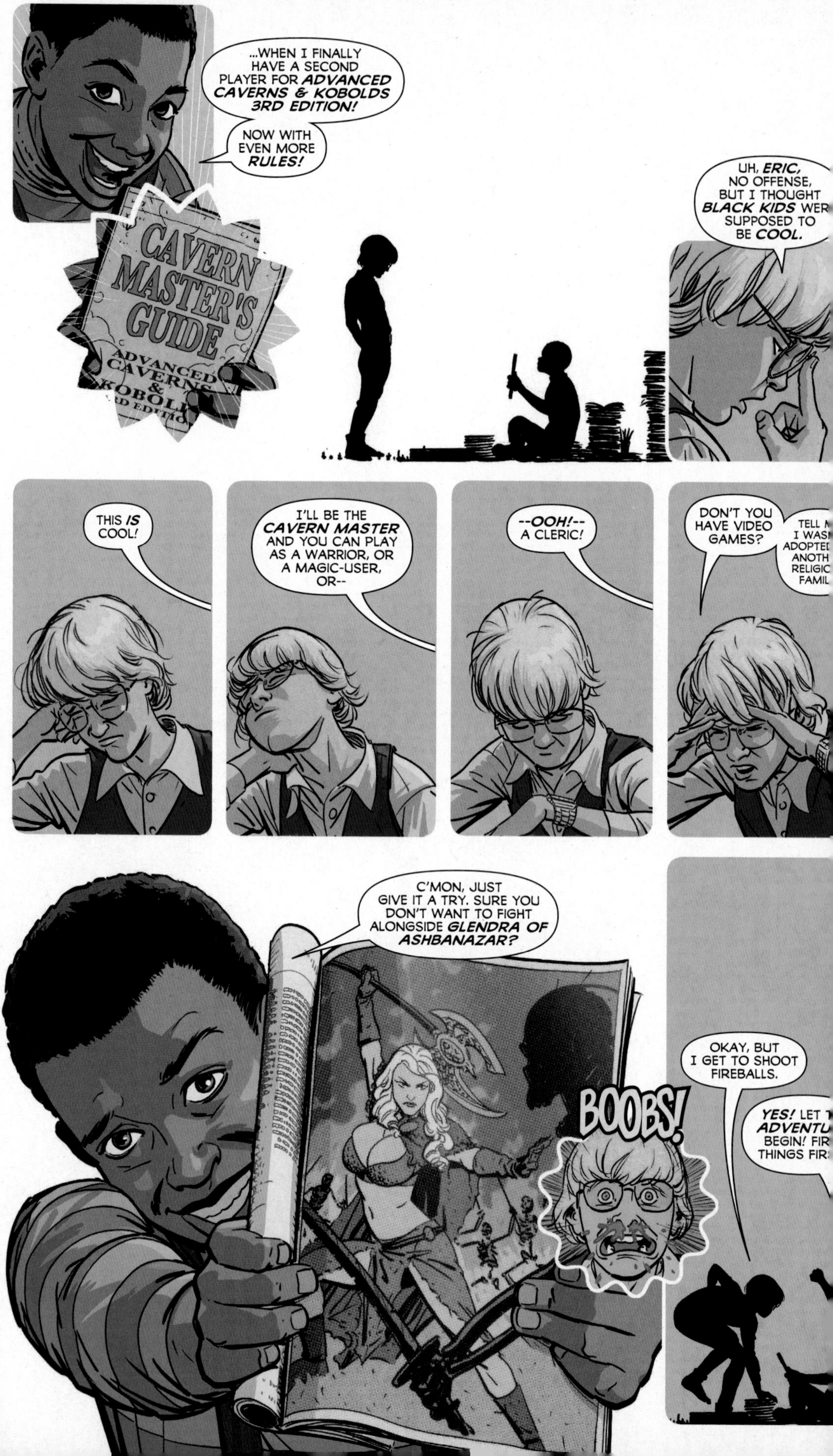

...WHEN I FINALLY HAVE A SECOND PLAYER FOR ADVANCED CAVERNS & KOBOLDS 3RD EDITION!
NOW WITH EVEN MORE RULES!
CAVERN MASTER'S GUIDE
UH, ERIC, NO OFFENSE, BUT I THOUGHT BLACK KIDS WER SUPPOSED TO BE COOL.
THIS IS COOL!
I'LL BE THE CAVERN MASTER AND YOU CAN PLAY AS A WARRIOR, OR A MAGIC-USER, OR--
--OOH!-- A CLERIC!
DON'T YOU HAVE VIDEO GAMES?
C'MON, JUST GIVE IT A TRY. SURE YOU DON'T WANT TO FIGHT ALONGSIDE GLENDRA OF ASHBANAZAR?
BOOBS!
OKAY, BUT I GET TO SHOOT FIREBALLS.

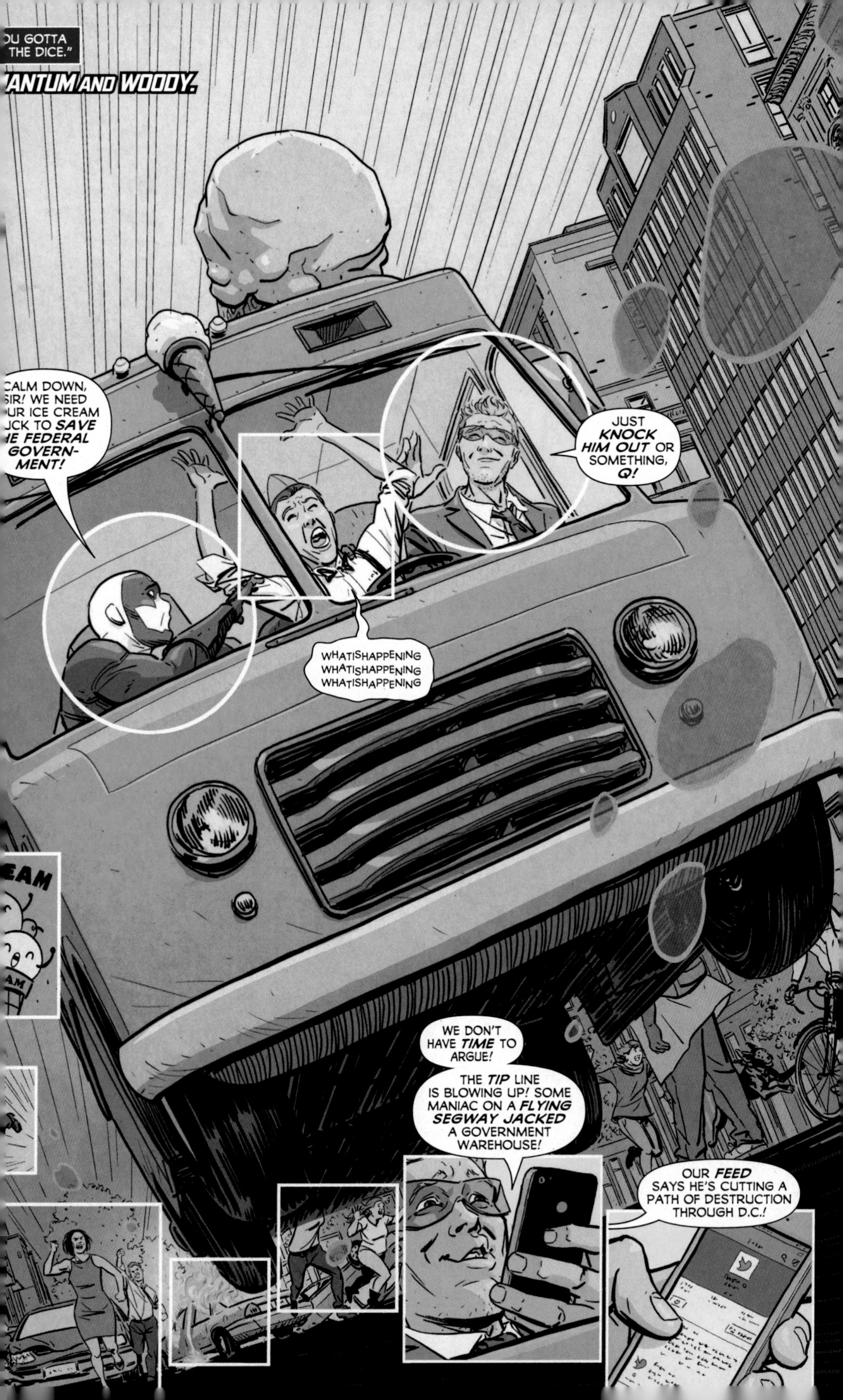

OU GOTTA
THE DICE."
ANTUM AND WOODY.
CALM DOWN, SIR! WE NEED UR ICE CREAM UCK TO SAVE IE FEDERAL GOVERN-MENT!
JUST KNOCK HIM OUT OR SOMETHING, Q!
WHATISHAPPENING WHATISHAPPENING WHATISHAPPENING
WE DON'T HAVE TIME TO ARGUE!
THE TIP LINE IS BLOWING UP! SOME MANIAC ON A FLYING SEGWAY JACKED A GOVERNMENT WAREHOUSE!
OUR FEED SAYS HE'S CUTTING A PATH OF DESTRUCTION THROUGH D.C.!

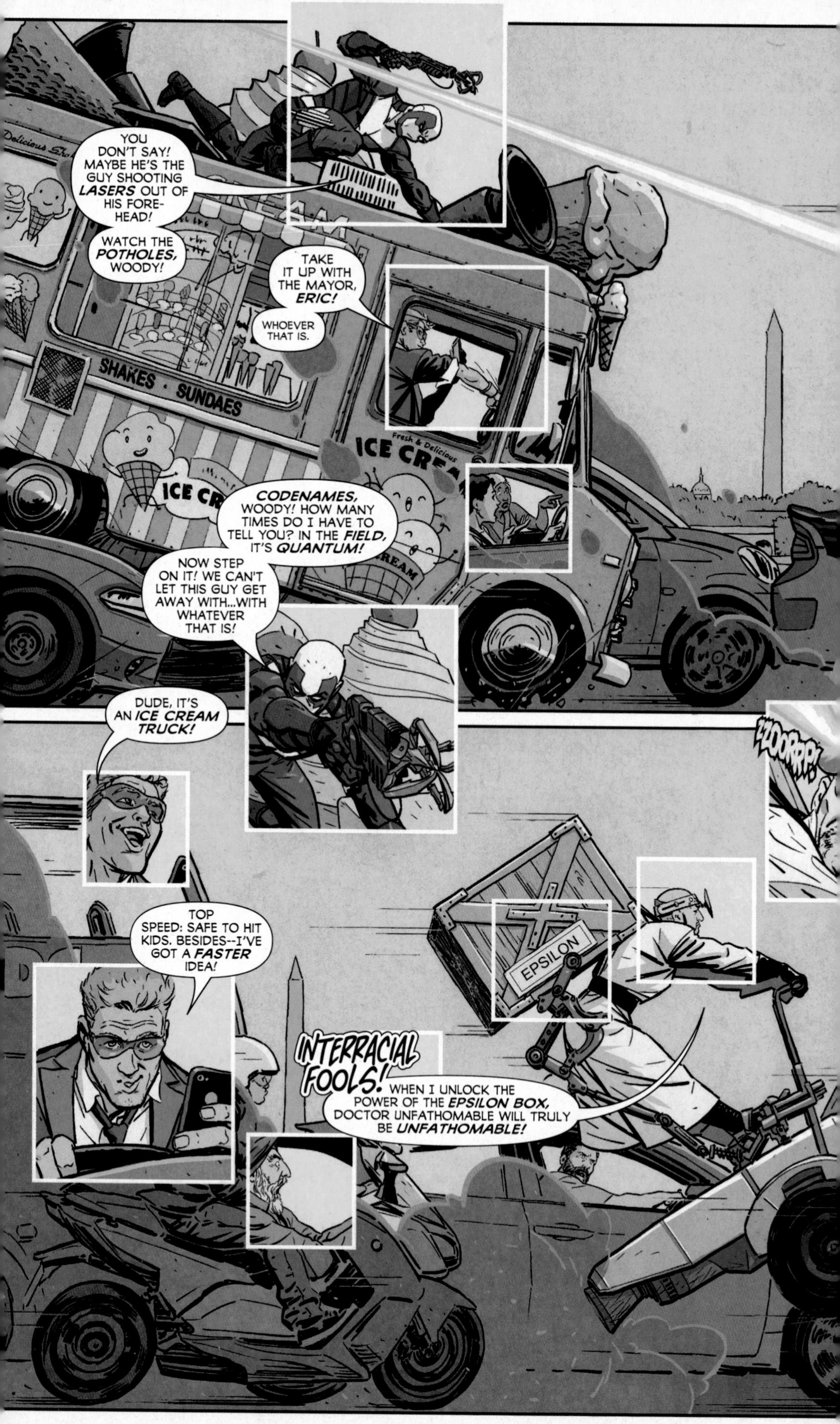

YOU DON'T SAY! MAYBE HE'S THE GUY SHOOTING LASERS OUT OF HIS FORE-HEAD!
WATCH THE POTHOLES, WOODY!
TAKE IT UP WITH THE MAYOR, ERIC!
WHOEVER THAT IS.
SHAKES · SUNDAES
Fresh & Delicious ICE CREAM
CODENAMES, WOODY! HOW MANY TIMES DO I HAVE TO TELL YOU? IN THE FIELD, IT'S QUANTUM!
NOW STEP ON IT! WE CAN'T LET THIS GUY GET AWAY WITH...WITH WHATEVER THAT IS!
DUDE, IT'S AN ICE CREAM TRUCK!
TOP SPEED: SAFE TO HIT KIDS. BESIDES--I'VE GOT A FASTER IDEA!
ZZOORRP!
EPSILON
INTERRACIAL FOOLS! WHEN I UNLOCK THE POWER OF THE EPSILON BOX, DOCTOR UNFATHOMABLE WILL TRULY BE UNFATHOMABLE!

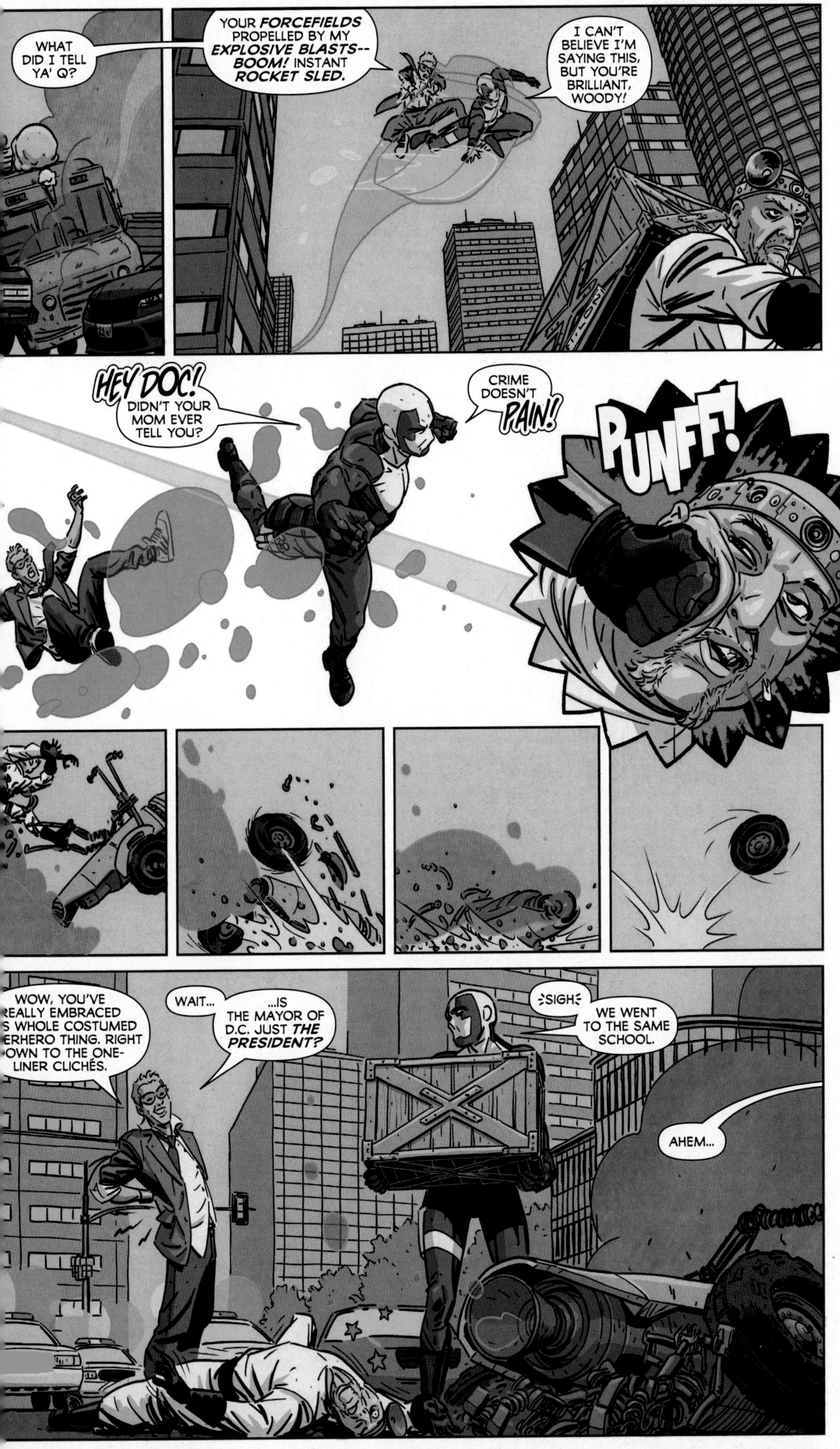
WHAT DID I TELL YA' Q?
YOUR FORCEFIELDS PROPELLED BY MY EXPLOSIVE BLASTS-- BOOM! INSTANT ROCKET SLED.
I CAN'T BELIEVE I'M SAYING THIS, BUT YOU'RE BRILLIANT, WOODY!
HEY DOC! DIDN'T YOUR MOM EVER TELL YOU?
CRIME DOESN'T PAIN!
PUNFF!
WOW, YOU'VE REALLY EMBRACED S WHOLE COSTUMED ERHERO THING. RIGHT OWN TO THE ONE-LINER CLICHÉS.
WAIT...
...IS THE MAYOR OF D.C. JUST THE PRESIDENT?
SIGH
WE WENT TO THE SAME SCHOOL.
AHEM...

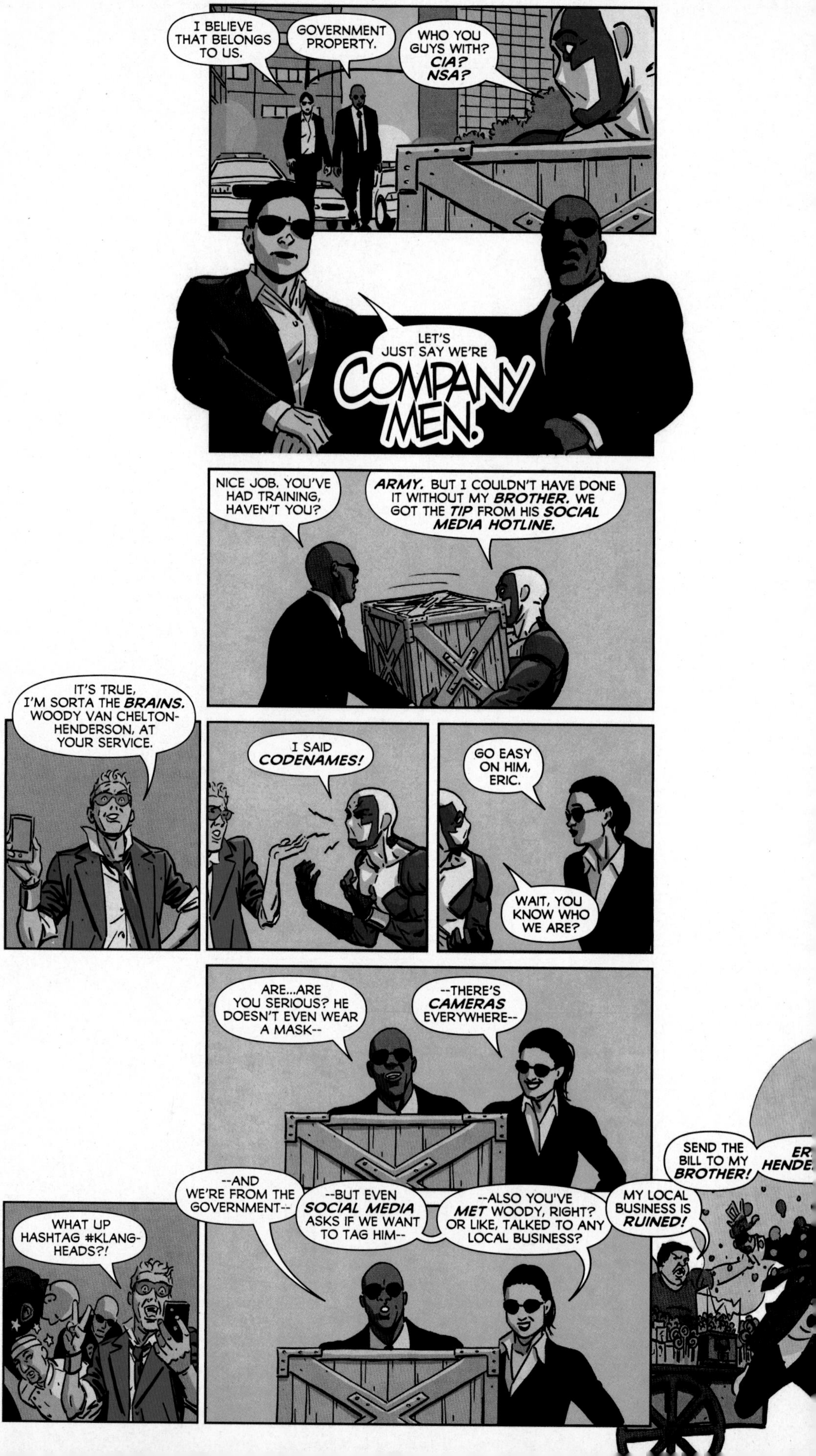
I BELIEVE THAT BELONGS TO US.
GOVERNMENT PROPERTY.
WHO YOU GUYS WITH? CIA? NSA?
LET'S JUST SAY WE'RE COMPANY MEN.
NICE JOB. YOU'VE HAD TRAINING, HAVEN'T YOU?
ARMY. BUT I COULDN'T HAVE DONE IT WITHOUT MY BROTHER. WE GOT THE TIP FROM HIS SOCIAL MEDIA HOTLINE.
IT'S TRUE, I'M SORTA THE BRAINS. WOODY VAN CHELTON-HENDERSON, AT YOUR SERVICE.
I SAID CODENAMES!
GO EASY ON HIM, ERIC.
WAIT, YOU KNOW WHO WE ARE?
ARE...ARE YOU SERIOUS? HE DOESN'T EVEN WEAR A MASK--
--THERE'S CAMERAS EVERYWHERE--
--AND WE'RE FROM THE GOVERNMENT--
--BUT EVEN SOCIAL MEDIA ASKS IF WE WANT TO TAG HIM--
--ALSO YOU'VE MET WOODY, RIGHT? OR LIKE, TALKED TO ANY LOCAL BUSINESS?
WHAT UP HASHTAG #KLANG-HEADS?!
MY LOCAL BUSINESS IS RUINED!
SEND THE BILL TO MY BROTHER!

OKAY, OKAY! I GET IT!

JUST KEEPING OUR NATION'S CAPITOL SAFE FROM AD SCIENTISTS AND KEEPING IT HASHTAG #WOODYLIFE!

YOU KNOW, WE'VE HAD OUR EYE ON YOU FOR A WHILE, MR. HENDERSON.

YOU HAVE?

THE DOCTOR UNFATHOMABLES OF THE WORLD WILL KEEP COMING, AND WE COULD USE SOMEONE WITH A FEW TRICKS UP THEIR SLEEVE.

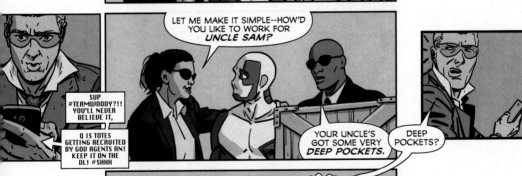

LET ME MAKE IT SIMPLE--HOW'D YOU LIKE TO WORK FOR UNCLE SAM?

SUP #TEAMWOODY?!! YOU'LL NEVER BELIEVE IT, Q IS TOTES GETTING RECRUITED BY GOV AGENTS RN! KEEP IT ON THE DL! #SHHH

YOUR UNCLE'S GOT SOME VERY DEEP POCKETS.

DEEP POCKETS?

WE'D LOVE TO!

ACTUALLY, THE OFFER ONLY EXTENDS TO--

THEN HE DECLINES! QUANTUM & WOODY ARE A PACKAGE DEAL!

...WOODY, CAN I TALK TO YOU FOR A SEC?

BUT...

WOODY, WE'RE BARELY COVERING THE OLD HOUSE AS IT IS.

BUT...

WOODY. C'MON, MAN. YOU KNOW THIS IS ALL I'VE EVER WANTED.

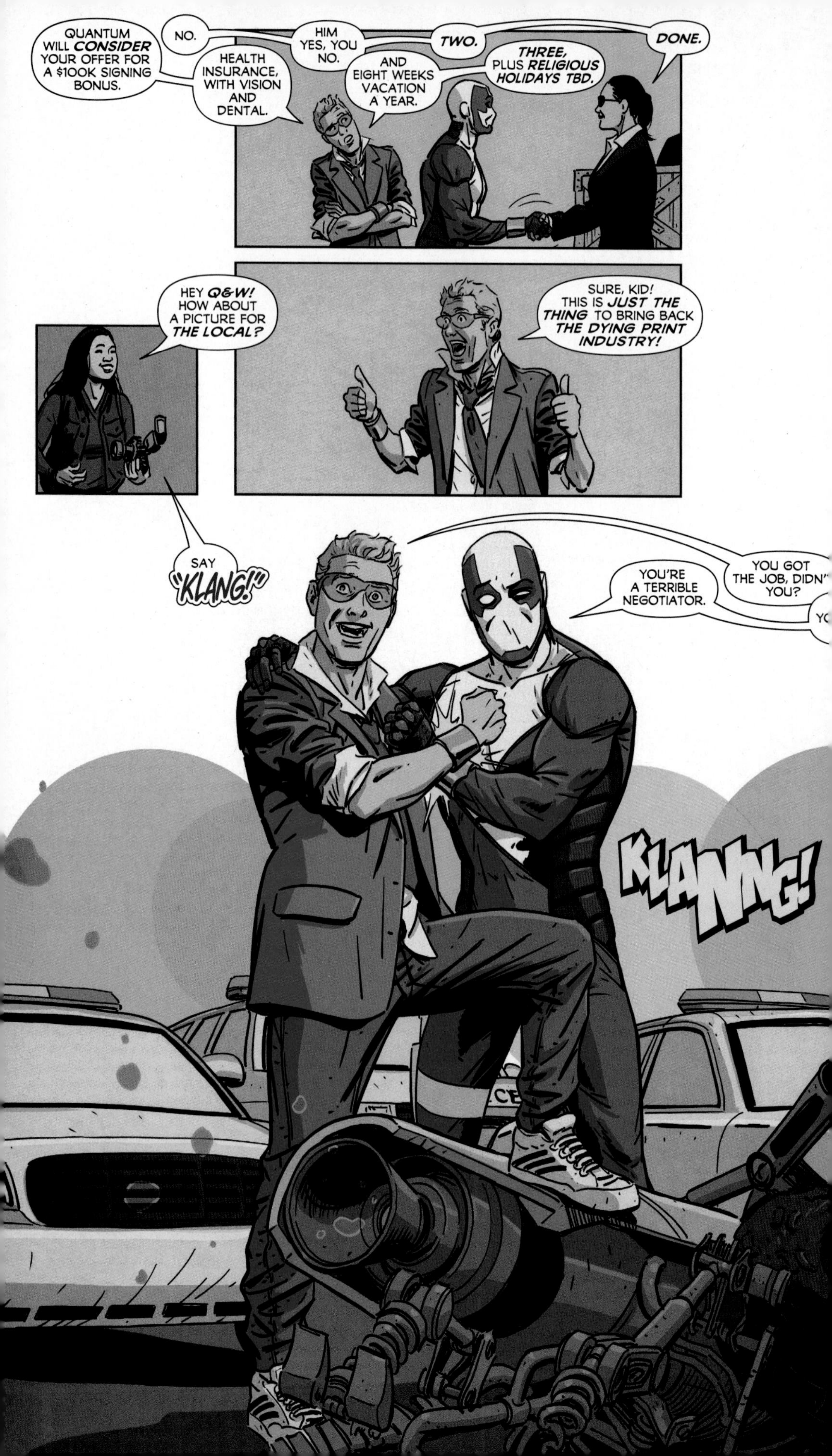
QUANTUM WILL CONSIDER YOUR OFFER FOR A $100K SIGNING BONUS.
NO.
HEALTH INSURANCE, WITH VISION AND DENTAL.
HIM YES, YOU NO.
AND EIGHT WEEKS VACATION A YEAR.
TWO.
THREE, PLUS RELIGIOUS HOLIDAYS TBD.
DONE.
HEY Q&W! HOW ABOUT A PICTURE FOR THE LOCAL?
SURE, KID! THIS IS JUST THE THING TO BRING BACK THE DYING PRINT INDUSTRY!
SAY "KLANG!"
YOU'RE A TERRIBLE NEGOTIATOR.
YOU GOT THE JOB, DIDN'T YOU?
KLANNNG!

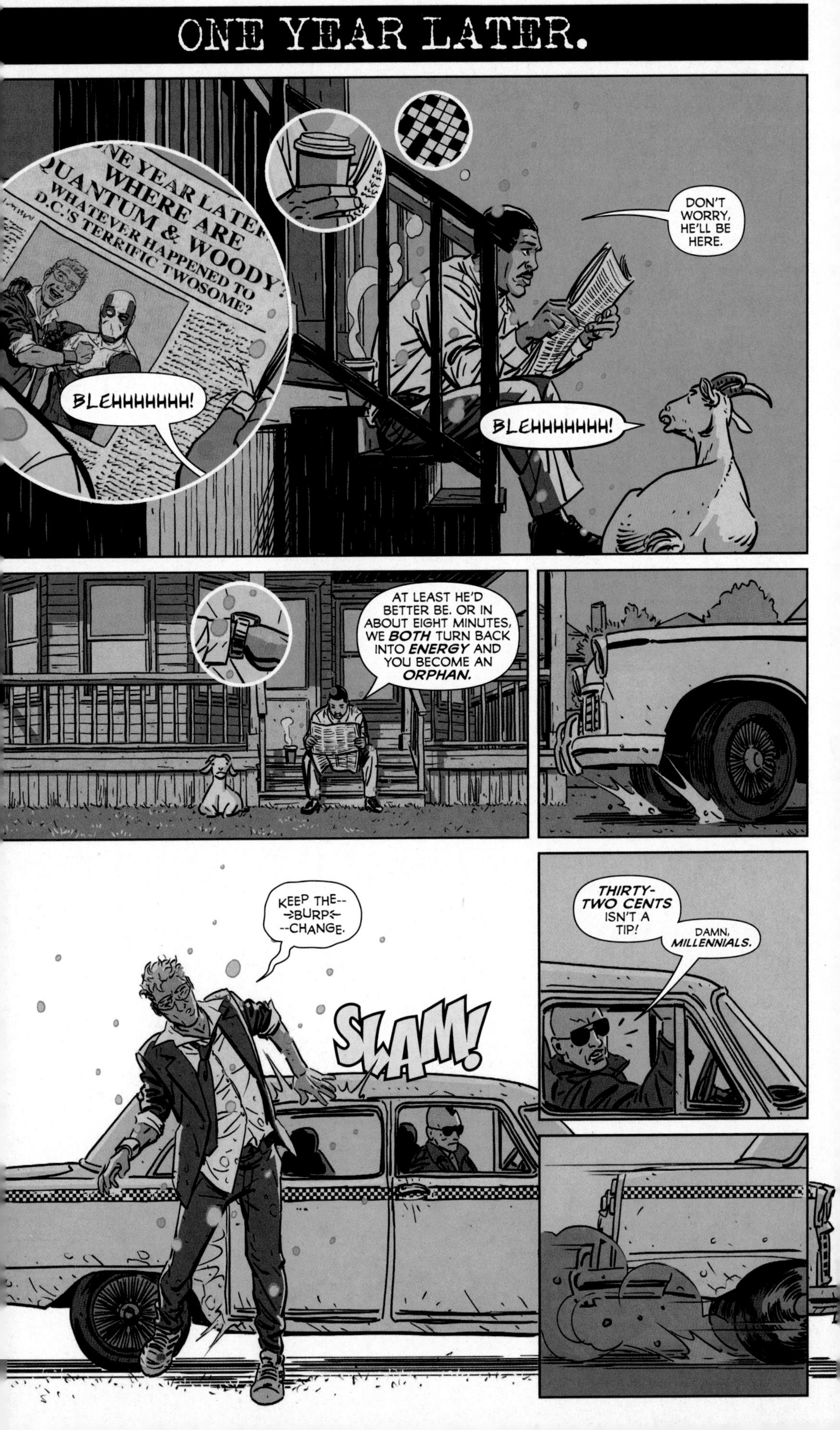
ONE YEAR LATER.
ONE YEAR LATER WHERE ARE QUANTUM & WOODY?
WHATEVER HAPPENED TO D.C.'S TERRIFIC TWOSOME?
DON'T WORRY, HE'LL BE HERE.
BLEHHHHHHH!
BLEHHHHHHH!
AT LEAST HE'D BETTER BE. OR IN ABOUT EIGHT MINUTES, WE BOTH TURN BACK INTO ENERGY AND YOU BECOME AN ORPHAN.
KEEP THE-- BURP --CHANGE.
SLAM!
THIRTY-TWO CENTS ISN'T A TIP!
DAMN, MILLENNIALS.

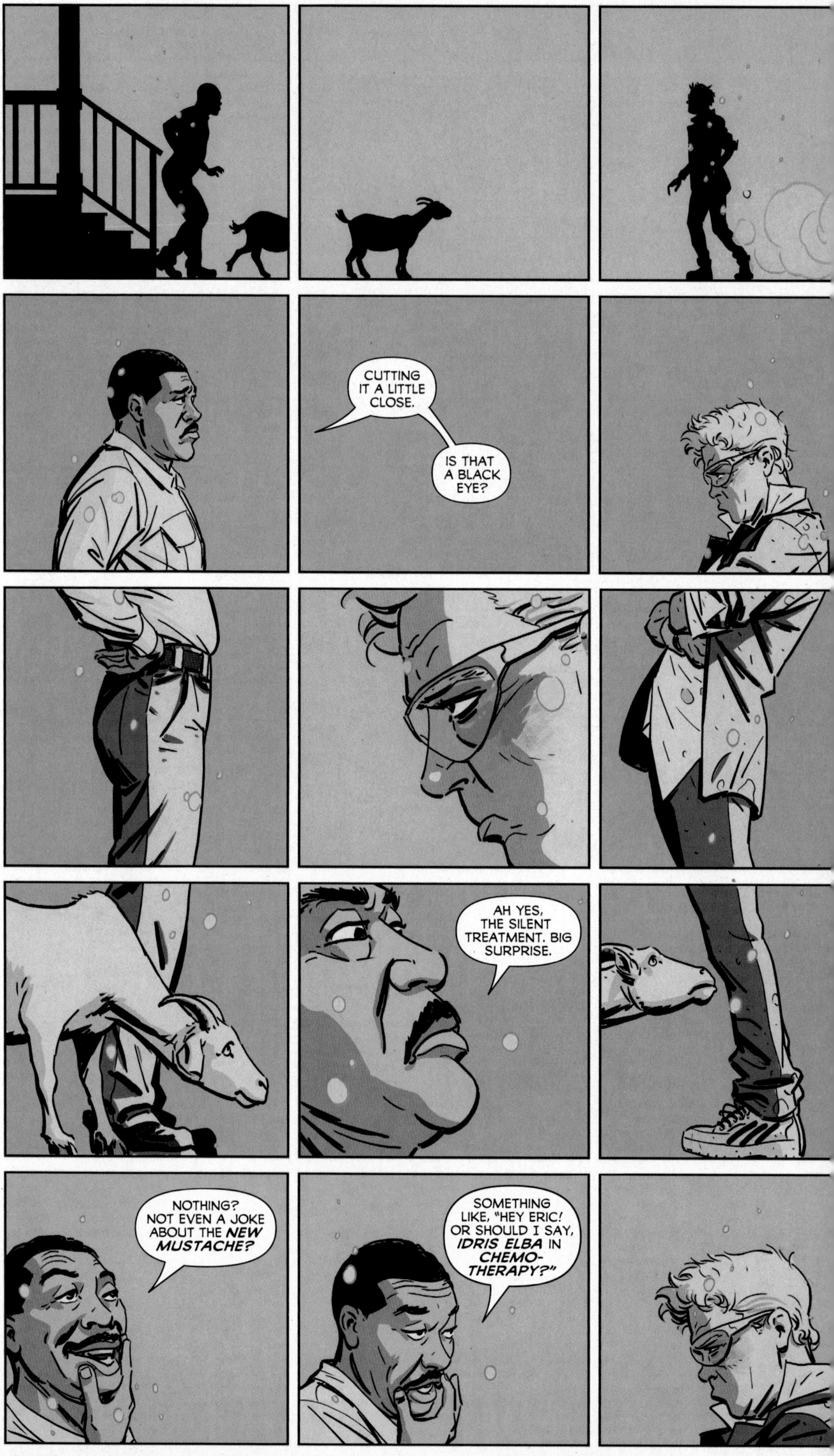
CUTTING IT A LITTLE CLOSE.
IS THAT A BLACK EYE?
AH YES, THE SILENT TREATMENT. BIG SURPRISE.
NOTHING? NOT EVEN A JOKE ABOUT THE *NEW MUSTACHE?*
SOMETHING LIKE, "HEY ERIC! OR SHOULD I SAY, *IDRIS ELBA* IN *CHEMO-THERAPY?"*

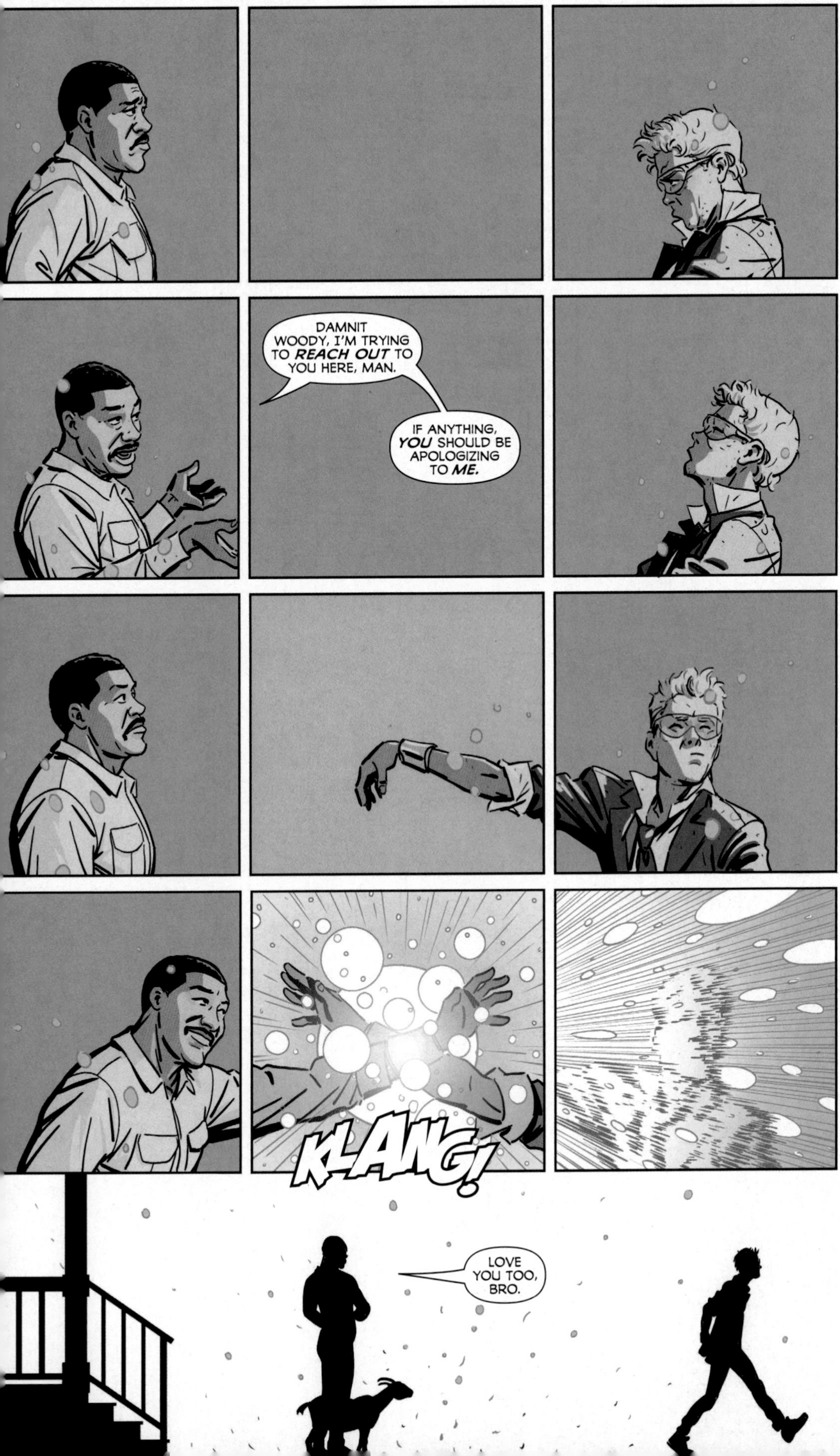
DAMNIT WOODY, I'M TRYING TO REACH OUT TO YOU HERE, MAN.
IF ANYTHING, YOU SHOULD BE APOLOGIZING TO ME.
KLANG!
LOVE YOU TOO, BRO.

SO, HOW WAS YOUR DAY?

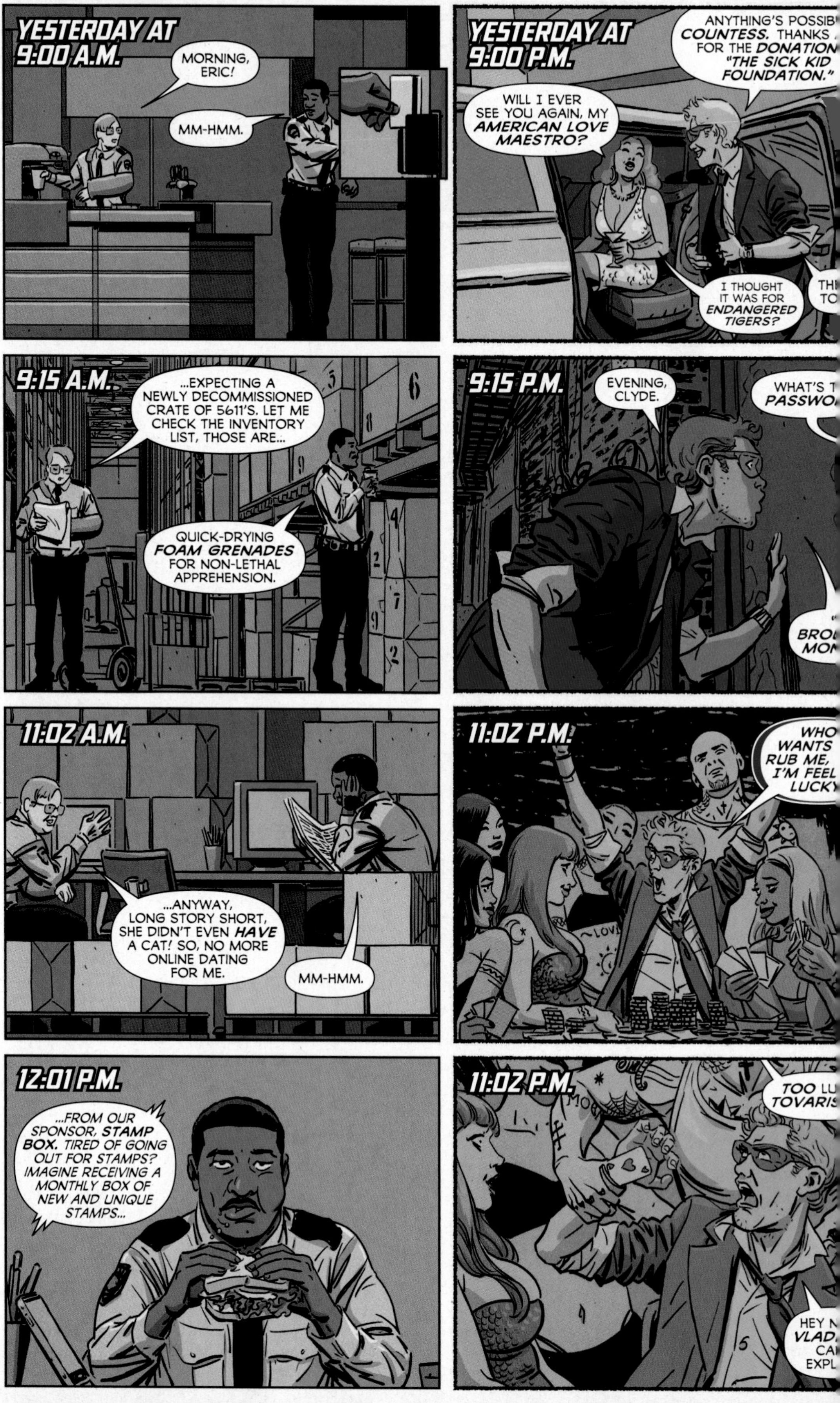
YESTERDAY AT 9:00 A.M.
MORNING, ERIC!
MM-HMM.
9:15 A.M.
...EXPECTING A NEWLY DECOMMISSIONED CRATE OF 5611'S. LET ME CHECK THE INVENTORY LIST, THOSE ARE...
QUICK-DRYING FOAM GRENADES FOR NON-LETHAL APPREHENSION.
11:02 A.M.
...ANYWAY, LONG STORY SHORT, SHE DIDN'T EVEN HAVE A CAT! SO, NO MORE ONLINE DATING FOR ME.
MM-HMM.
12:01 P.M.
...FROM OUR SPONSOR, STAMP BOX. TIRED OF GOING OUT FOR STAMPS? IMAGINE RECEIVING A MONTHLY BOX OF NEW AND UNIQUE STAMPS...
YESTERDAY AT 9:00 P.M.
ANYTHING'S POSSIB COUNTESS. THANKS FOR THE DONATION "THE SICK KID FOUNDATION."
WILL I EVER SEE YOU AGAIN, MY AMERICAN LOVE MAESTRO?
I THOUGHT IT WAS FOR ENDANGERED TIGERS?
9:15 P.M.
EVENING, CLYDE.
WHAT'S T PASSWO
11:02 P.M.
WHO WANTS RUB ME, I'M FEEL LUCKY
11:02 P.M.
TOO LU TOVARIS
HEY N VLAD CA EXPL

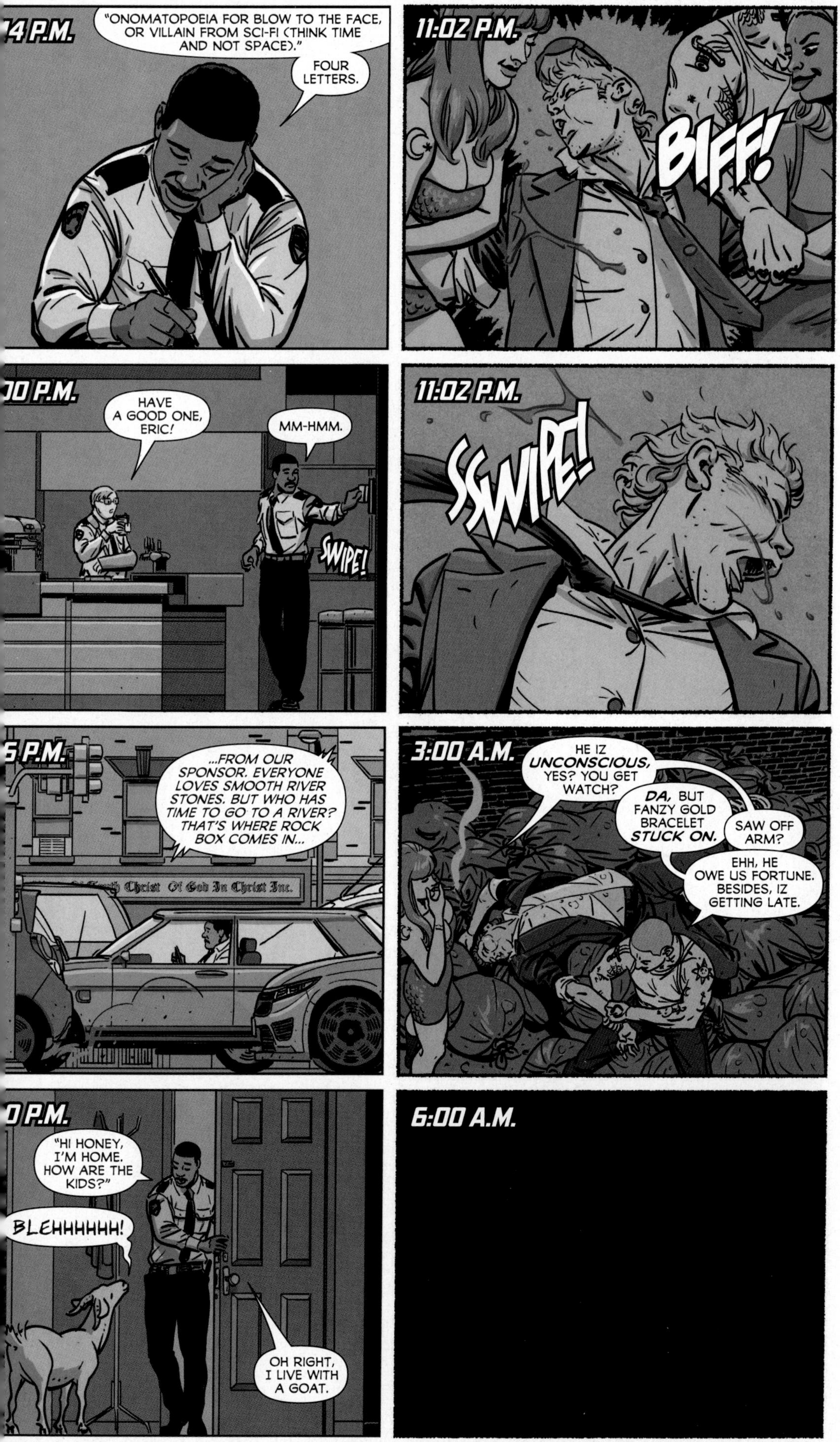

4 P.M.
"ONOMATOPOEIA FOR BLOW TO THE FACE, OR VILLAIN FROM SCI-FI (THINK TIME AND NOT SPACE)."
FOUR LETTERS.
11:02 P.M.
BIFF!
00 P.M.
HAVE A GOOD ONE, ERIC!
MM-HMM.
SWIPE!
11:02 P.M.
SSWIPE!
5 P.M.
...FROM OUR SPONSOR. EVERYONE LOVES SMOOTH RIVER STONES. BUT WHO HAS TIME TO GO TO A RIVER? THAT'S WHERE ROCK BOX COMES IN...
Christ Of God In Christ Inc.
3:00 A.M.
HE IZ UNCONSCIOUS, YES? YOU GET WATCH?
DA, BUT FANZY GOLD BRACELET STUCK ON.
SAW OFF ARM?
EHH, HE OWE US FORTUNE. BESIDES, IZ GETTING LATE.
0 P.M.
"HI HONEY, I'M HOME. HOW ARE THE KIDS?"
BLEHHHHHH!
OH RIGHT, I LIVE WITH A GOAT.
6:00 A.M.

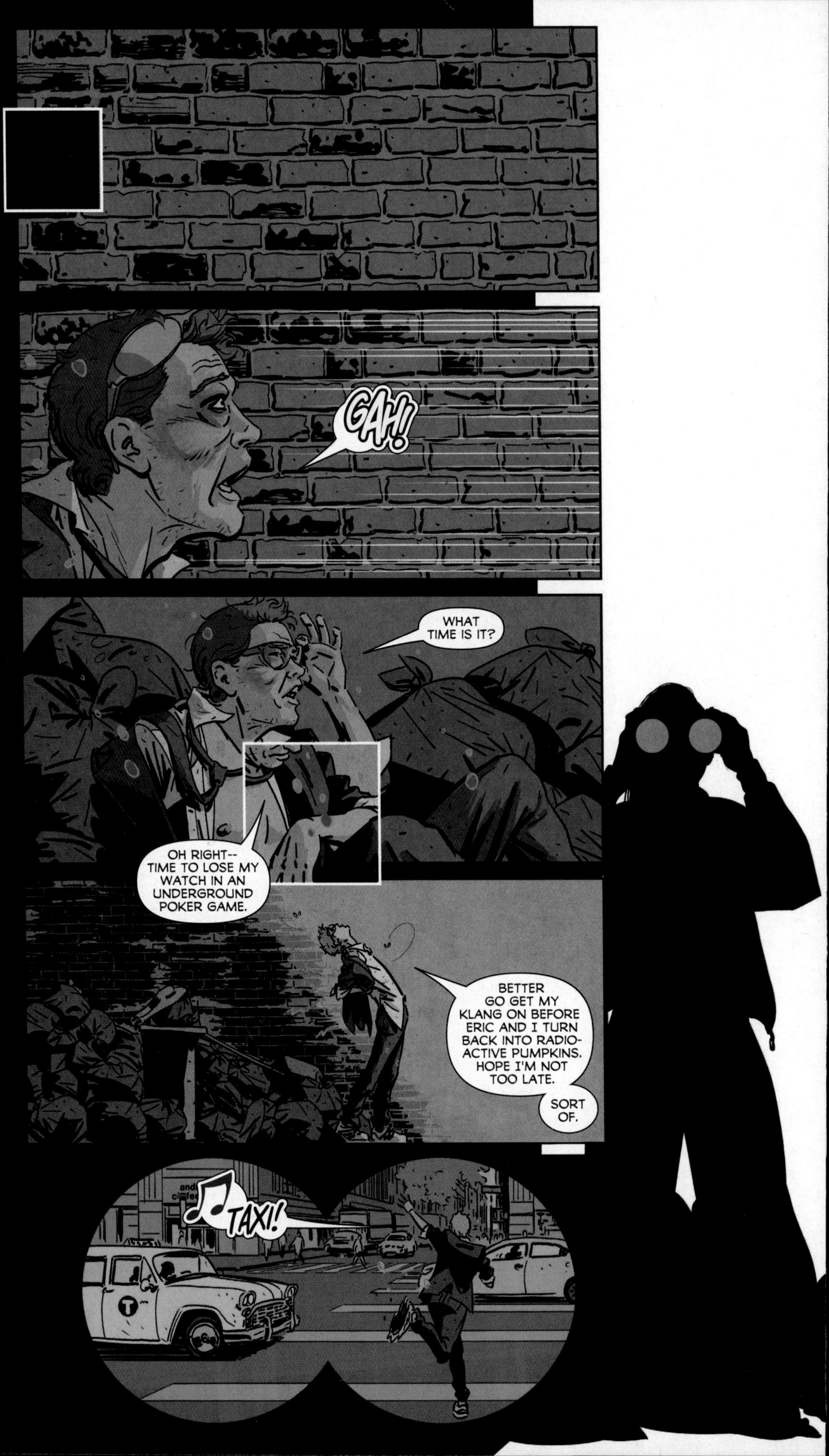
GAH!
WHAT TIME IS IT?
OH RIGHT-- TIME TO LOSE MY WATCH IN AN UNDERGROUND POKER GAME.
BETTER GO GET MY KLANG ON BEFORE ERIC AND I TURN BACK INTO RADIO-ACTIVE PUMPKINS. HOPE I'M NOT TOO LATE.
SORT OF.
TAXI!

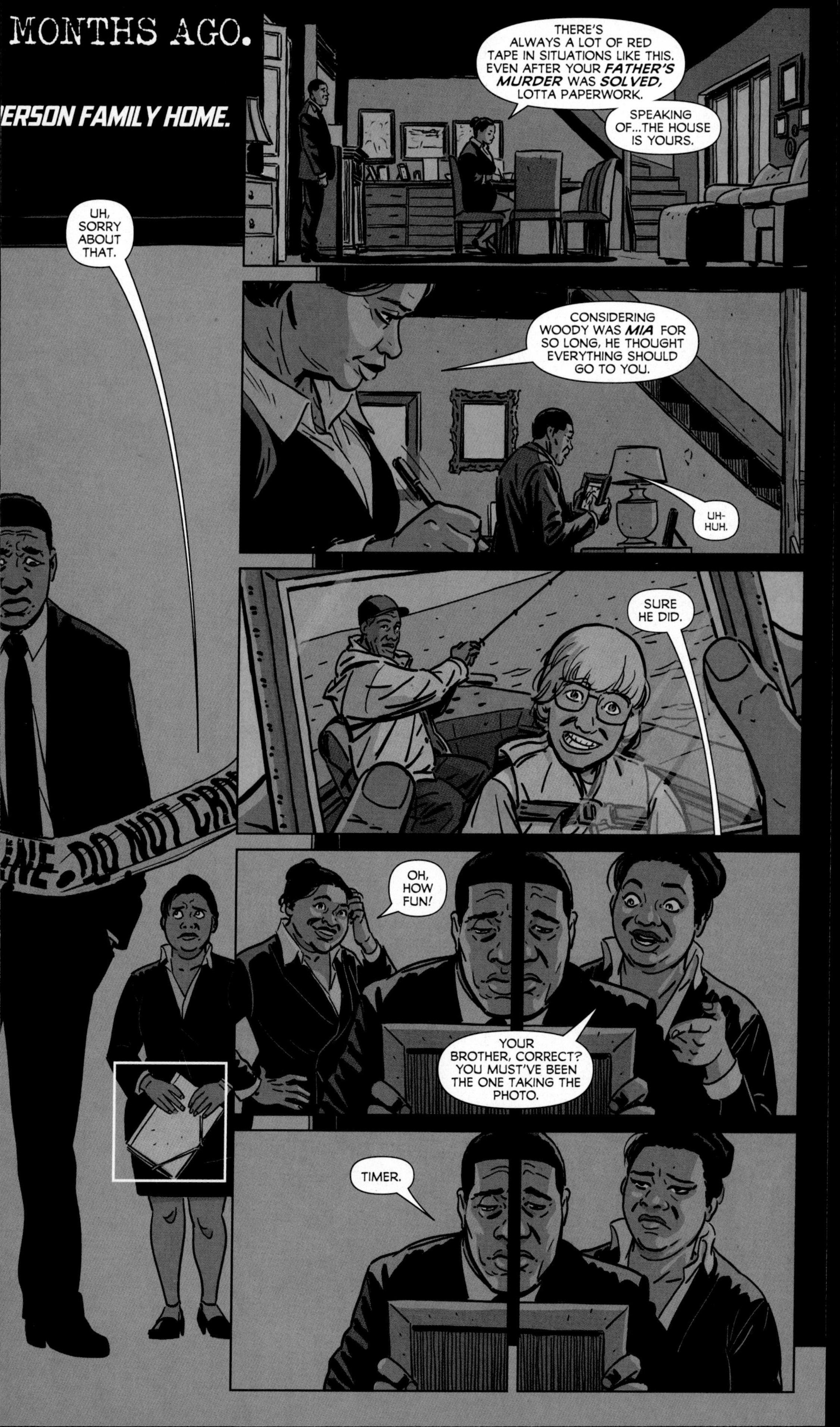
MONTHS AGO.
ERSON FAMILY HOME.
THERE'S ALWAYS A LOT OF RED TAPE IN SITUATIONS LIKE THIS. EVEN AFTER YOUR FATHER'S MURDER WAS SOLVED, LOTTA PAPERWORK.
SPEAKING OF...THE HOUSE IS YOURS.
UH, SORRY ABOUT THAT.
CONSIDERING WOODY WAS MIA FOR SO LONG, HE THOUGHT EVERYTHING SHOULD GO TO YOU.
UH-HUH.
SURE HE DID.
NE. DO NOT CR
OH, HOW FUN!
YOUR BROTHER, CORRECT? YOU MUST'VE BEEN THE ONE TAKING THE PHOTO.
TIMER.

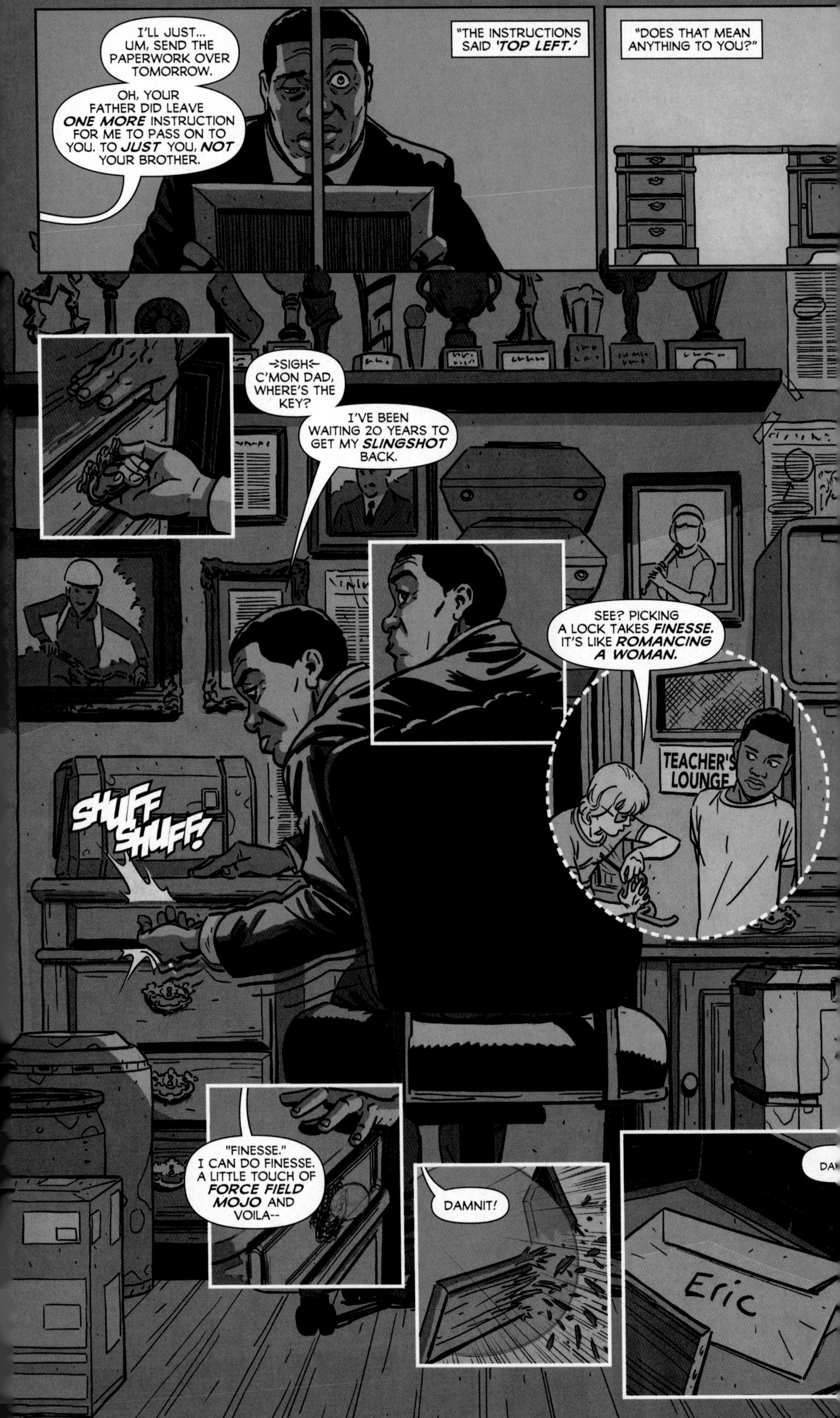
I'LL JUST... UM, SEND THE PAPERWORK OVER TOMORROW.
OH, YOUR FATHER DID LEAVE ONE MORE INSTRUCTION FOR ME TO PASS ON TO YOU. TO JUST YOU, NOT YOUR BROTHER.
"THE INSTRUCTIONS SAID 'TOP LEFT.'
"DOES THAT MEAN ANYTHING TO YOU?"
>SIGH< C'MON DAD, WHERE'S THE KEY?
I'VE BEEN WAITING 20 YEARS TO GET MY SLINGSHOT BACK.
SEE? PICKING A LOCK TAKES FINESSE. IT'S LIKE ROMANCING A WOMAN.
TEACHER'S LOUNGE
SHUFF SHUFF!
"FINESSE." I CAN DO FINESSE. A LITTLE TOUCH OF FORCE FIELD MOJO AND VOILA--
DAMNIT!
Eric

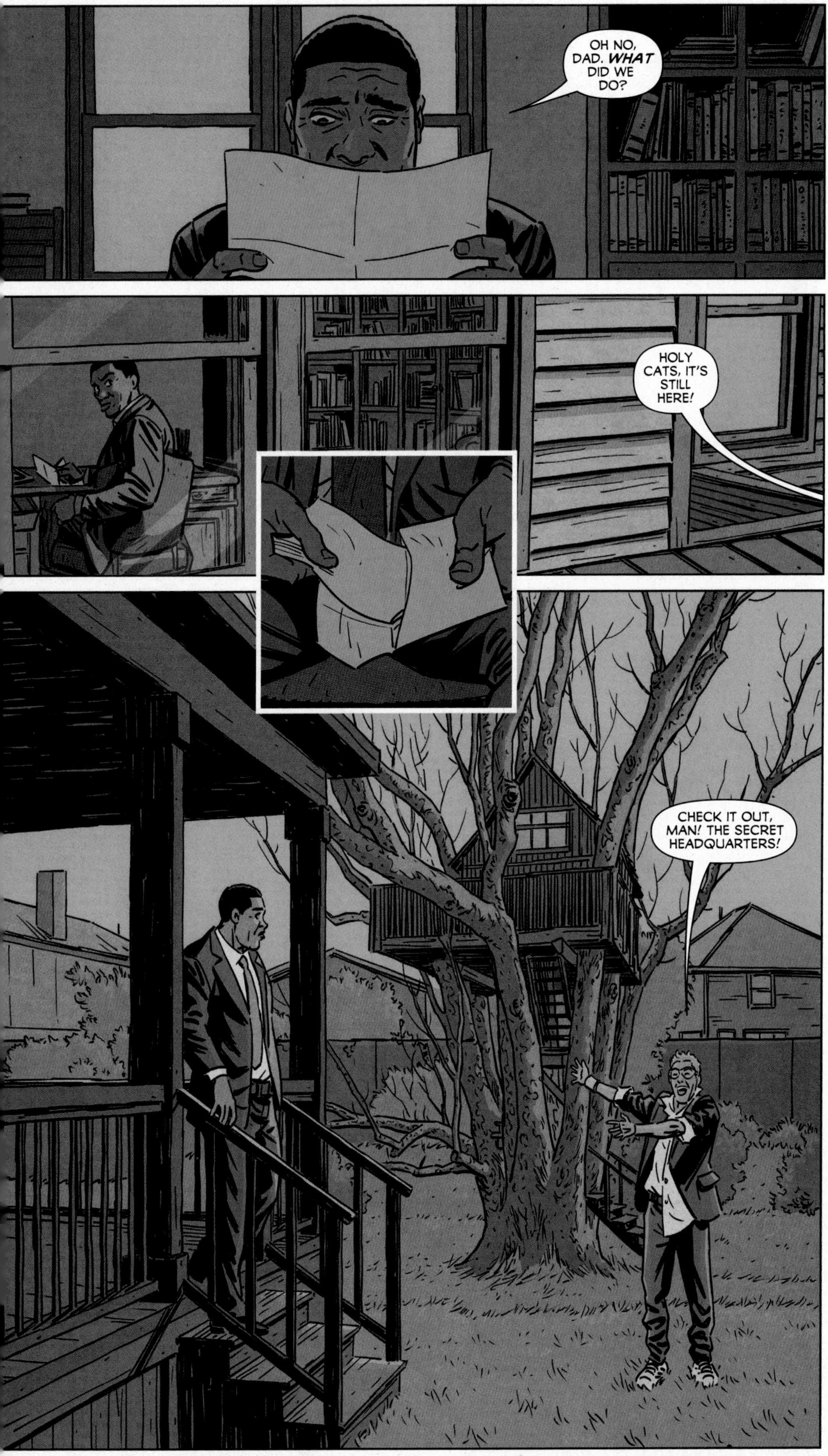
OH NO, DAD. ***WHAT*** DID WE DO?
HOLY CATS, IT'S STILL HERE!
CHECK IT OUT, MAN! THE SECRET HEADQUARTERS!

Dear, Mr. Henderson...

SORRY I'M LATE. DID I MISS ANYTHING?

...NOPE. NOT A THING.

Or maybe I should call you Derek, seeing as how we're sort of family now.

CAN YOU BELIEVE IT? DAD SURE BUILT THINGS STURDY, DIDN'T HE?

HARDER FOR US TO BREAK, I GUESS.

The caseworkers got word to me about what happened.

To Woody.

EH, WE STILL MANAGED.

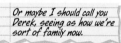

To Woody's N

You must think I'm a real coward, and you'd be right.

SO...WHO GETS DAD'S ROOM?

Leaving Lucy behind that. Telling her to my own boy I was

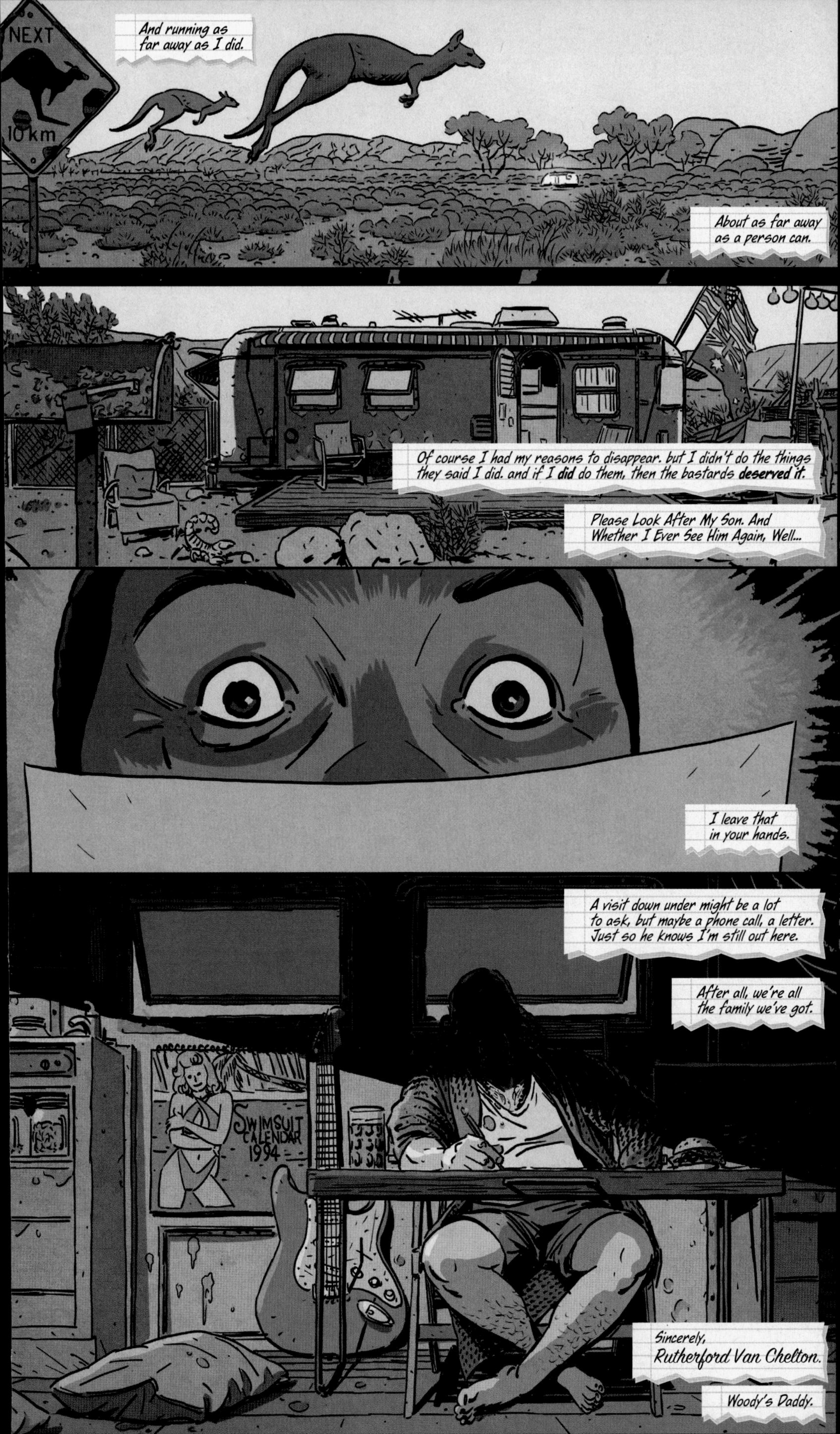
NEXT
10 km
And running as far away as I did.
About as far away as a person can.
Of course I had my reasons to disappear. but I didn't do the things they said I did. and if I **did** do them, then the bastards **deserved it**.
Please Look After My Son. And Whether I Ever See Him Again, Well...
I leave that in your hands.
A visit down under might be a lot to ask, but maybe a phone call, a letter. Just so he knows I'm still out here.
After all, we're all the family we've got.
SWIMSUIT CALENDAR 1994
Sincerely, Rutherford Van Chelton.
Woody's Daddy.

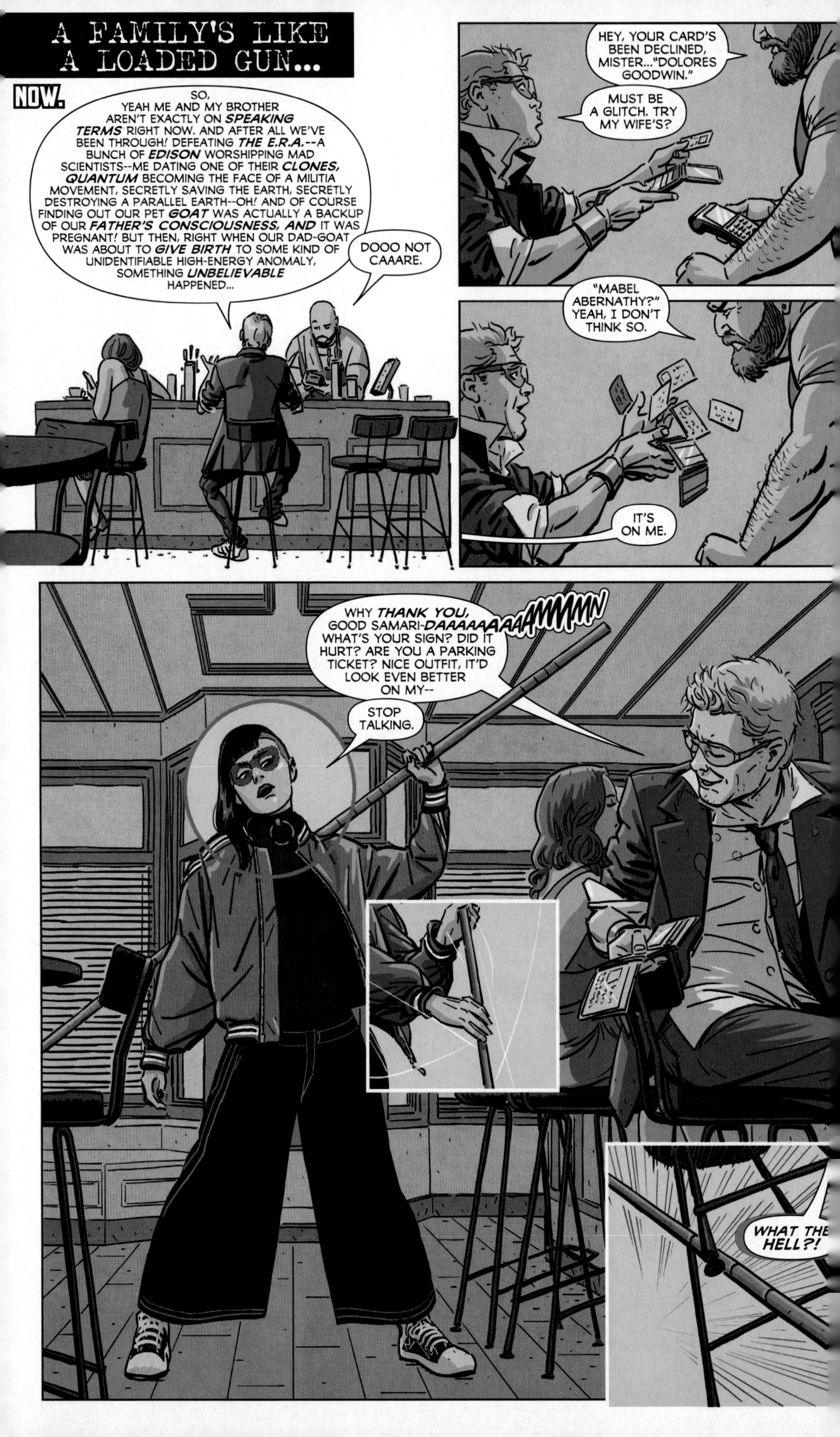
A FAMILY'S LIKE A LOADED GUN...
NOW.
SO, YEAH ME AND MY BROTHER AREN'T EXACTLY ON SPEAKING TERMS RIGHT NOW. AND AFTER ALL WE'VE BEEN THROUGH! DEFEATING THE E.R.A.--A BUNCH OF EDISON WORSHIPPING MAD SCIENTISTS--ME DATING ONE OF THEIR CLONES, QUANTUM BECOMING THE FACE OF A MILITIA MOVEMENT, SECRETLY SAVING THE EARTH, SECRETLY DESTROYING A PARALLEL EARTH--OH! AND OF COURSE FINDING OUT OUR PET GOAT WAS ACTUALLY A BACKUP OF OUR FATHER'S CONSCIOUSNESS, AND IT WAS PREGNANT! BUT THEN, RIGHT WHEN OUR DAD-GOAT WAS ABOUT TO GIVE BIRTH TO SOME KIND OF UNIDENTIFIABLE HIGH-ENERGY ANOMALY, SOMETHING UNBELIEVABLE HAPPENED...
DOOO NOT CAAARE.
HEY, YOUR CARD'S BEEN DECLINED, MISTER..."DOLORES GOODWIN."
MUST BE A GLITCH. TRY MY WIFE'S?
"MABEL ABERNATHY?" YEAH, I DON'T THINK SO.
IT'S ON ME.
WHY THANK YOU, GOOD SAMARI-DAAAAAAAAAMMMN
WHAT'S YOUR SIGN? DID IT HURT? ARE YOU A PARKING TICKET? NICE OUTFIT, IT'D LOOK EVEN BETTER ON MY--
STOP TALKING.
WHAT THE HELL?!

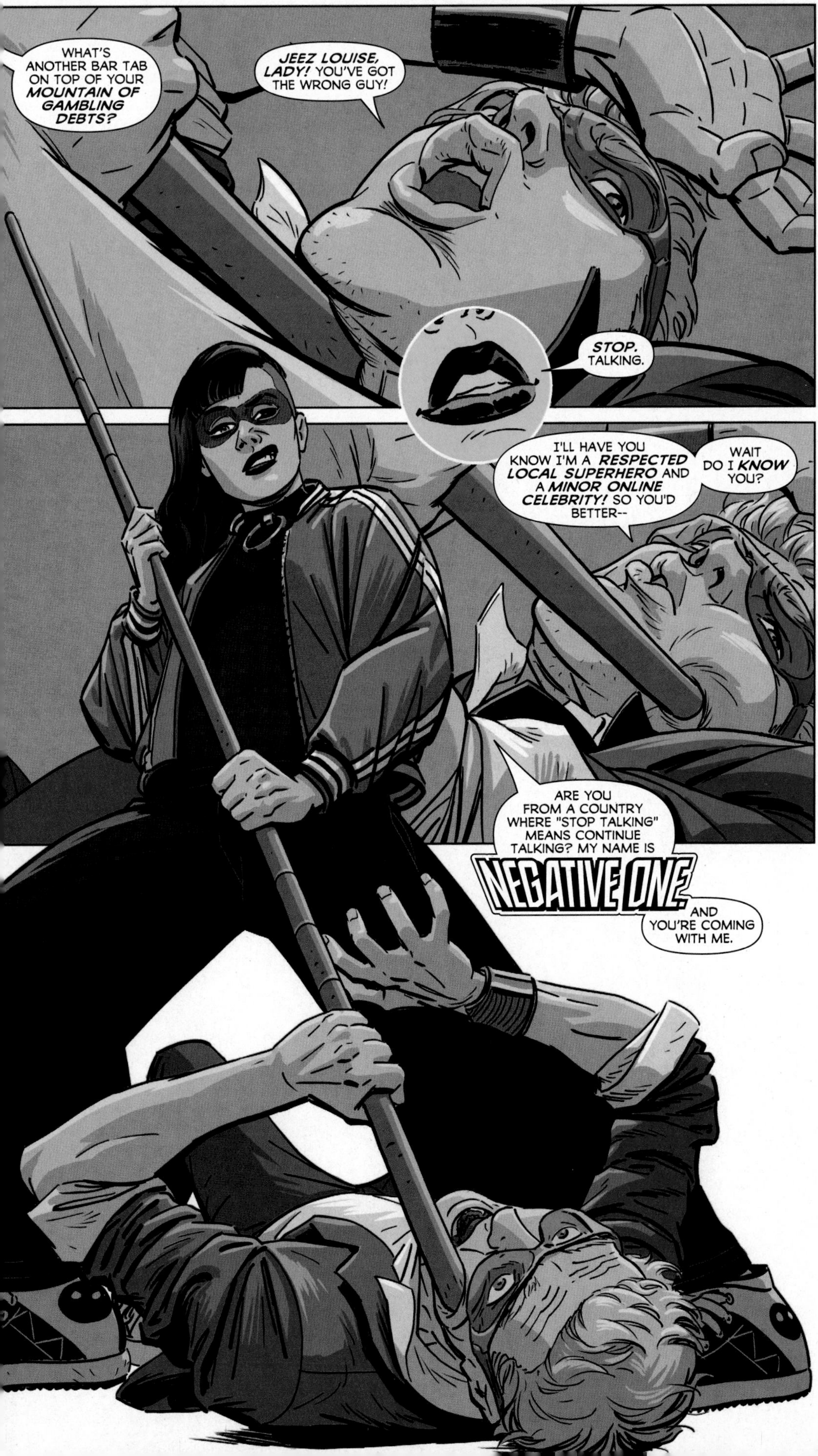
WHAT'S ANOTHER BAR TAB ON TOP OF YOUR *MOUNTAIN OF GAMBLING DEBTS?*
JEEZ LOUISE, LADY! YOU'VE GOT THE WRONG GUY!
STOP. TALKING.
I'LL HAVE YOU KNOW I'M A *RESPECTED LOCAL SUPERHERO* AND A *MINOR ONLINE CELEBRITY!* SO YOU'D BETTER--
WAIT DO I *KNOW* YOU?
ARE YOU FROM A COUNTRY WHERE "STOP TALKING" MEANS CONTINUE TALKING? MY NAME IS
NEGATIVE ONE
AND YOU'RE COMING WITH ME.

KEEP THE CHANGE. HE'LL BE PAYING IT OFF TO **US** FROM NOW ON.

LOOK LADY, I MIGHT OWE A COUPLE BUCKS TO SOME PEOPLE, BUT IT SURE AS HECK AIN'T--

GENTS

HEY **TOVARISHCH**, EES VLADDY! NICE LADY COME BUY UP ALL YOUR DEBTS. YOU **LUCKY** AFTER ALL, HUH?

OKAY, H— DO I PRESS RECORDIN—

IF I HAD MY WAY, YOU'D ALREADY BE DEAD. BUT MY EMPLOYER WANTS YOU ALIVE.

WELL THEN I GUESS THERE'S ONLY ONE THING LEFT TO DO...

GOODBYENICEMEETINGYOU!

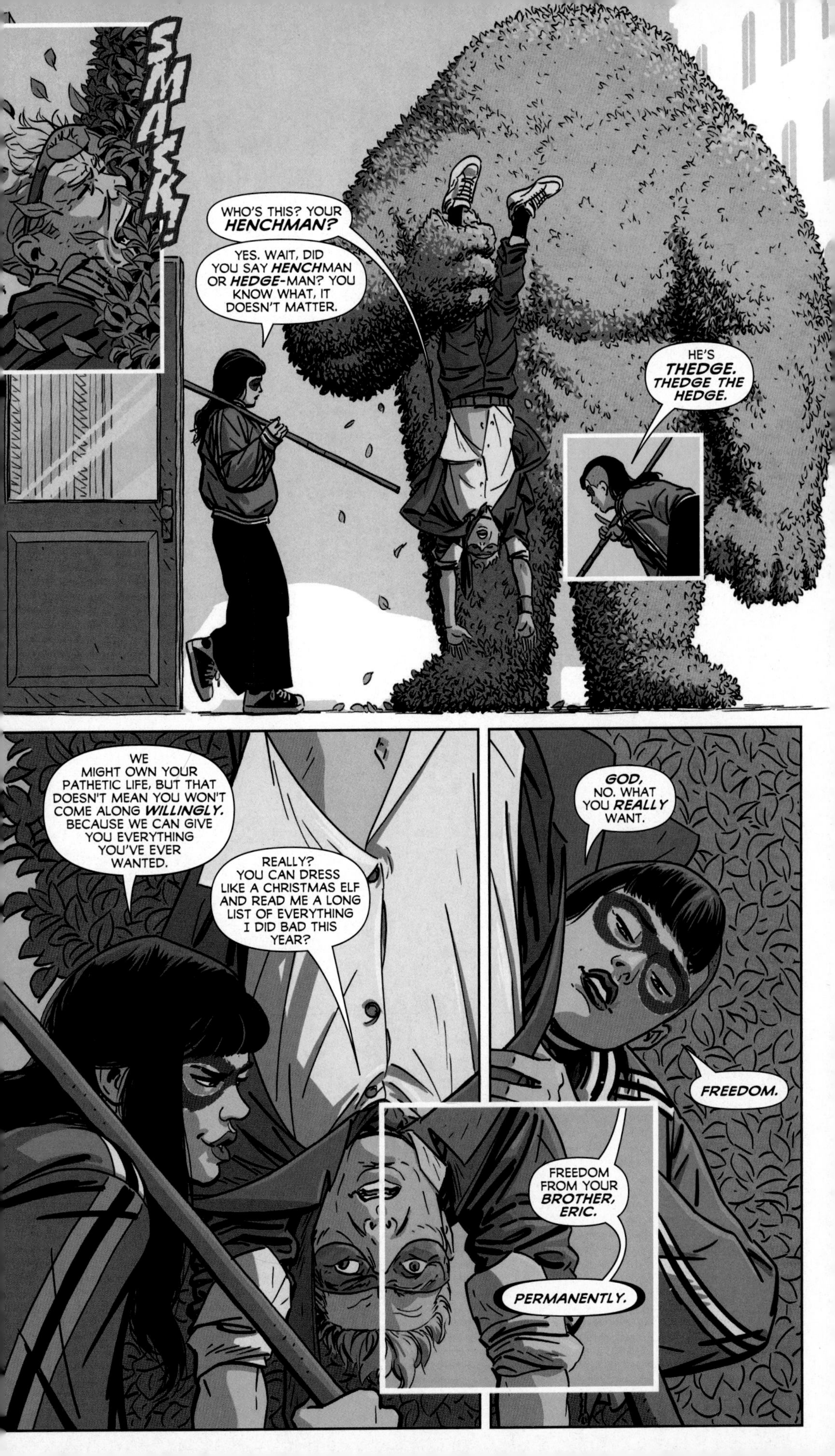
SMAKK!
WHO'S THIS? YOUR HENCHMAN?
YES. WAIT, DID YOU SAY HENCHMAN OR HEDGE-MAN? YOU KNOW WHAT, IT DOESN'T MATTER.
HE'S THEDGE. THEDGE THE HEDGE.
WE MIGHT OWN YOUR PATHETIC LIFE, BUT THAT DOESN'T MEAN YOU WON'T COME ALONG WILLINGLY. BECAUSE WE CAN GIVE YOU EVERYTHING YOU'VE EVER WANTED.
REALLY? YOU CAN DRESS LIKE A CHRISTMAS ELF AND READ ME A LONG LIST OF EVERYTHING I DID BAD THIS YEAR?
GOD, NO. WHAT YOU REALLY WANT.
FREEDOM.
FREEDOM FROM YOUR BROTHER, ERIC.
PERMANENTLY.

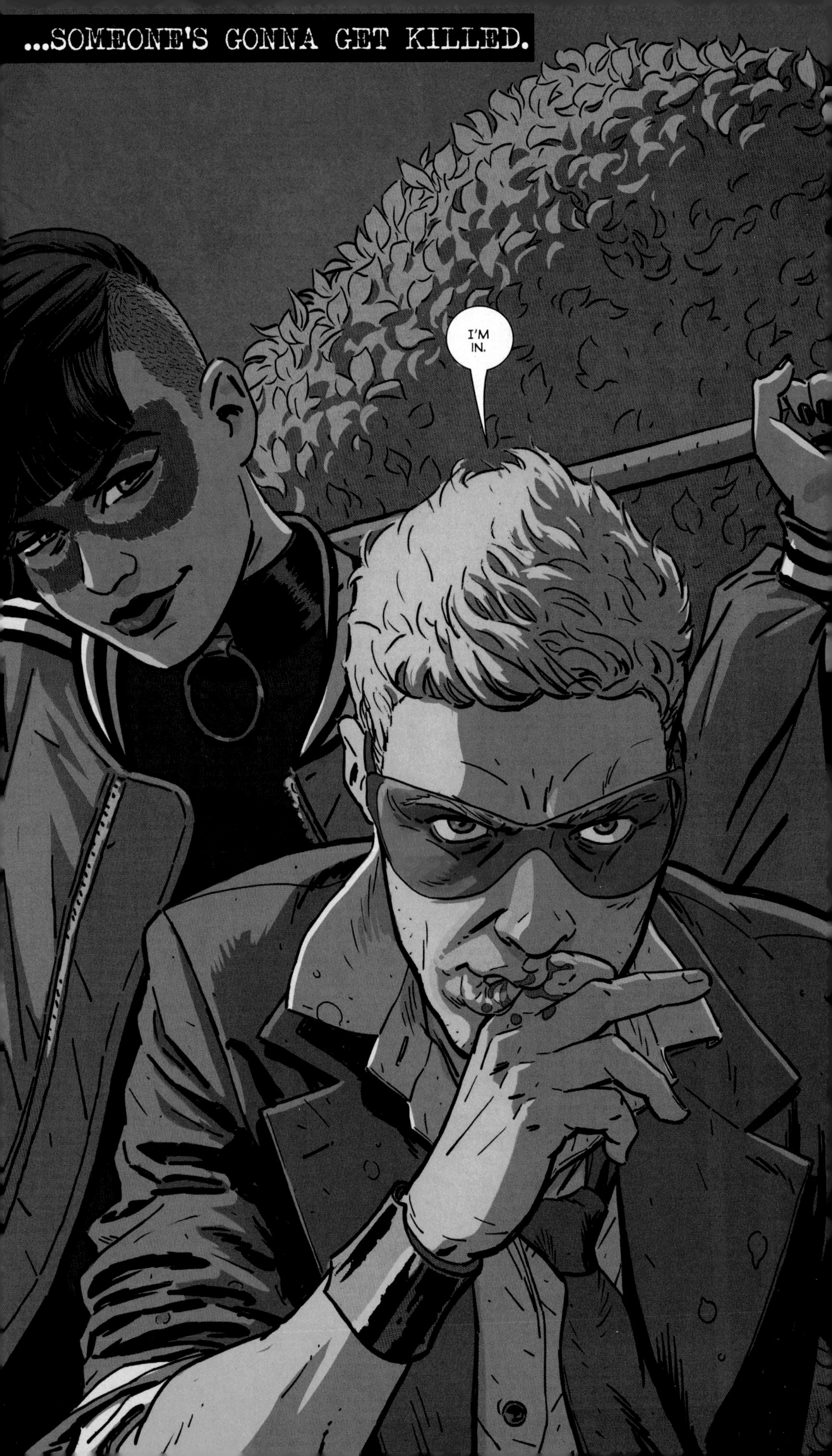
...SOMEONE'S GONNA GET KILLED.
I'M IN.

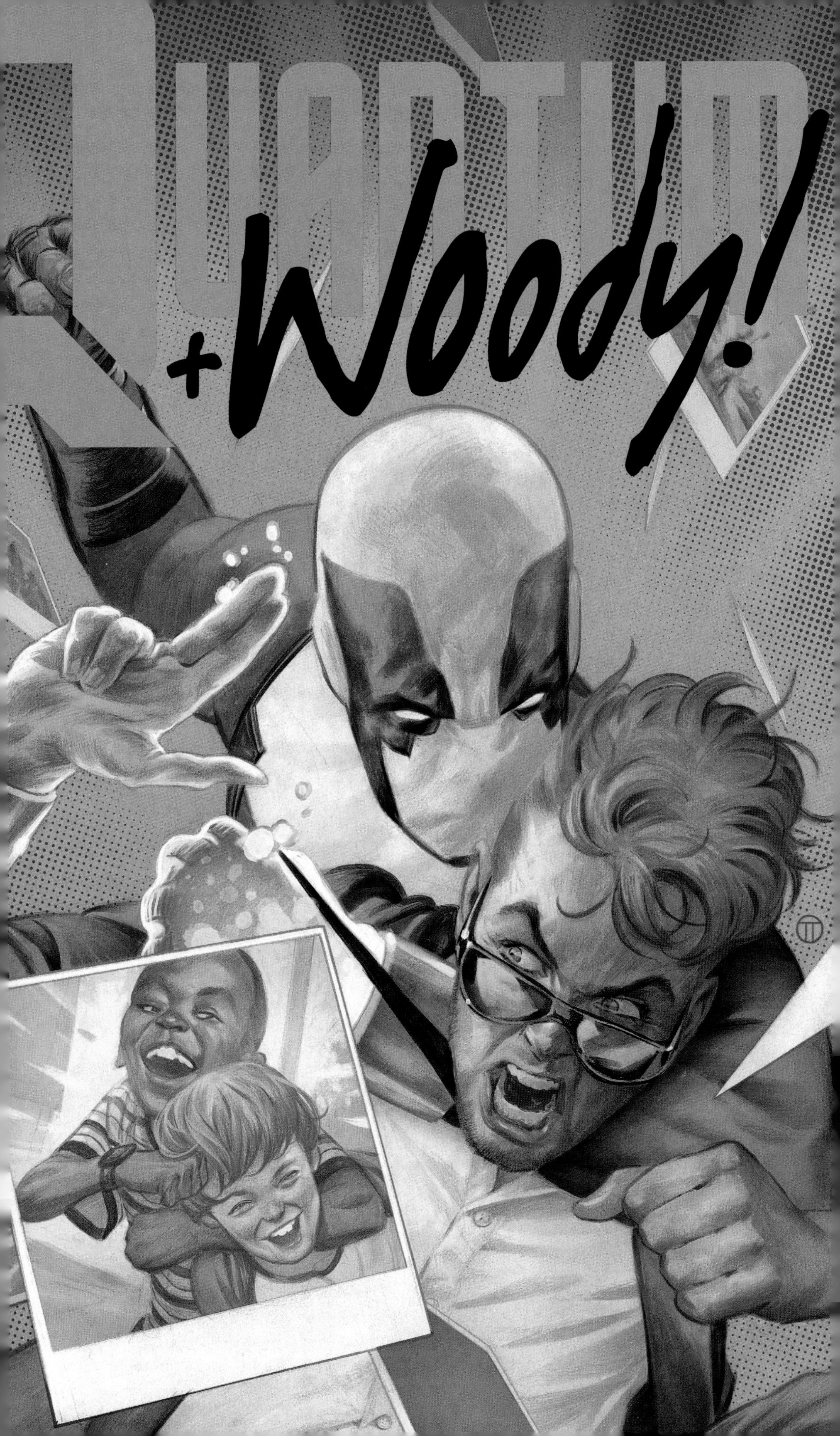
+Woody!

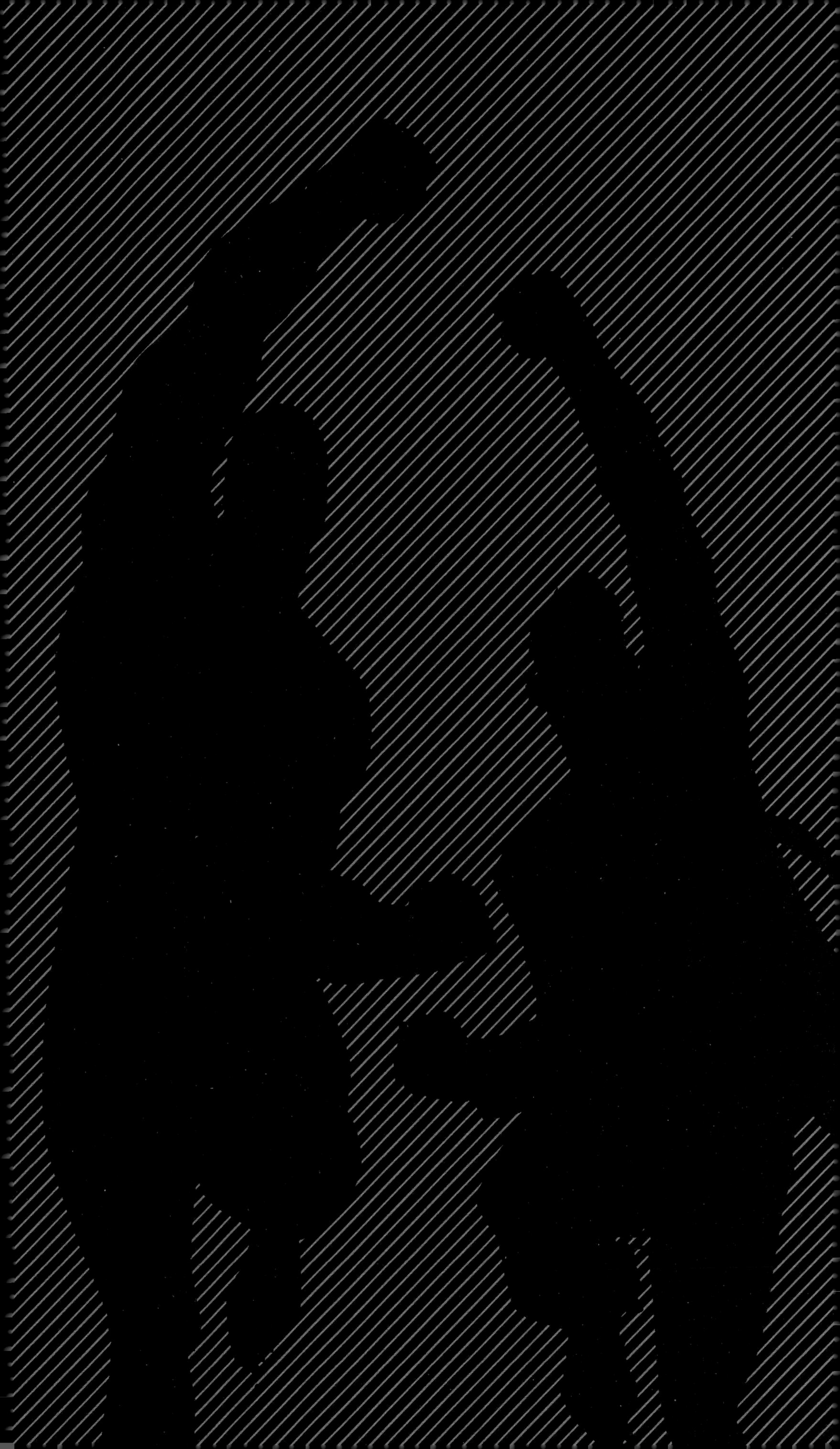

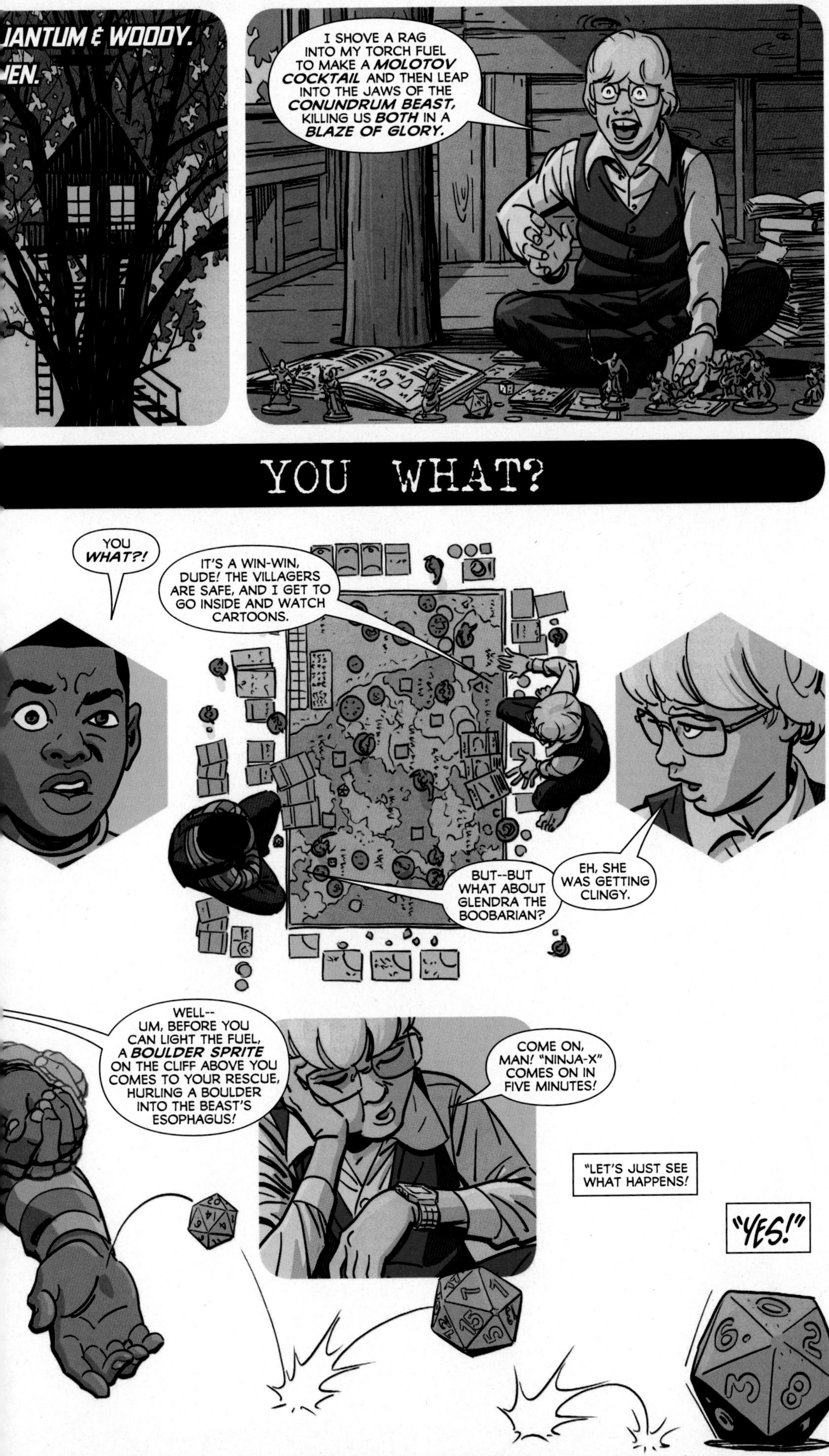

JANTUM & WOODY.
EN.
I SHOVE A RAG INTO MY TORCH FUEL TO MAKE A MOLOTOV COCKTAIL AND THEN LEAP INTO THE JAWS OF THE CONUNDRUM BEAST, KILLING US BOTH IN A BLAZE OF GLORY.
YOU WHAT?
YOU WHAT?!
IT'S A WIN-WIN, DUDE! THE VILLAGERS ARE SAFE, AND I GET TO GO INSIDE AND WATCH CARTOONS.
BUT--BUT WHAT ABOUT GLENDRA THE BOOBARIAN?
EH, SHE WAS GETTING CLINGY.
WELL-- UM, BEFORE YOU CAN LIGHT THE FUEL, A BOULDER SPRITE ON THE CLIFF ABOVE YOU COMES TO YOUR RESCUE, HURLING A BOULDER INTO THE BEAST'S ESOPHAGUS!
COME ON, MAN! "NINJA-X" COMES ON IN FIVE MINUTES!
"LET'S JUST SEE WHAT HAPPENS!
"YES!"

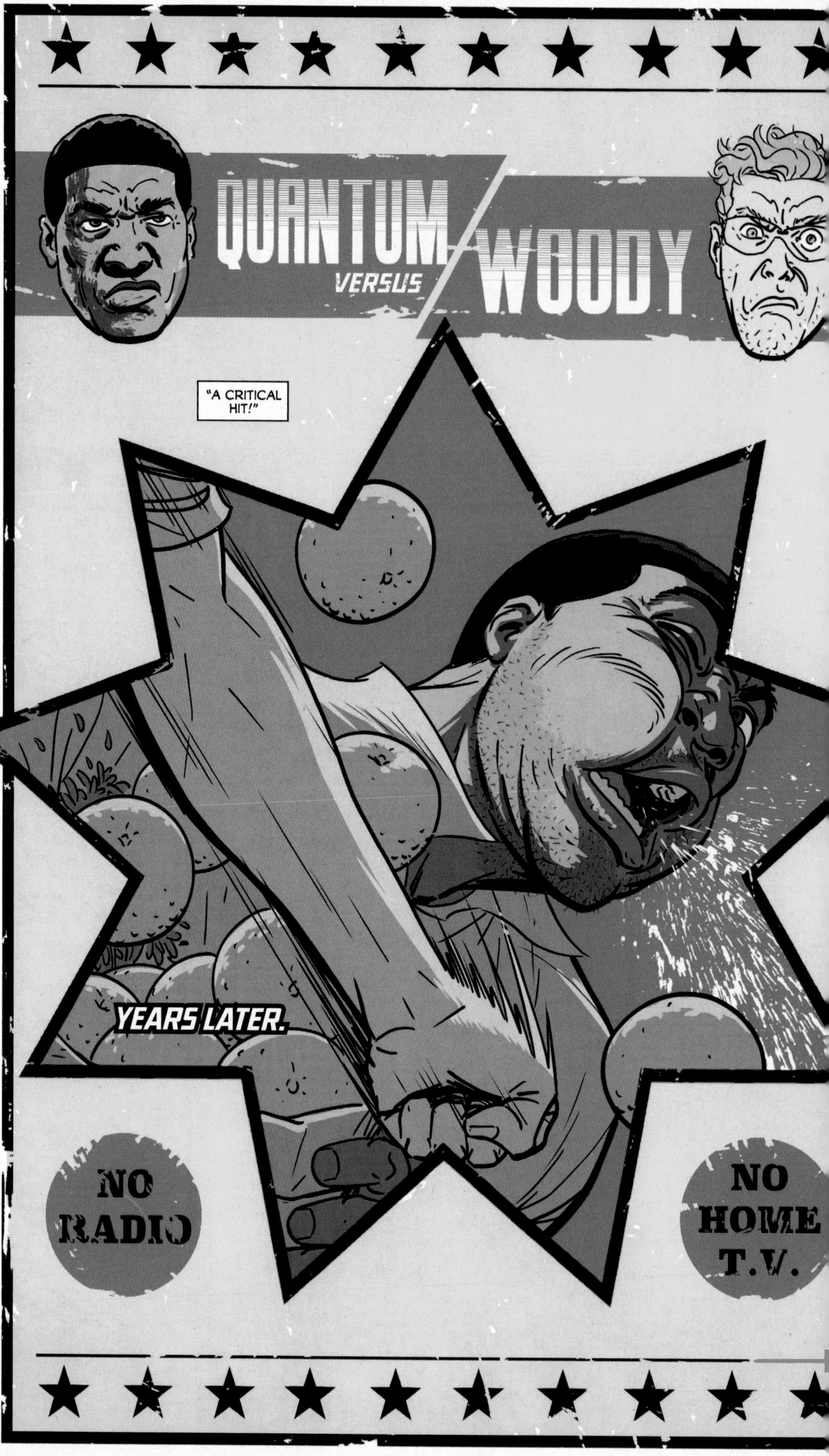
QUANTUM
VERSUS
WOODY
"A CRITICAL HIT!"
YEARS LATER.
NO RADIO
NO HOME T.V.

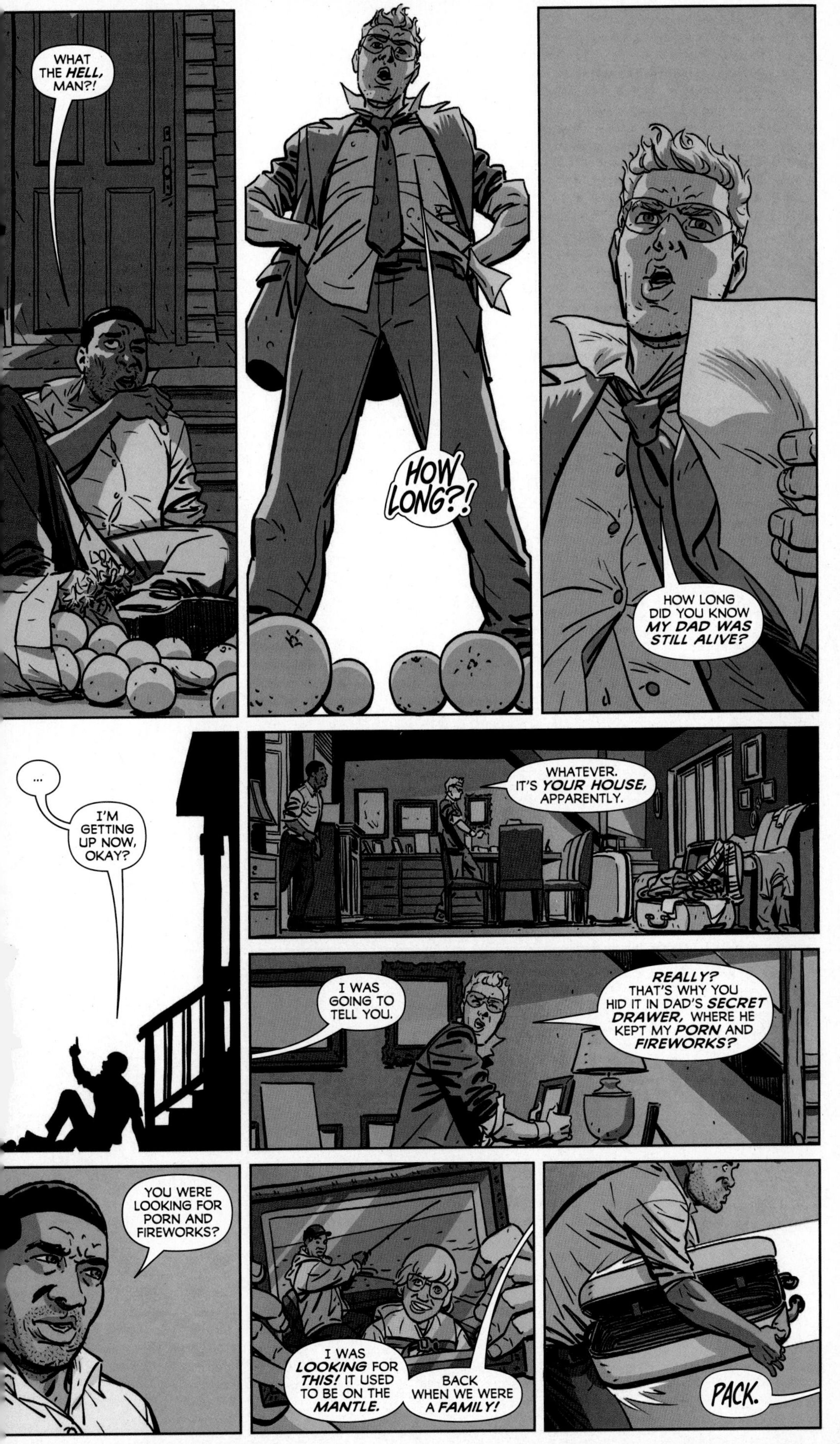

WHAT THE *HELL,* MAN?!
HOW LONG?!
HOW LONG DID YOU KNOW *MY DAD WAS STILL ALIVE?*
...
I'M GETTING UP NOW, OKAY?
WHATEVER. IT'S *YOUR HOUSE,* APPARENTLY.
I WAS GOING TO TELL YOU.
REALLY? THAT'S WHY YOU HID IT IN DAD'S *SECRET DRAWER,* WHERE HE KEPT MY *PORN* AND *FIREWORKS?*
YOU WERE LOOKING FOR PORN AND FIREWORKS?
I WAS *LOOKING* FOR *THIS!* IT USED TO BE ON THE *MANTLE.*
BACK WHEN WE WERE A *FAMILY!*
PACK.

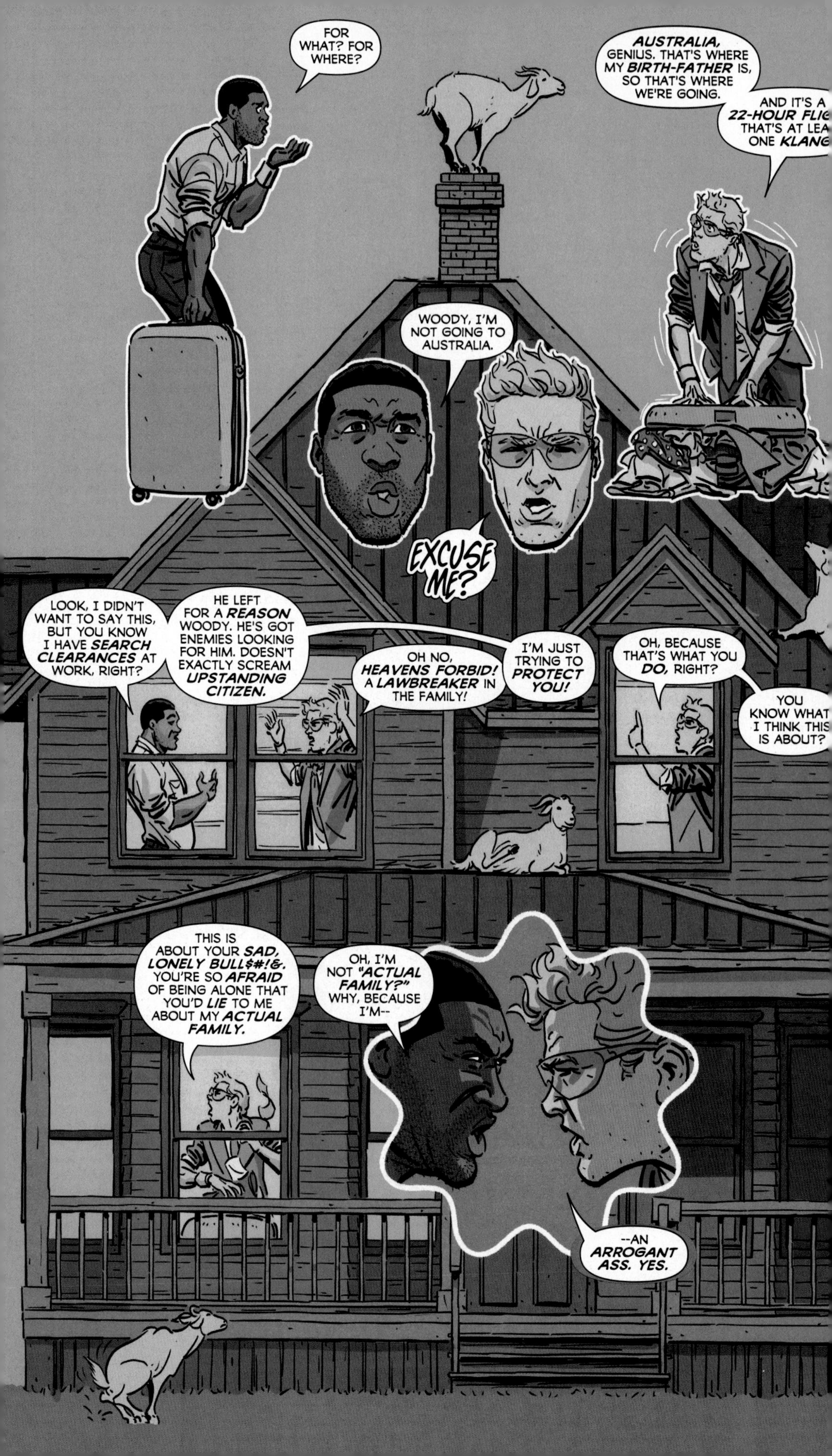
FOR WHAT? FOR WHERE?
AUSTRALIA, GENIUS. THAT'S WHERE MY BIRTH-FATHER IS, SO THAT'S WHERE WE'RE GOING.
AND IT'S A 22-HOUR FLIG THAT'S AT LEA ONE KLANG
WOODY, I'M NOT GOING TO AUSTRALIA.
EXCUSE ME?
LOOK, I DIDN'T WANT TO SAY THIS, BUT YOU KNOW I HAVE SEARCH CLEARANCES AT WORK, RIGHT?
HE LEFT FOR A REASON WOODY. HE'S GOT ENEMIES LOOKING FOR HIM. DOESN'T EXACTLY SCREAM UPSTANDING CITIZEN.
OH NO, HEAVENS FORBID! A LAWBREAKER IN THE FAMILY!
I'M JUST TRYING TO PROTECT YOU!
OH, BECAUSE THAT'S WHAT YOU DO, RIGHT?
YOU KNOW WHAT I THINK THIS IS ABOUT?
THIS IS ABOUT YOUR SAD, LONELY BULL$#!&. YOU'RE SO AFRAID OF BEING ALONE THAT YOU'D LIE TO ME ABOUT MY ACTUAL FAMILY.
OH, I'M NOT "ACTUAL FAMILY?" WHY, BECAUSE I'M--
--AN ARROGANT ASS. YES.

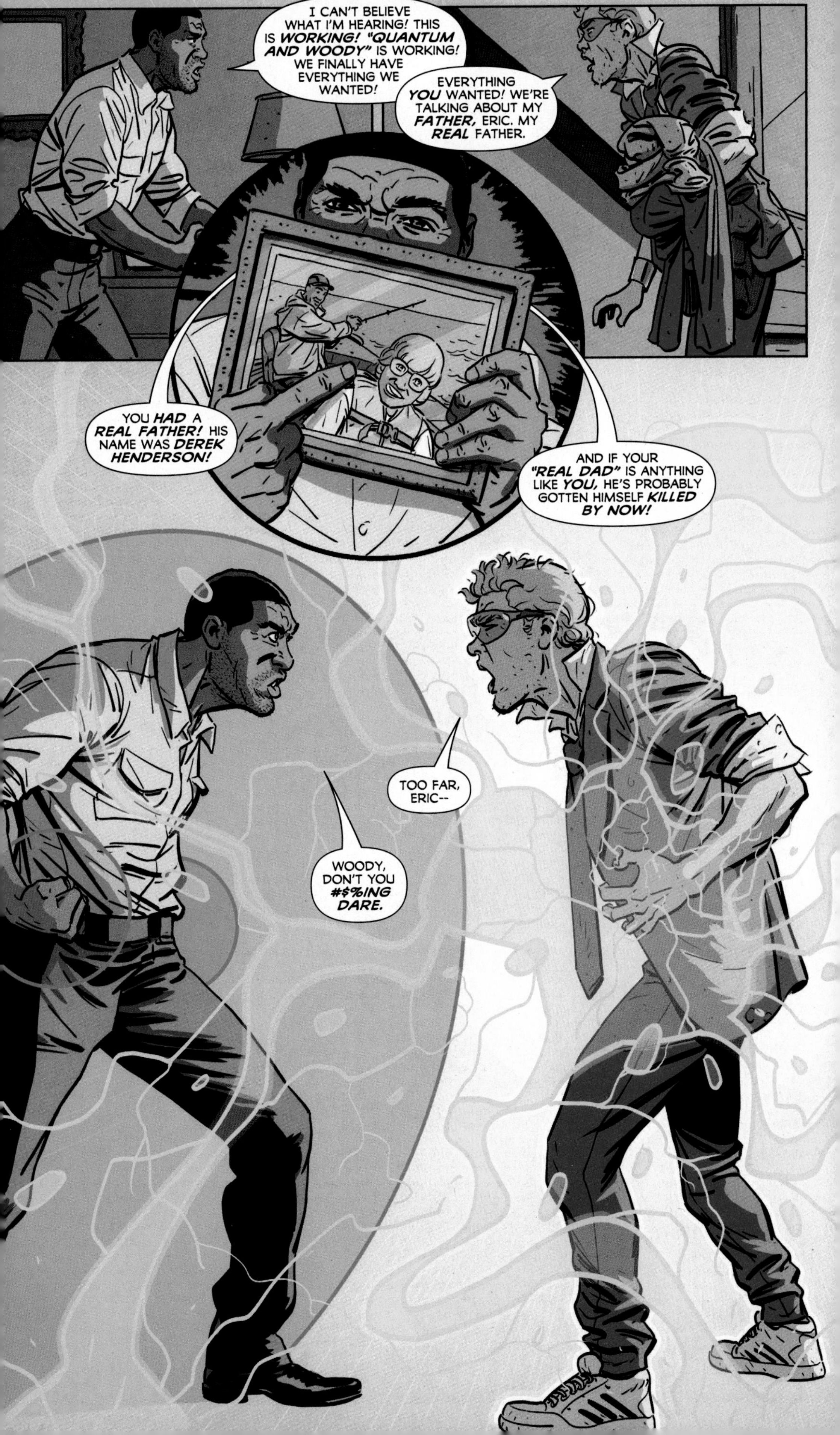
I CAN'T BELIEVE WHAT I'M HEARING! THIS IS WORKING! "QUANTUM AND WOODY" IS WORKING! WE FINALLY HAVE EVERYTHING WE WANTED!
EVERYTHING YOU WANTED! WE'RE TALKING ABOUT MY FATHER, ERIC. MY REAL FATHER.
YOU HAD A REAL FATHER! HIS NAME WAS DEREK HENDERSON!
AND IF YOUR "REAL DAD" IS ANYTHING LIKE YOU, HE'S PROBABLY GOTTEN HIMSELF KILLED BY NOW!
TOO FAR, ERIC--
WOODY, DON'T YOU #$%ING DARE.

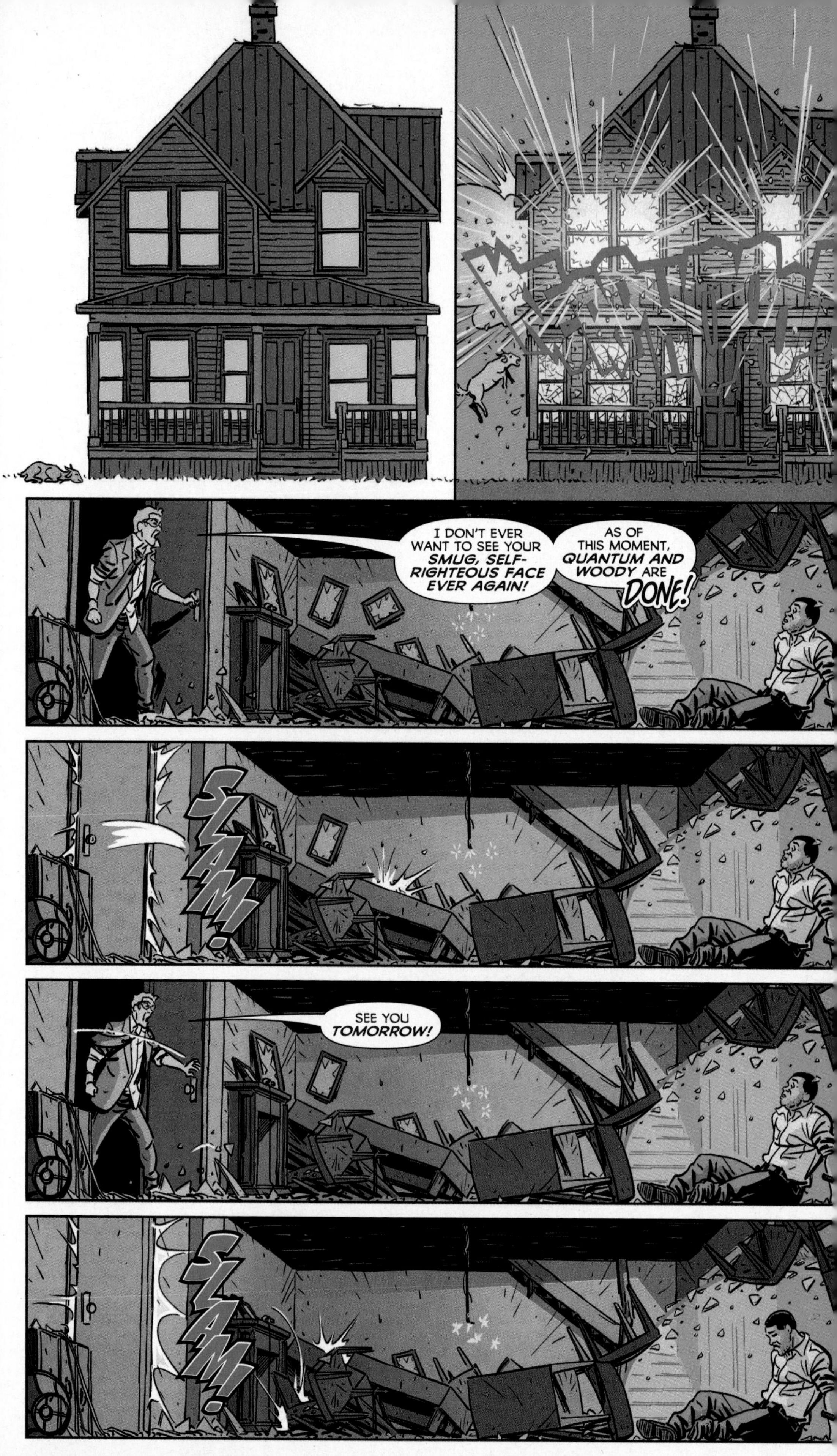
I DON'T EVER WANT TO SEE YOUR SMUG, SELF-RIGHTEOUS FACE EVER AGAIN!
AS OF THIS MOMENT, QUANTUM AND WOODY ARE DONE!
SLAM!
SEE YOU TOMORROW!
SLAM!

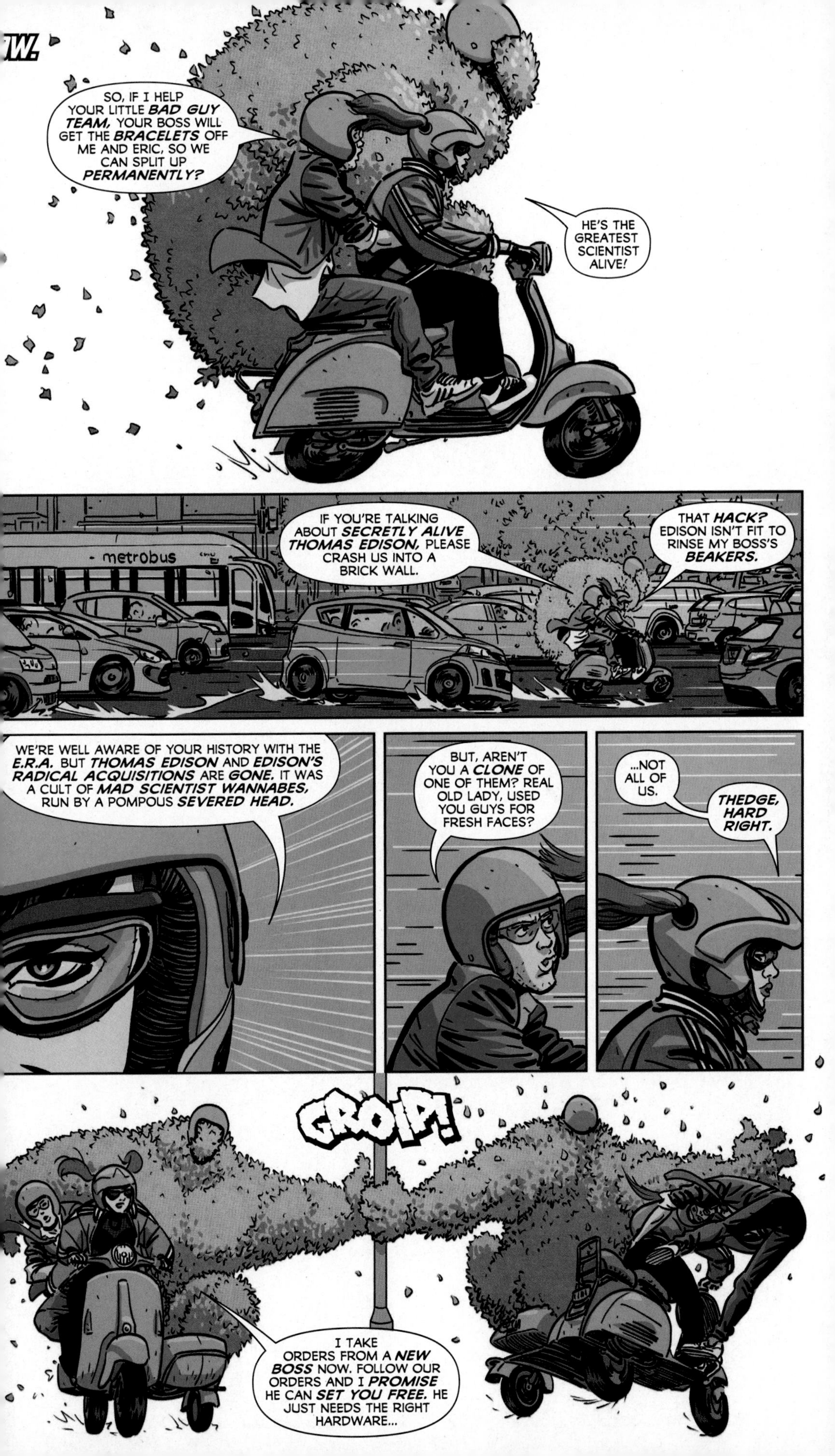

SO, IF I HELP YOUR LITTLE BAD GUY TEAM, YOUR BOSS WILL GET THE BRACELETS OFF ME AND ERIC, SO WE CAN SPLIT UP PERMANENTLY?
HE'S THE GREATEST SCIENTIST ALIVE!
metrobus
IF YOU'RE TALKING ABOUT SECRETLY ALIVE THOMAS EDISON, PLEASE CRASH US INTO A BRICK WALL.
THAT HACK? EDISON ISN'T FIT TO RINSE MY BOSS'S BEAKERS.
WE'RE WELL AWARE OF YOUR HISTORY WITH THE E.R.A. BUT THOMAS EDISON AND EDISON'S RADICAL ACQUISITIONS ARE GONE. IT WAS A CULT OF MAD SCIENTIST WANNABES, RUN BY A POMPOUS SEVERED HEAD.
BUT, AREN'T YOU A CLONE OF ONE OF THEM? REAL OLD LADY, USED YOU GUYS FOR FRESH FACES?
...NOT ALL OF US.
THEDGE, HARD RIGHT.
GROIP!
I TAKE ORDERS FROM A NEW BOSS NOW. FOLLOW OUR ORDERS AND I PROMISE HE CAN SET YOU FREE. HE JUST NEEDS THE RIGHT HARDWARE...

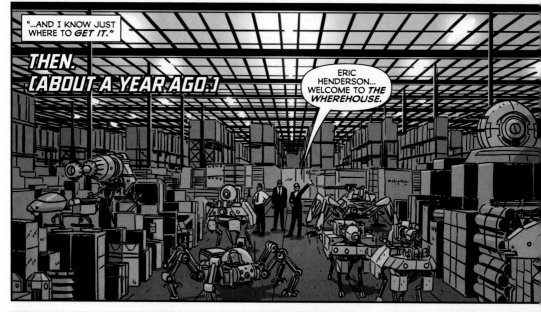

"...AND I KNOW JUST WHERE TO *GET IT.*"

THEN. [ABOUT A YEAR AGO.]

ERIC HENDERSON... WELCOME TO *THE WHEREHOUSE.*

EVERY *SUPERWEAPON,* EVERY *DOOMSDAY DEVICE* CONFISCATED BY THE AUTHORITIES FROM A *SCIENCE TERRORIST* ENDS UP HERE.

--AND WE'VE BEEN LOOKING FOR A MAN LIKE *YOU* TO BE OUR *LAST LINE OF DEFENSE.*

HOLY MOLY. WHAT'S THAT ONE DO?

QUICK-DRYING *FOAM GRENADES* FOR NON-LETHAL APPREHENSION.

AND THAT ONE?

"THE SWAY GUN INDUCES *MIL... SUGGESTIV...* FOR CROWD DISPERSAL.

...AND *THAT* ONE?

EPSILON

THE ONE YOU *RECOVERED* FOR US FROM DOCTOR UNFATHOMABLE... *THE EPSILON BOX.*

--AND YOU DO NOT *ASK* ABOUT *THE EPSILON BOX!*

OKAY, OKAY, *JEEZ.*

FREEZE, PIGS! I'M AN EV... MAD SCIENTIST AND THIS IS A--

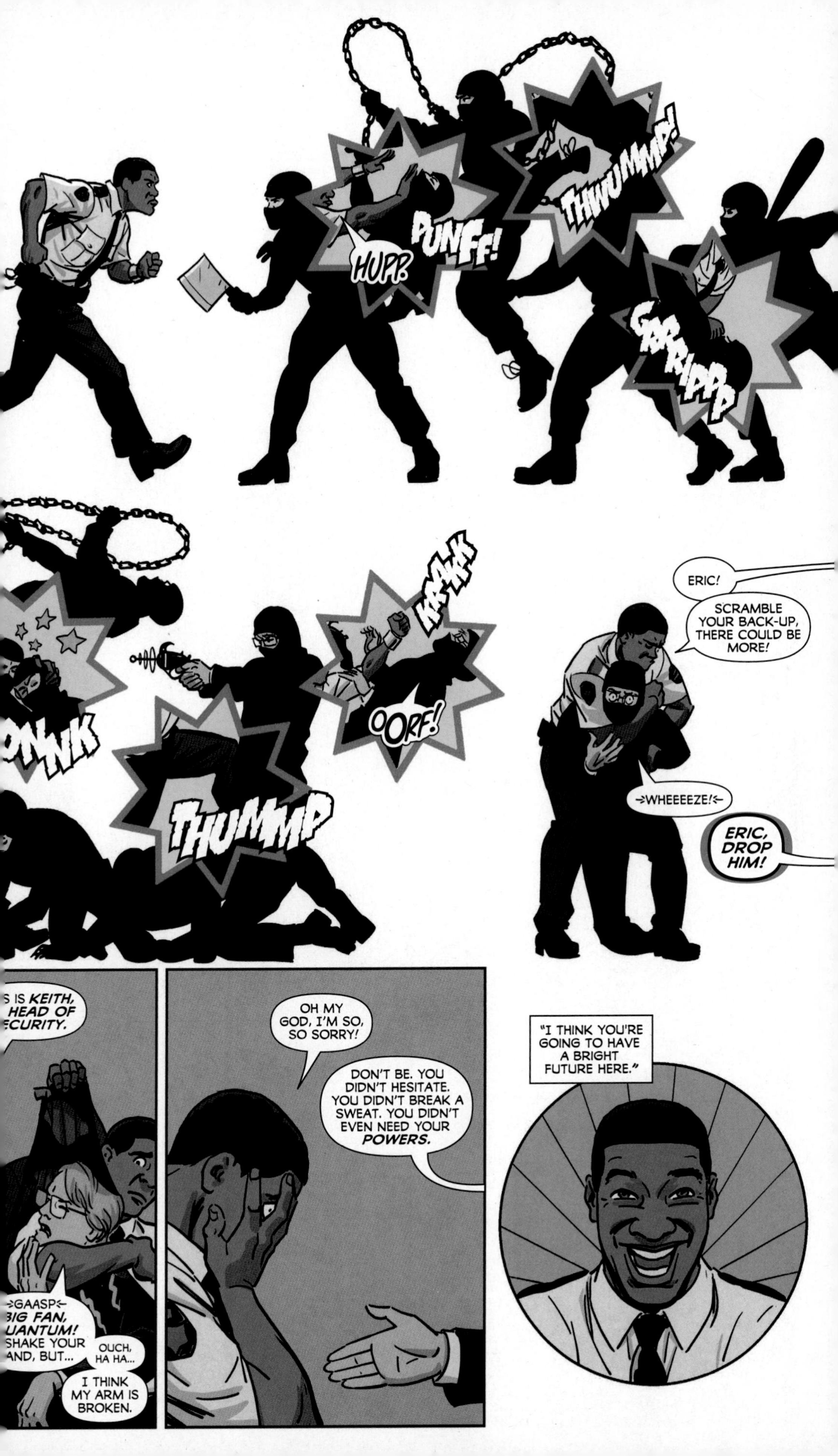
HUPP.
PUNFF!
THWUMMP!
GRRIPPP
ONK
KRAKK
OORF!
THUMMP
ERIC!
SCRAMBLE YOUR BACK-UP, THERE COULD BE MORE!
WHEEEEZE!
ERIC, DROP HIM!
S IS KEITH, HEAD OF ECURITY.
GAASP
BIG FAN, UANTUM!
SHAKE YOUR AND, BUT...
OUCH, HA HA...
I THINK MY ARM IS BROKEN.
OH MY GOD, I'M SO, SO SORRY!
DON'T BE. YOU DIDN'T HESITATE. YOU DIDN'T BREAK A SWEAT. YOU DIDN'T EVEN NEED YOUR POWERS.
"I THINK YOU'RE GOING TO HAVE A BRIGHT FUTURE HERE."

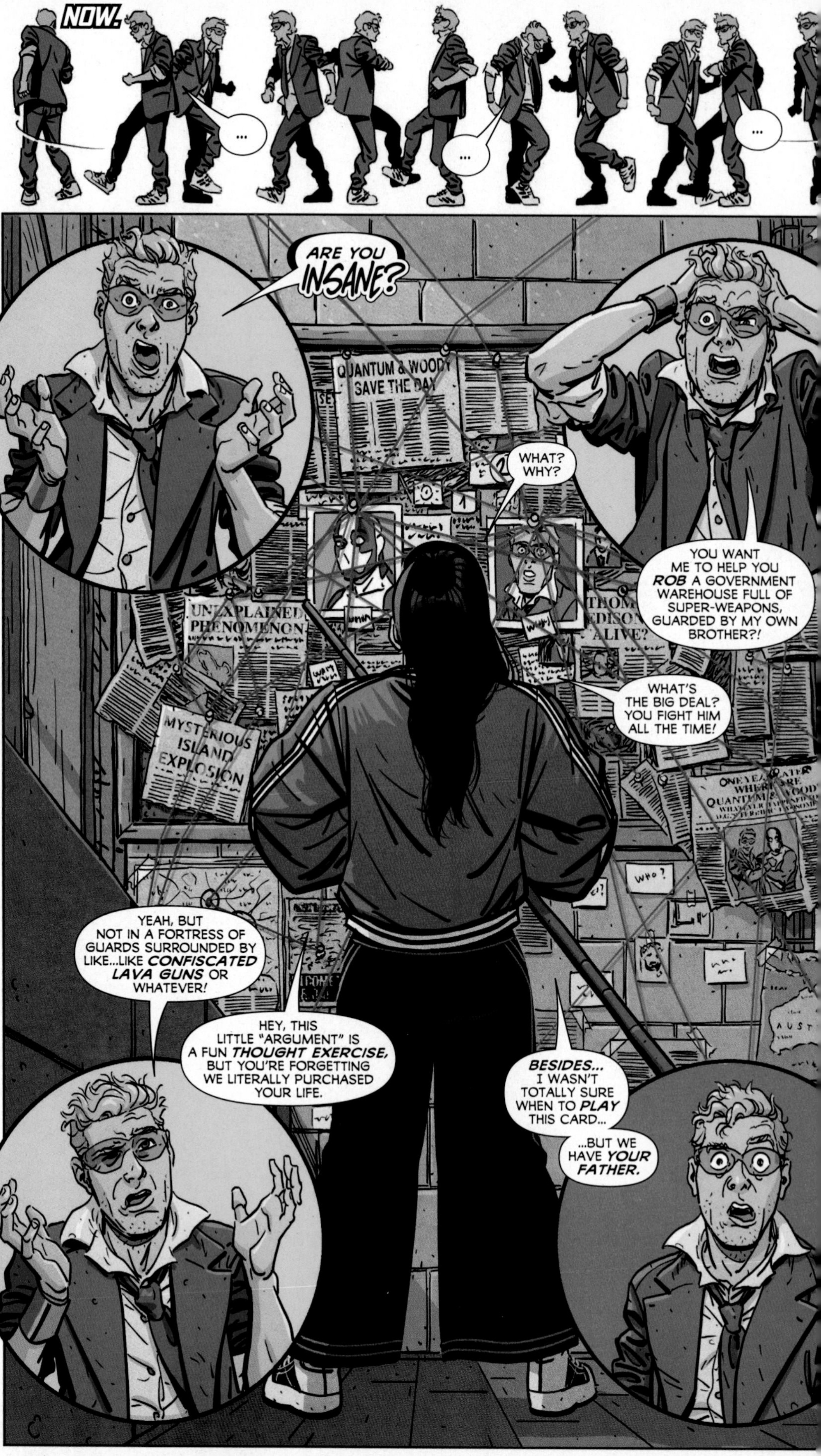
NOW.
...
...
...
ARE YOU INSANE?
WHAT? WHY?
YOU WANT ME TO HELP YOU ROB A GOVERNMENT WAREHOUSE FULL OF SUPER-WEAPONS, GUARDED BY MY OWN BROTHER?!
WHAT'S THE BIG DEAL? YOU FIGHT HIM ALL THE TIME!
YEAH, BUT NOT IN A FORTRESS OF GUARDS SURROUNDED BY LIKE...LIKE CONFISCATED LAVA GUNS OR WHATEVER!
HEY, THIS LITTLE "ARGUMENT" IS A FUN THOUGHT EXERCISE, BUT YOU'RE FORGETTING WE LITERALLY PURCHASED YOUR LIFE.
BESIDES... I WASN'T TOTALLY SURE WHEN TO PLAY THIS CARD...
...BUT WE HAVE YOUR FATHER.
QUANTUM & WOODY SAVE THE DAY
UNEXPLAINED PHENOMENON
MYSTERIOUS ISLAND EXPLOSION
WHO?

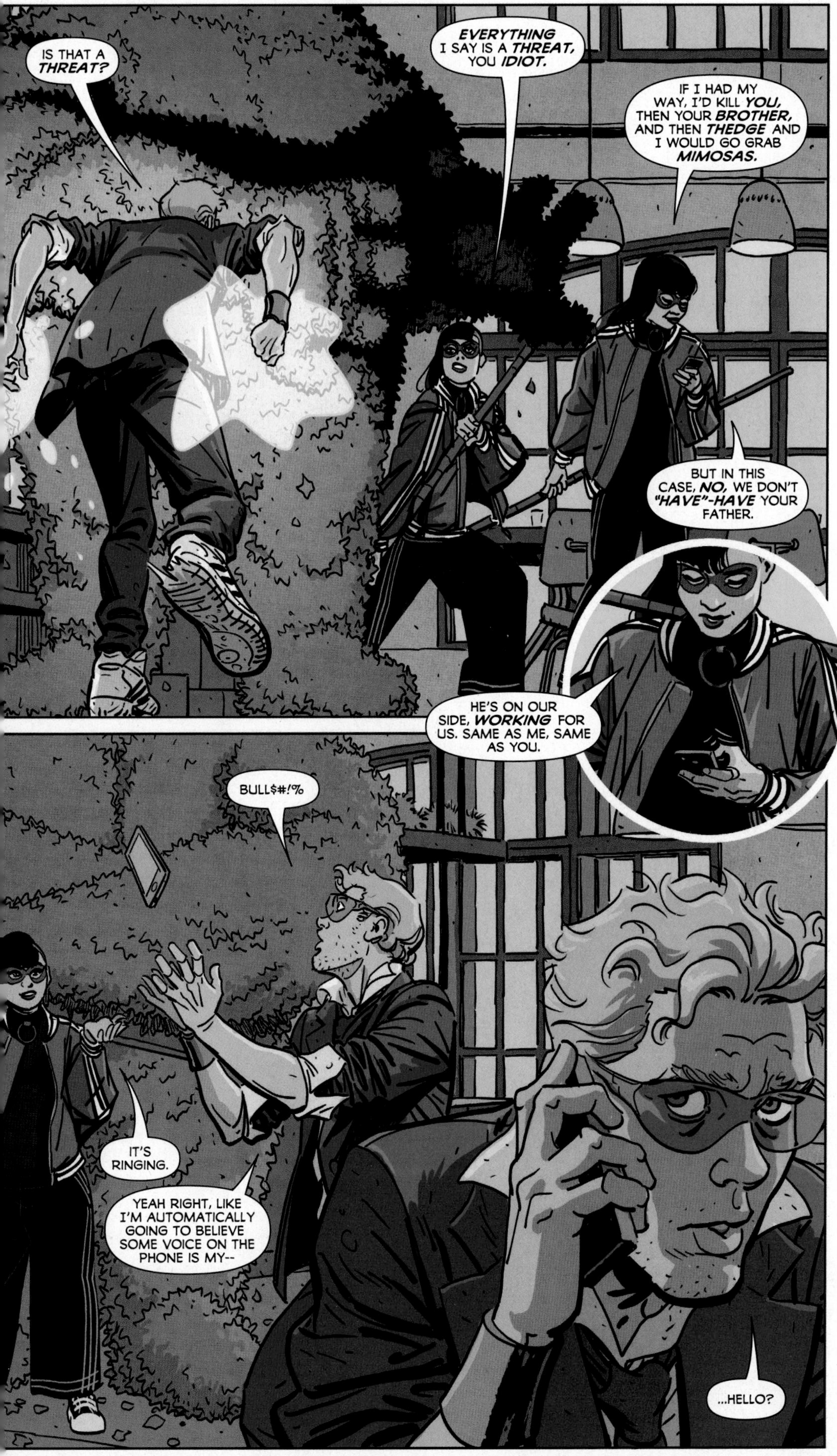
IS THAT A THREAT?
EVERYTHING I SAY IS A THREAT, YOU IDIOT.
IF I HAD MY WAY, I'D KILL YOU, THEN YOUR BROTHER, AND THEN THEDGE AND I WOULD GO GRAB MIMOSAS.
BUT IN THIS CASE, NO, WE DON'T "HAVE"-HAVE YOUR FATHER.
HE'S ON OUR SIDE, WORKING FOR US. SAME AS ME, SAME AS YOU.
BULL$#!%
IT'S RINGING.
YEAH RIGHT, LIKE I'M AUTOMATICALLY GOING TO BELIEVE SOME VOICE ON THE PHONE IS MY--
...HELLO?

UM... YEAH, IT'S *ME.*

AND I GUESS YOU'RE SUPPOSED TO BE *YOU.*

OKAY, WISE YOU'RE REAL IF YOU'RE F *WHO YO YOU ARE, MOM'S* NAME

...*NO CLUE,* HUH? GUESS THAT ACTUALLY CHECKS OUT.

OKAY, THEN... WHERE WAS I *BORN?*

SERIOUSLY? NOT EVEN A *GUESS?*

...YES, I CAN SEE HOW *PROVING* YOU'RE A DEADBEAT DAD IS "A REAL CATCH-22." *OKAY,* I GOT ONE...WHERE WAS I *CONCEIVED?*

OKAY, OKAY, *ENOUGH!* THAT'S *DISGUSTING!*

I'M *HANGING UP* NOW!

CONVINCED?

HE DESCRIBED MY MOM'S BURNT-ORANGE *1982 HATCHBACK CAVALIER* RIGHT DOWN TO THE *FUZZY DICE.*

ARE SOME OF THOSE *EUPHEMISMS?*

WAIT--HE SAI "SEE US BOTH WHO'S *BO*

WH DO YOU GEN

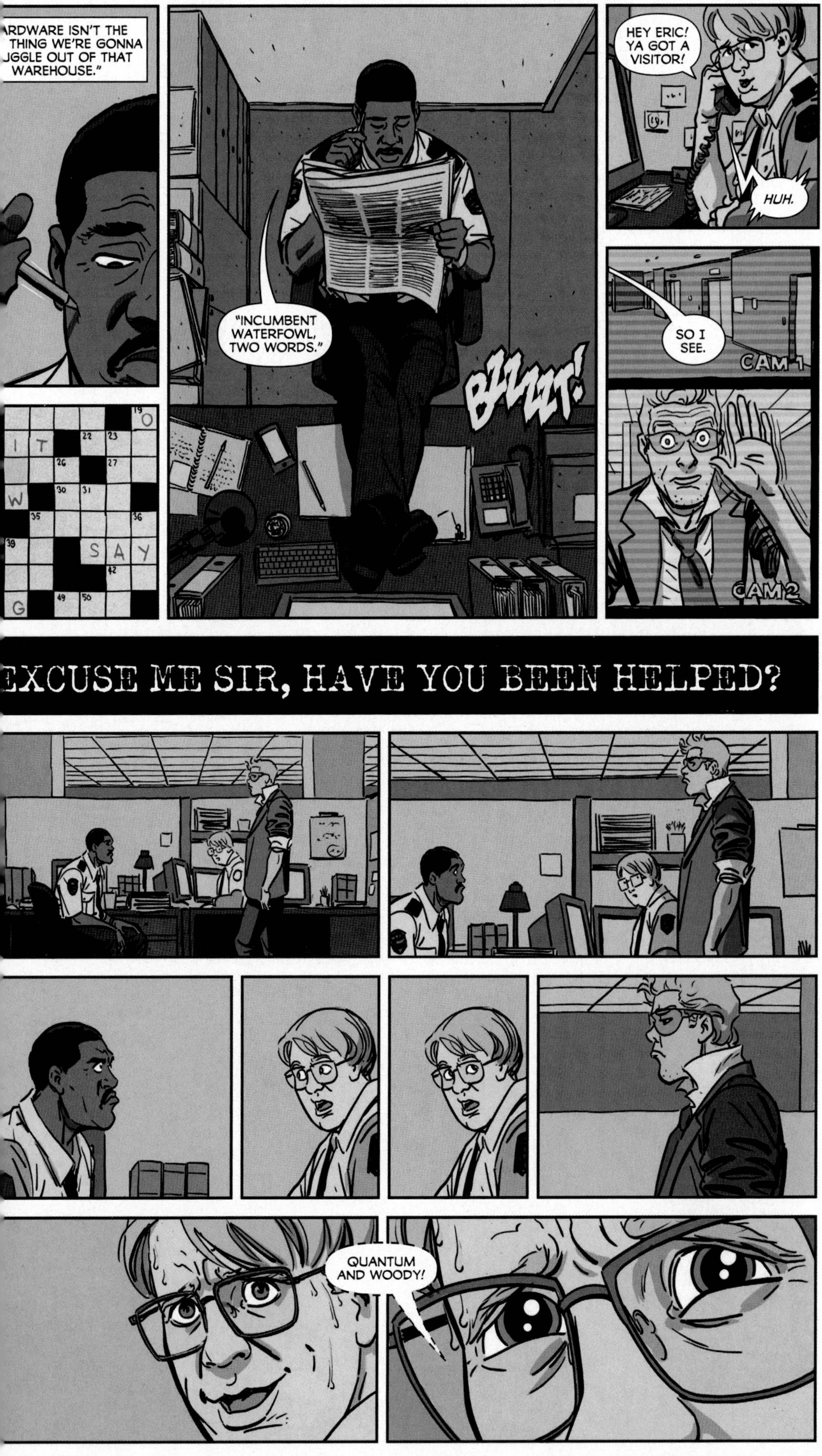

RDWARE ISN'T THE
THING WE'RE GONNA
UGGLE OUT OF THAT
WAREHOUSE."
"INCUMBENT WATERFOWL, TWO WORDS."
BZZZZT!
HEY ERIC! YA GOT A VISITOR!
HUH.
SO I SEE.
CAM 1
CAM 2
EXCUSE ME SIR, HAVE YOU BEEN HELPED?
QUANTUM AND WOODY!

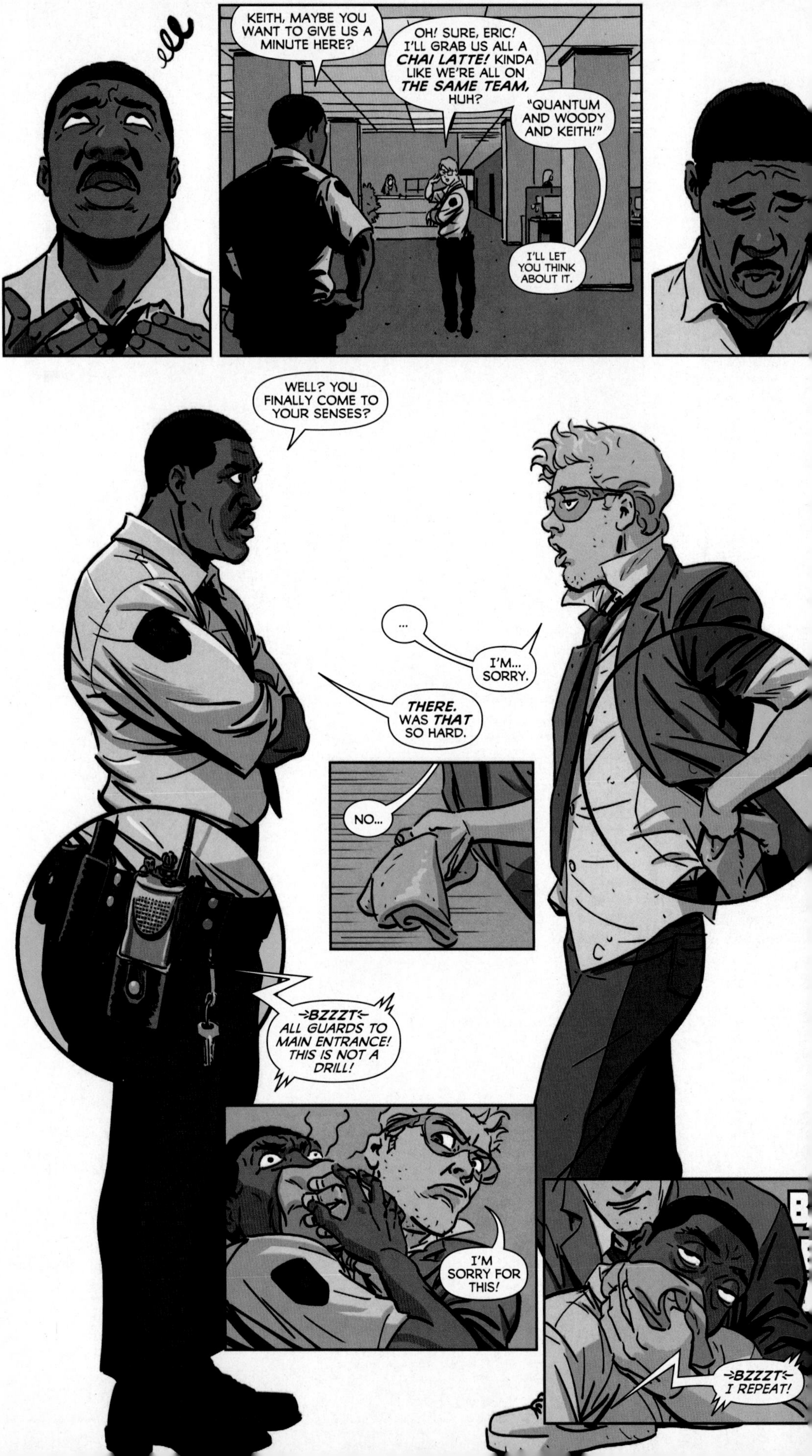
KEITH, MAYBE YOU WANT TO GIVE US A MINUTE HERE?
OH! SURE, ERIC! I'LL GRAB US ALL A *CHAI LATTE!* KINDA LIKE WE'RE ALL ON *THE SAME TEAM,* HUH?
"QUANTUM AND WOODY AND KEITH!"
I'LL LET YOU THINK ABOUT IT.
WELL? YOU FINALLY COME TO YOUR SENSES?
...
I'M... SORRY.
THERE. WAS *THAT* SO HARD.
NO...
BZZZT ALL GUARDS TO MAIN ENTRANCE! THIS IS NOT A DRILL!
I'M SORRY FOR THIS!
BZZZT I REPEAT!

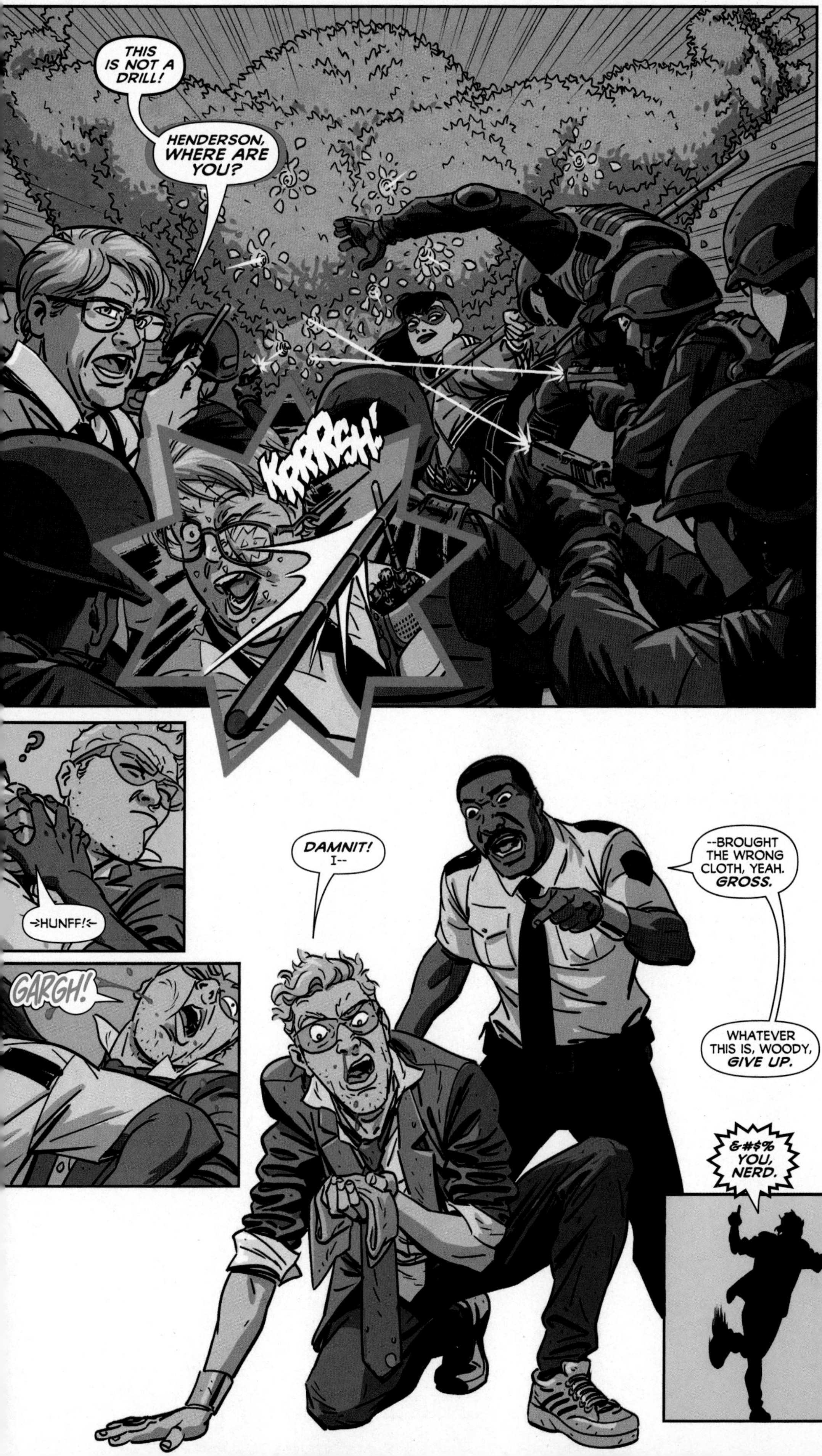
THIS IS NOT A DRILL!
HENDERSON, WHERE ARE YOU?
KRRRSH!
?
HUNFF!
GARGH!
DAMNIT! I--
--BROUGHT THE WRONG CLOTH, YEAH. GROSS.
WHATEVER THIS IS, WOODY, GIVE UP.
&#$% YOU, NERD.

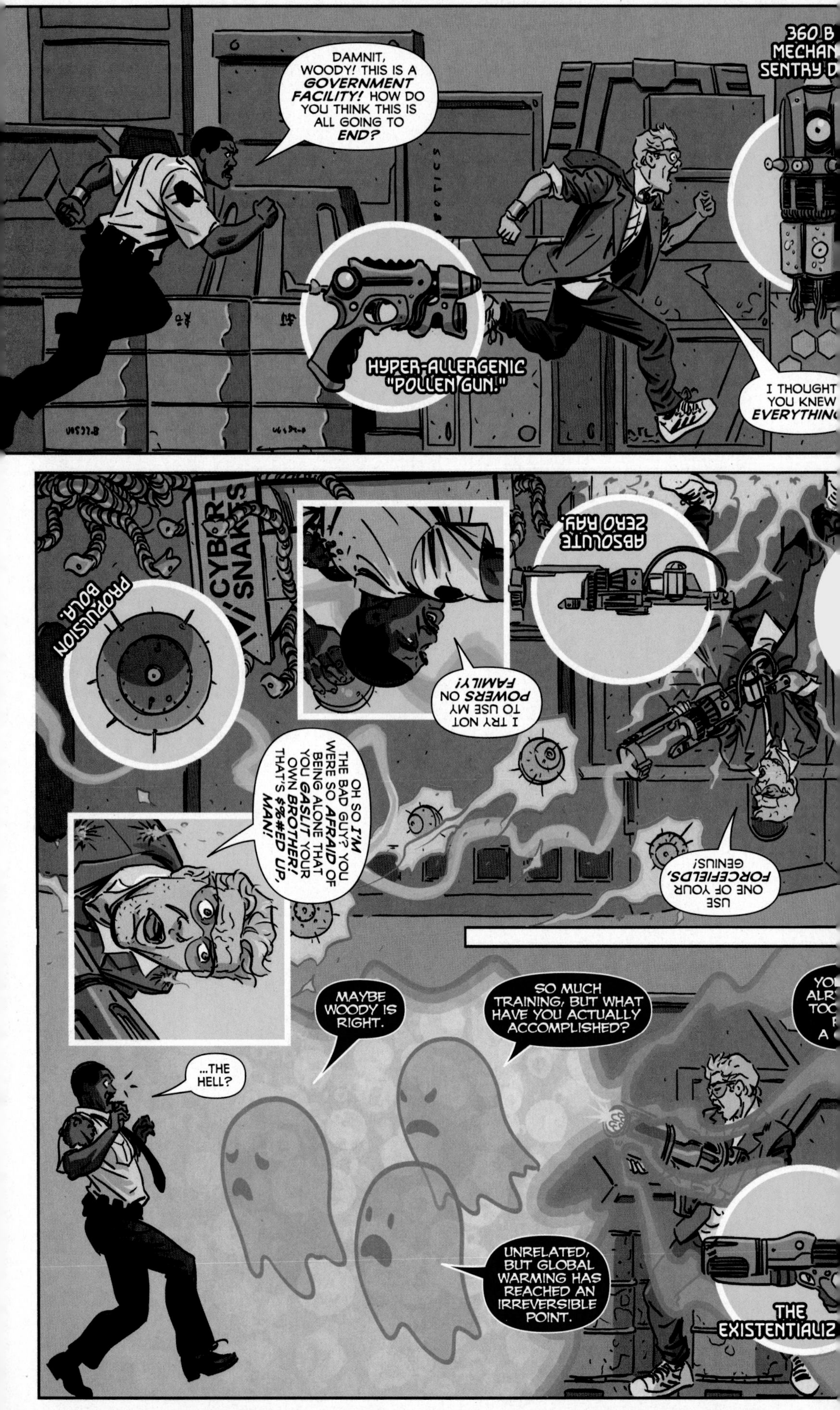
DAMNIT, WOODY! THIS IS A GOVERNMENT FACILITY! HOW DO YOU THINK THIS IS ALL GOING TO END?
HYPER-ALLERGENIC "POLLEN GUN."
360 B
MECHAN
SENTRY D
I THOUGHT YOU KNEW EVERYTHIN
CYBER-SNAKES
PROPULSION BOLA.
I TRY NOT TO USE MY POWERS ON FAMILY!
ABSOLUTE ZERO RAY.
OH SO I'M THE BAD GUY? YOU WERE SO AFRAID OF BEING ALONE THAT YOU GASLIT YOUR OWN BROTHER! THAT'S $%#ED UP, MAN!
USE ONE OF YOUR FORCEFIELDS, GENIUS!
MAYBE WOODY IS RIGHT.
SO MUCH TRAINING, BUT WHAT HAVE YOU ACTUALLY ACCOMPLISHED?
...THE HELL?
UNRELATED, BUT GLOBAL WARMING HAS REACHED AN IRREVERSIBLE POINT.
THE EXISTENTIALIZ

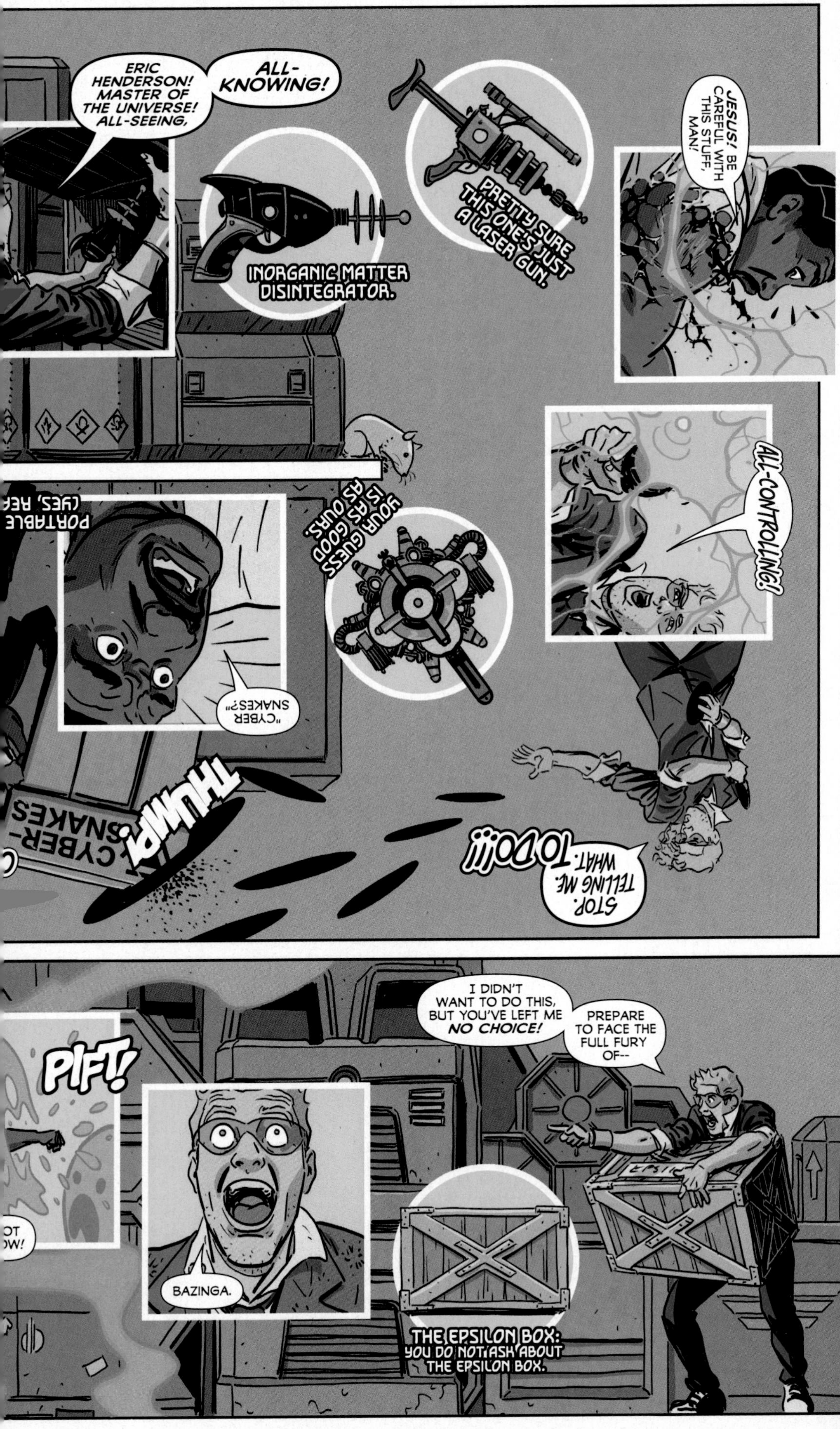

ERIC HENDERSON! MASTER OF THE UNIVERSE! ALL-SEEING,
ALL-KNOWING!
INORGANIC MATTER DISINTEGRATOR.
PRETTY SURE THIS ONE'S JUST A LASER GUN.
JESUS! BE CAREFUL WITH THIS STUFF, MAN!
ALL-CONTROLLING!
YOUR GUESS IS AS GOOD AS OURS.
"CYBER SNAKES?"
STOP. TELLING ME. WHAT. TO DO!!!
THUMP!
CYBER-SNAKES
I DIDN'T WANT TO DO THIS, BUT YOU'VE LEFT ME NO CHOICE!
PREPARE TO FACE THE FULL FURY OF--
PIFT!
BAZINGA.
THE EPSILON BOX: YOU DO NOT ASK ABOUT THE EPSILON BOX.

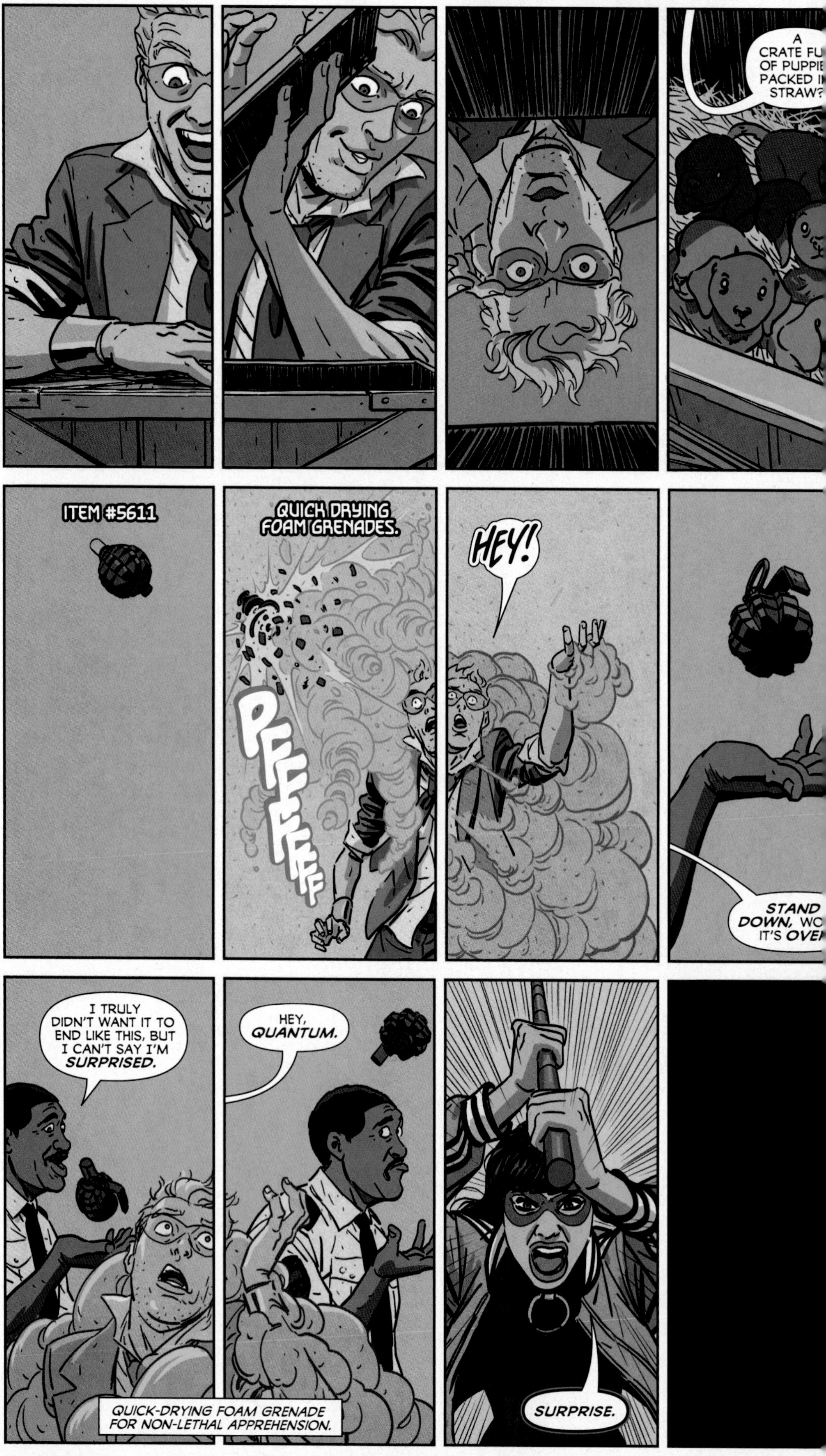

A CRATE FU OF PUPPIE PACKED I STRAW?
ITEM #5611
QUICK DRYING FOAM GRENADES.
PFFFFFF
HEY!
STAND DOWN, WO IT'S OVE
I TRULY DIDN'T WANT IT TO END LIKE THIS, BUT I CAN'T SAY I'M SURPRISED.
HEY, QUANTUM.
QUICK-DRYING FOAM GRENADE FOR NON-LETHAL APPREHENSION.
SURPRISE.

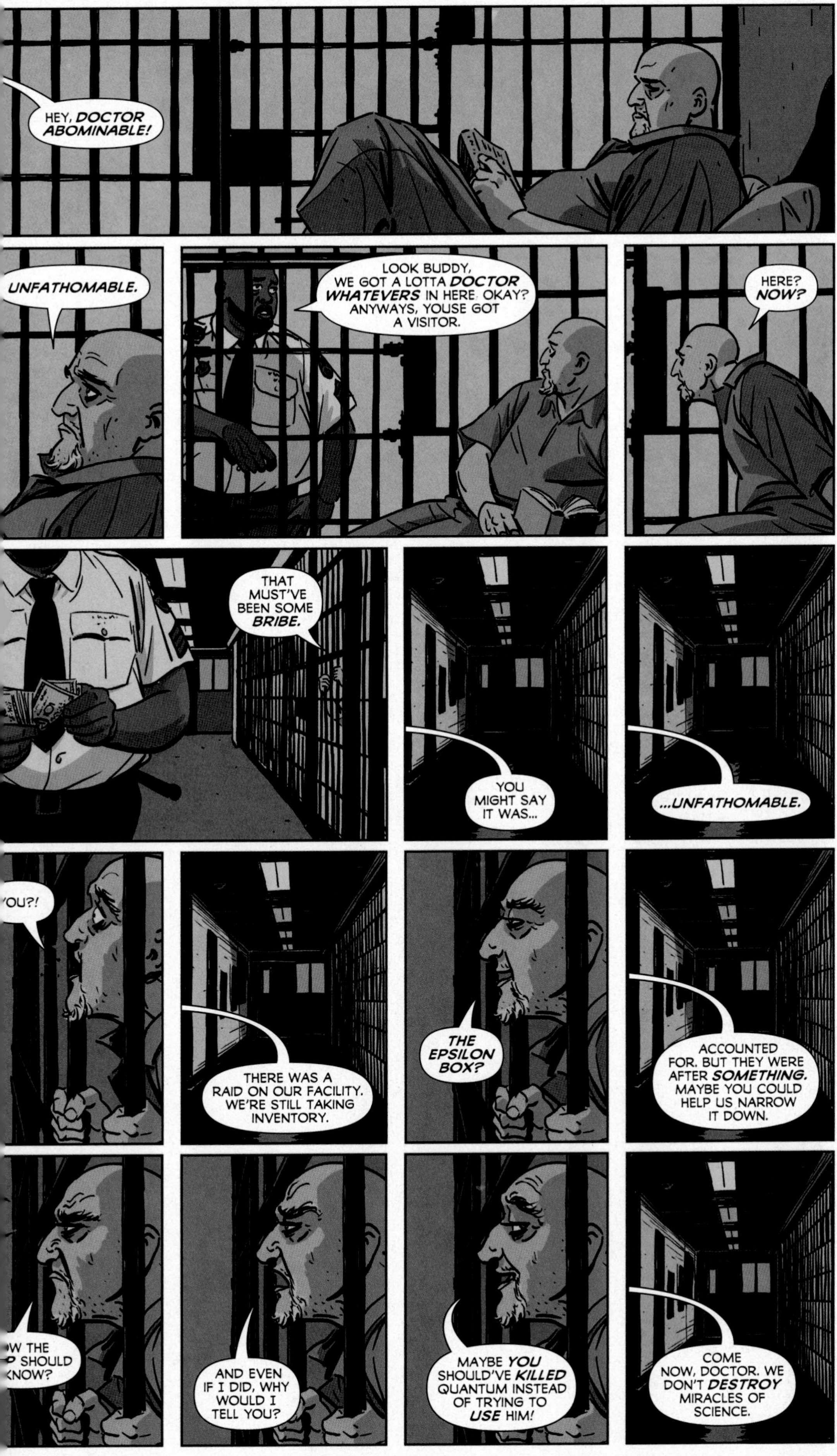
HEY, DOCTOR ABOMINABLE!
UNFATHOMABLE.
LOOK BUDDY, WE GOT A LOTTA DOCTOR WHATEVERS IN HERE. OKAY? ANYWAYS, YOUSE GOT A VISITOR.
HERE? NOW?
THAT MUST'VE BEEN SOME BRIBE.
YOU MIGHT SAY IT WAS...
...UNFATHOMABLE.
OU?!
THERE WAS A RAID ON OUR FACILITY. WE'RE STILL TAKING INVENTORY.
THE EPSILON BOX?
ACCOUNTED FOR. BUT THEY WERE AFTER SOMETHING. MAYBE YOU COULD HELP US NARROW IT DOWN.
W THE SHOULD NOW?
AND EVEN IF I DID, WHY WOULD I TELL YOU?
MAYBE YOU SHOULD'VE KILLED QUANTUM INSTEAD OF TRYING TO USE HIM!
COME NOW, DOCTOR. WE DON'T DESTROY MIRACLES OF SCIENCE.

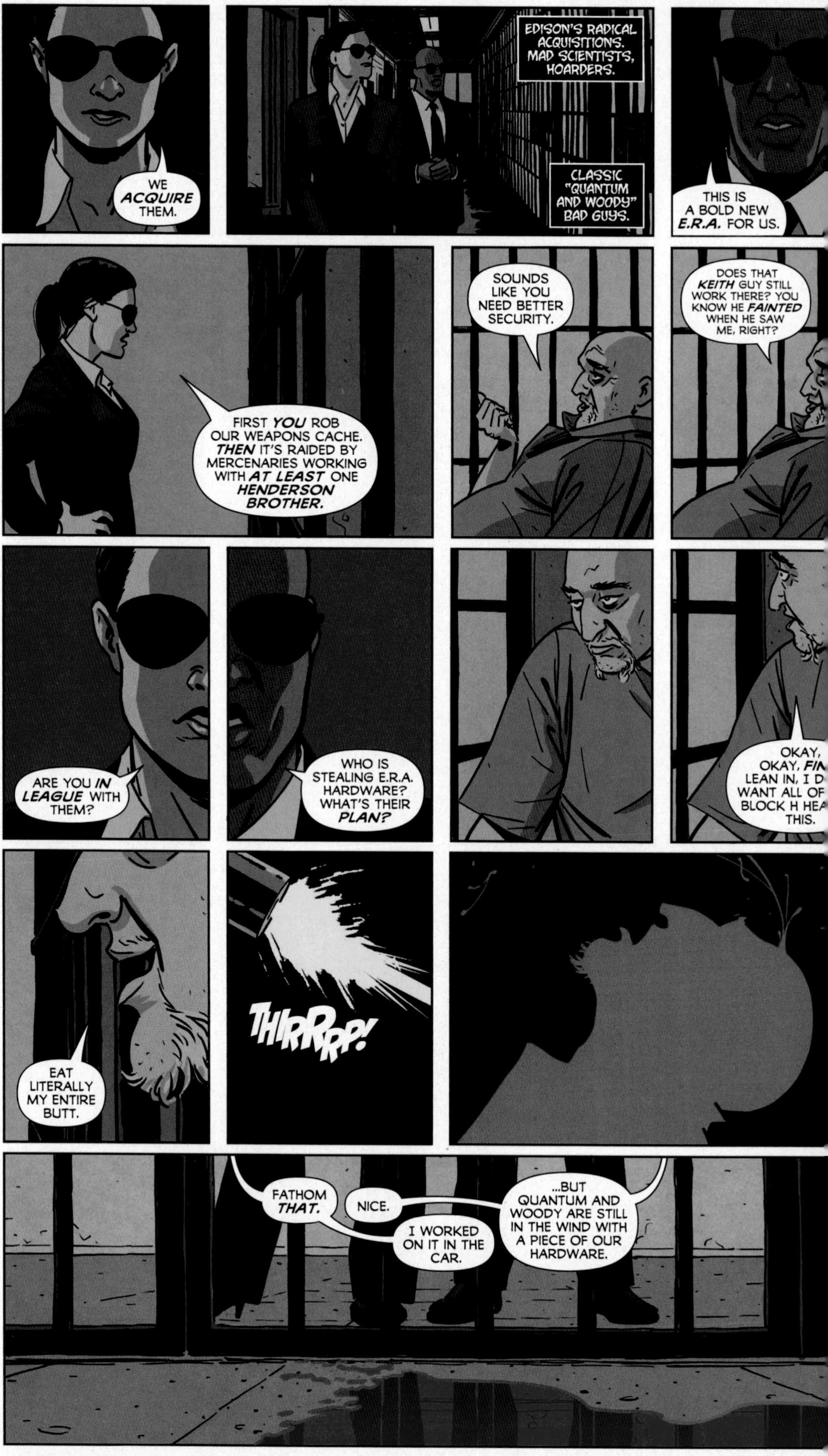
WE ACQUIRE THEM.
EDISON'S RADICAL ACQUISITIONS. MAD SCIENTISTS, HOARDERS.
CLASSIC "QUANTUM AND WOODY" BAD GUYS.
THIS IS A BOLD NEW E.R.A. FOR US.
FIRST YOU ROB OUR WEAPONS CACHE. THEN IT'S RAIDED BY MERCENARIES WORKING WITH AT LEAST ONE HENDERSON BROTHER.
SOUNDS LIKE YOU NEED BETTER SECURITY.
DOES THAT KEITH GUY STILL WORK THERE? YOU KNOW HE FAINTED WHEN HE SAW ME, RIGHT?
ARE YOU IN LEAGUE WITH THEM?
WHO IS STEALING E.R.A. HARDWARE? WHAT'S THEIR PLAN?
OKAY, OKAY, FIN LEAN IN, I D WANT ALL OF BLOCK H HEA THIS.
EAT LITERALLY MY ENTIRE BUTT.
THIRRRP!
FATHOM THAT.
NICE.
I WORKED ON IT IN THE CAR.
...BUT QUANTUM AND WOODY ARE STILL IN THE WIND WITH A PIECE OF OUR HARDWARE.

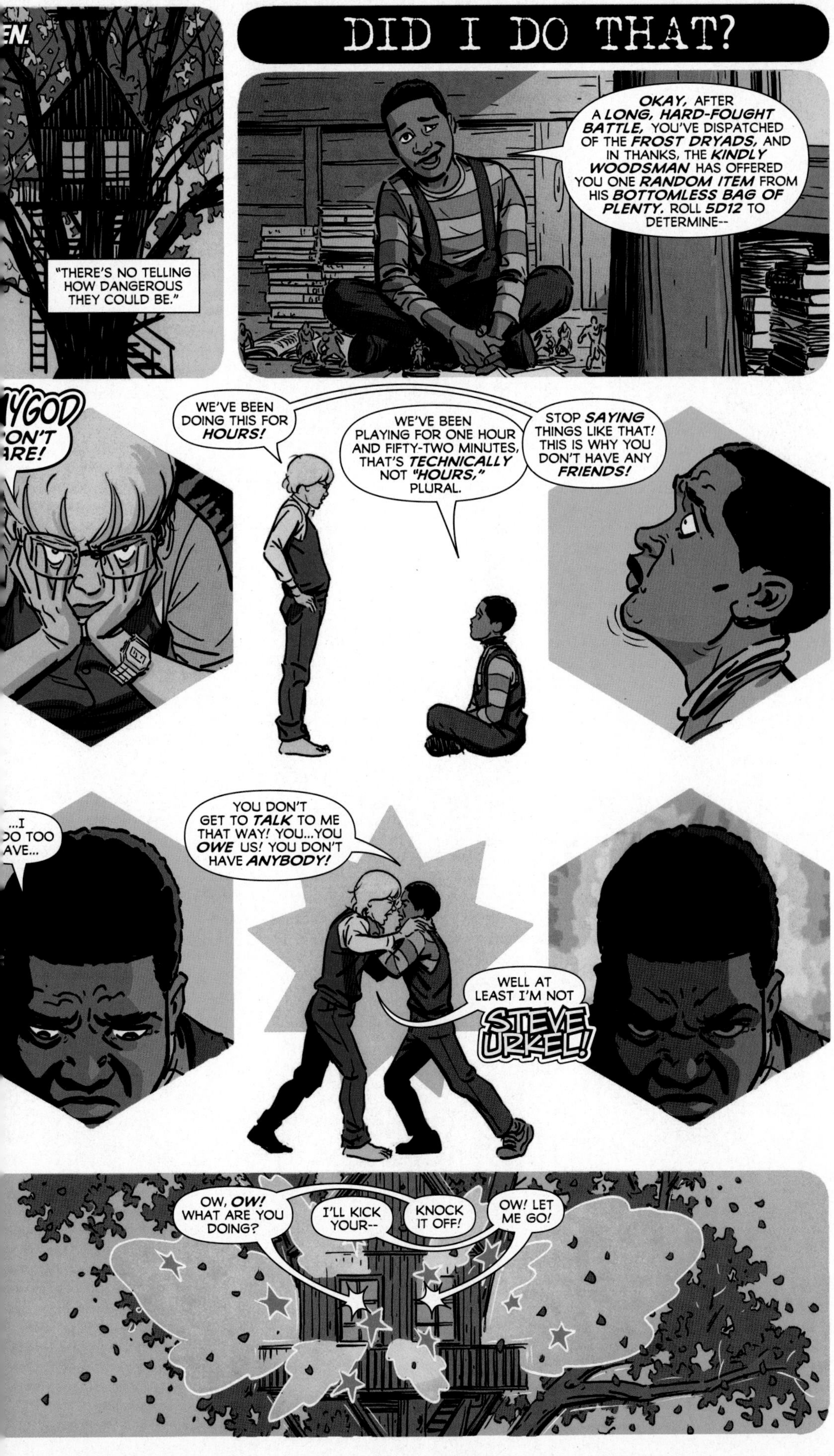
DID I DO THAT?
"THERE'S NO TELLING HOW DANGEROUS THEY COULD BE."
OKAY, AFTER A LONG, HARD-FOUGHT BATTLE, YOU'VE DISPATCHED OF THE FROST DRYADS, AND IN THANKS, THE KINDLY WOODSMAN HAS OFFERED YOU ONE RANDOM ITEM FROM HIS BOTTOMLESS BAG OF PLENTY. ROLL 5D12 TO DETERMINE--
WE'VE BEEN DOING THIS FOR HOURS!
WE'VE BEEN PLAYING FOR ONE HOUR AND FIFTY-TWO MINUTES, THAT'S TECHNICALLY NOT "HOURS," PLURAL.
STOP SAYING THINGS LIKE THAT! THIS IS WHY YOU DON'T HAVE ANY FRIENDS!
YOU DON'T GET TO TALK TO ME THAT WAY! YOU...YOU OWE US! YOU DON'T HAVE ANYBODY!
WELL AT LEAST I'M NOT STEVE URKEL!
OW, OW! WHAT ARE YOU DOING?
I'LL KICK YOUR--
KNOCK IT OFF!
OW! LET ME GO!

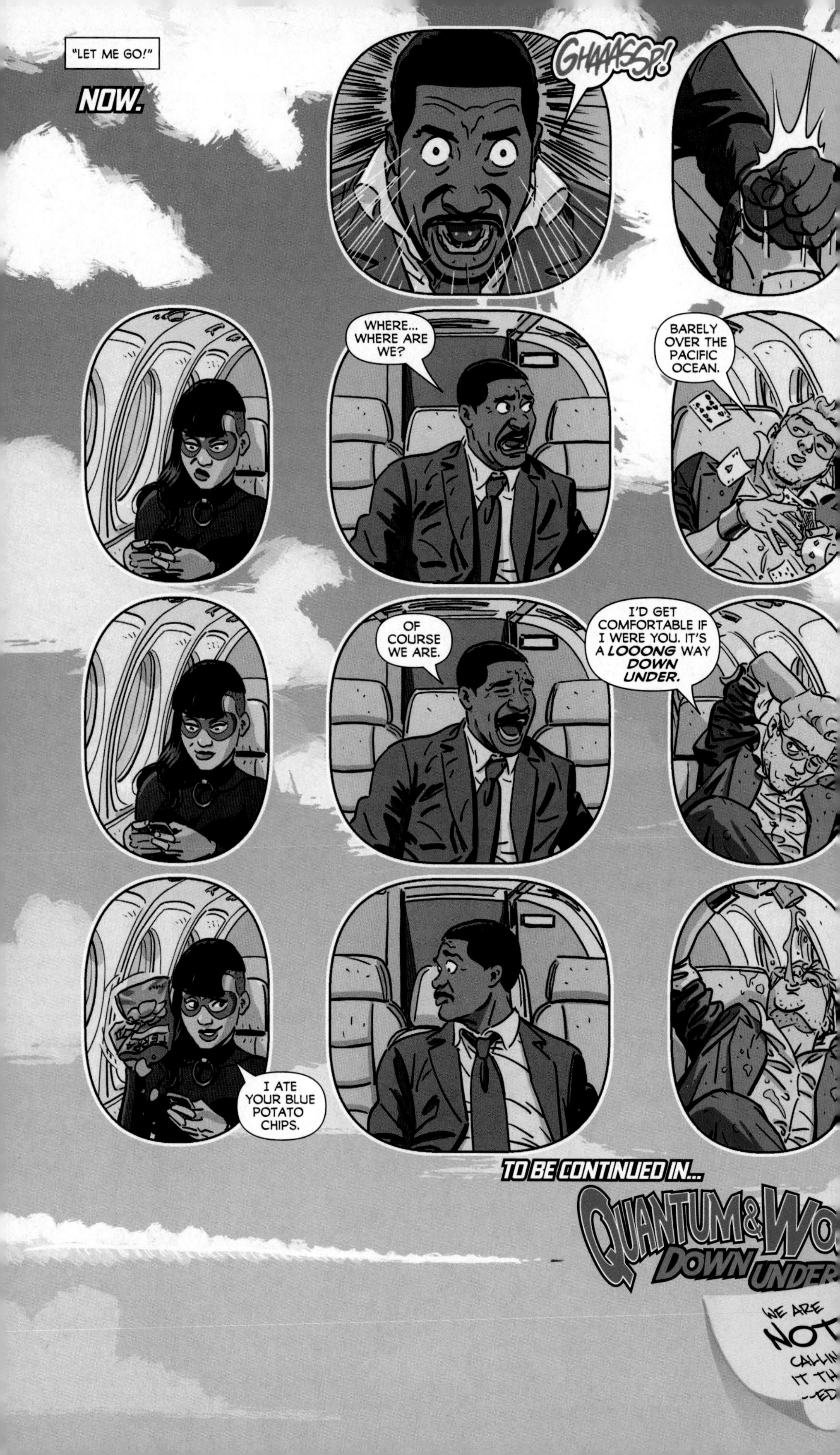
"LET ME GO!"
NOW.
GHAAASSP!
WHERE... WHERE ARE WE?
BARELY OVER THE PACIFIC OCEAN.
OF COURSE WE ARE.
I'D GET COMFORTABLE IF I WERE YOU. IT'S A LOOONG WAY DOWN UNDER.
I ATE YOUR BLUE POTATO CHIPS.
TO BE CONTINUED IN...
DOWN UNDER
WE ARE NOT

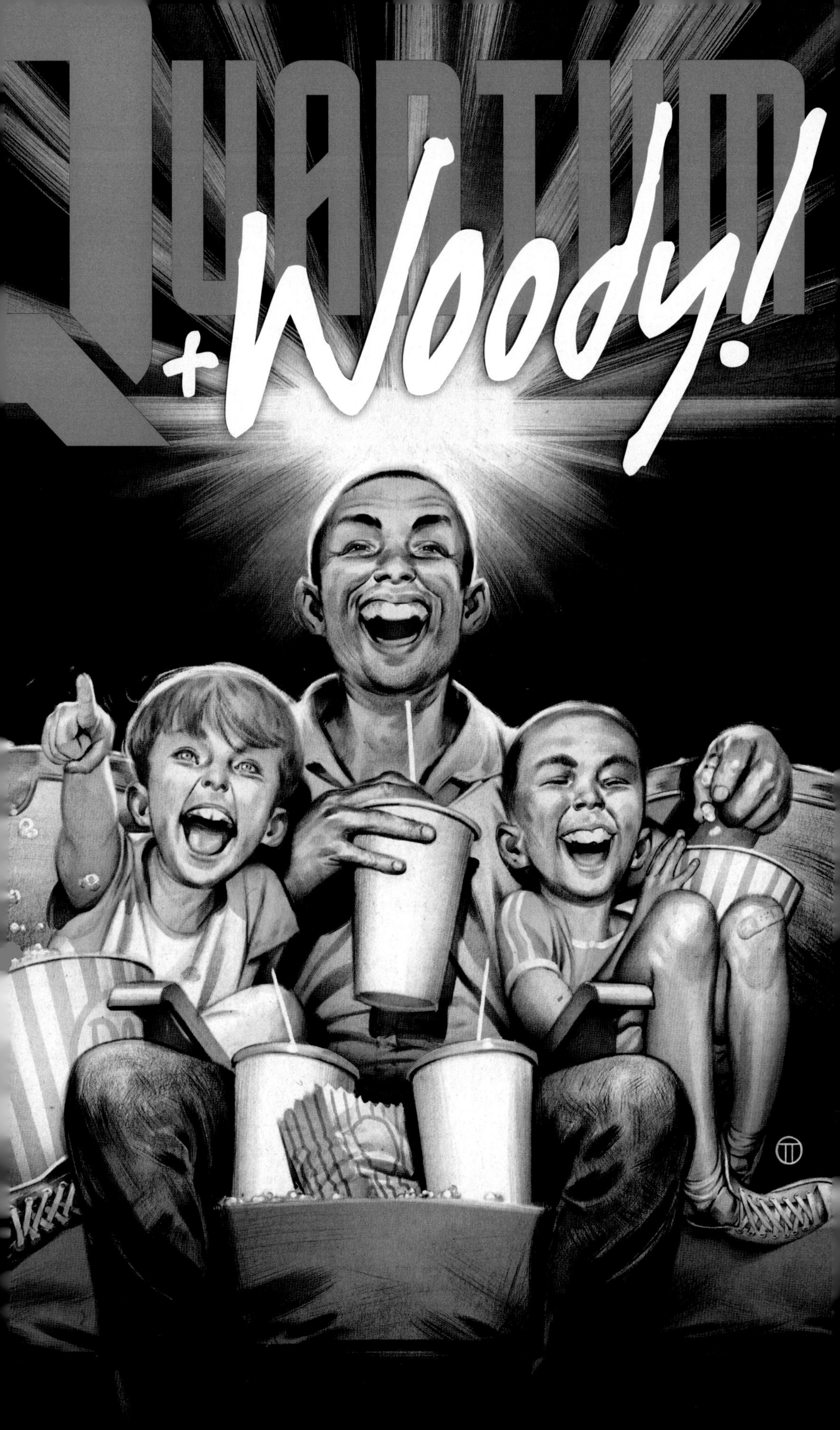
QUANTUM
+Woody!

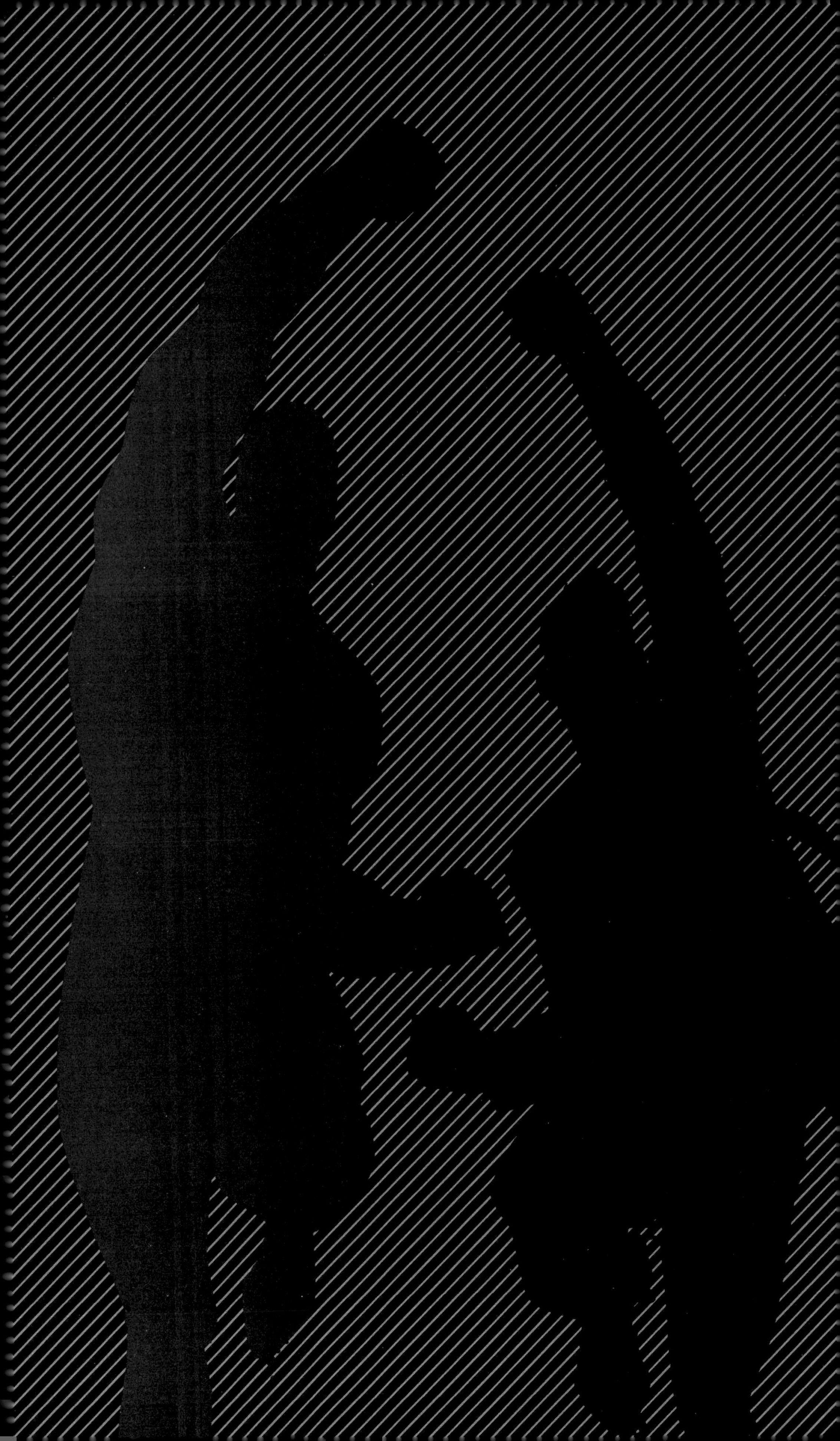

SO ... WHAT'S THE DEAL WITH THE GOAT?

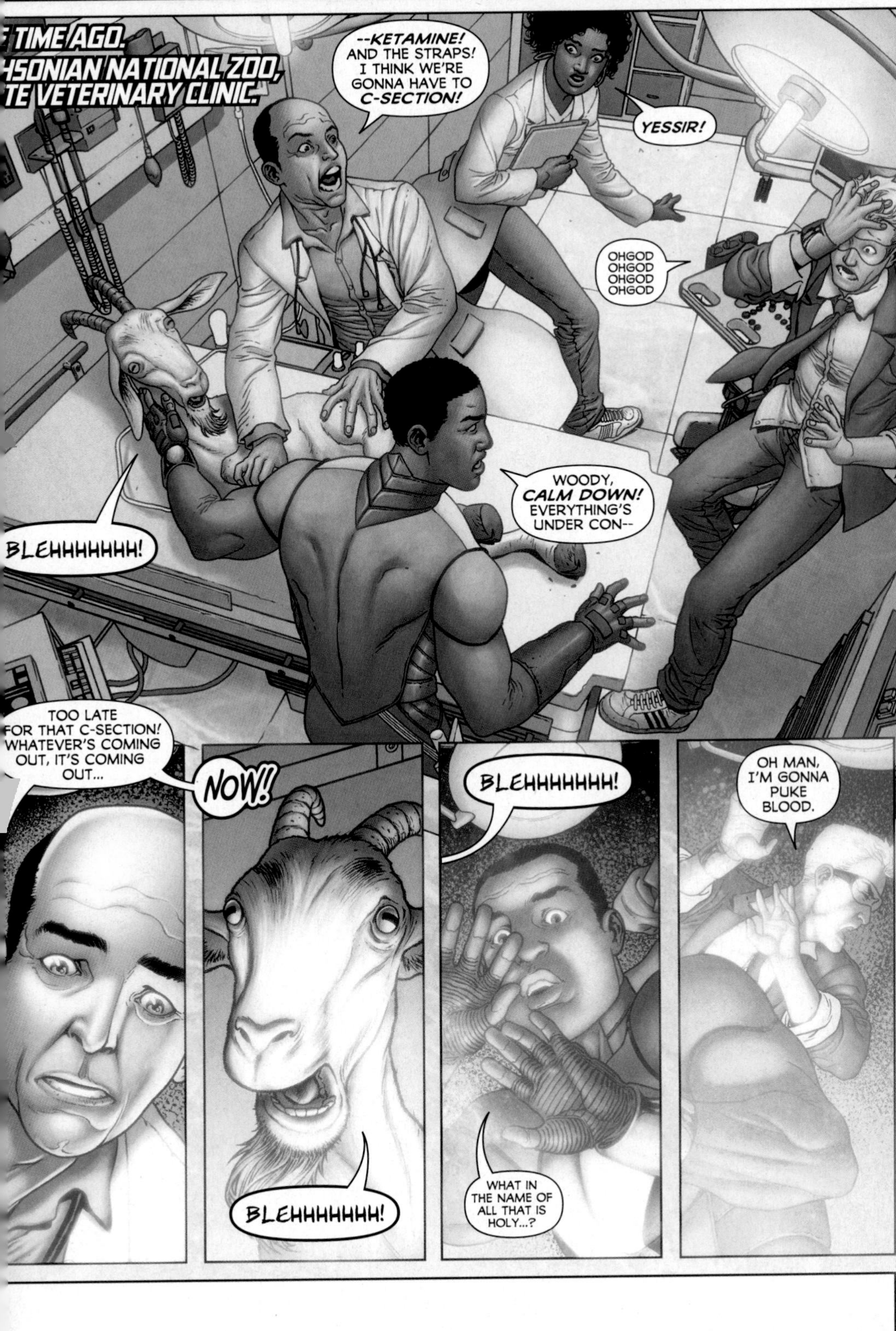

E TIME AGO.
HSONIAN NATIONAL ZOO,
TE VETERINARY CLINIC.
--KETAMINE! AND THE STRAPS! I THINK WE'RE GONNA HAVE TO C-SECTION!
YESSIR!
OHGOD OHGOD OHGOD OHGOD
BLEHHHHHHH!
WOODY, CALM DOWN! EVERYTHING'S UNDER CON--
TOO LATE FOR THAT C-SECTION! WHATEVER'S COMING OUT, IT'S COMING OUT...
NOW!
BLEHHHHHHH!
BLEHHHHHHH!
WHAT IN THE NAME OF ALL THAT IS HOLY...?
OH MAN, I'M GONNA PUKE BLOOD.

MIDNIGHT DOUBLE FEATURE

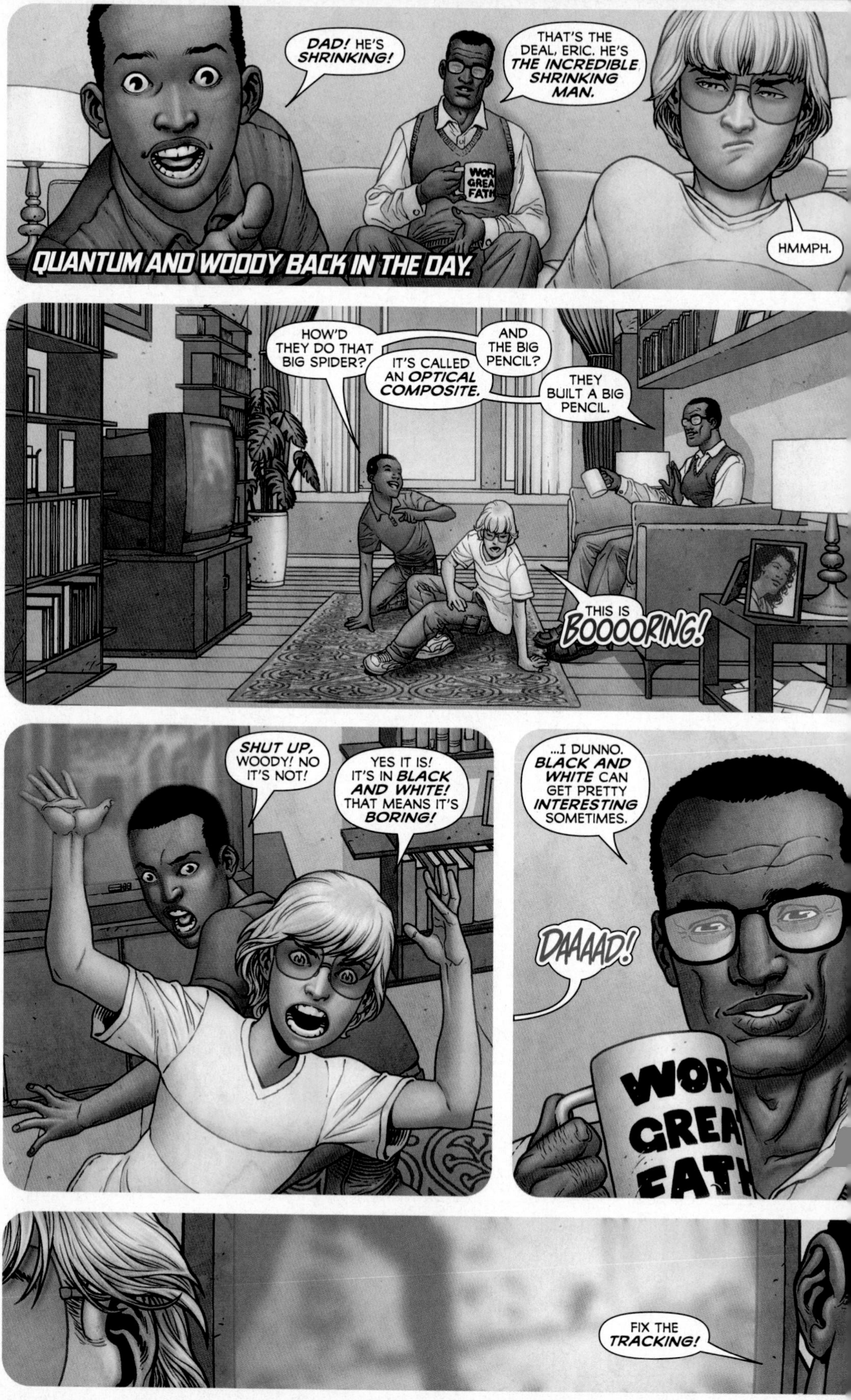

QUANTUM AND WOODY BACK IN THE DAY.
DAD! HE'S SHRINKING!
THAT'S THE DEAL, ERIC. HE'S THE INCREDIBLE SHRINKING MAN.
HMMPH.
HOW'D THEY DO THAT BIG SPIDER?
IT'S CALLED AN OPTICAL COMPOSITE.
AND THE BIG PENCIL?
THEY BUILT A BIG PENCIL.
THIS IS BOOOORING!
SHUT UP, WOODY! NO IT'S NOT!
YES IT IS! IT'S IN BLACK AND WHITE! THAT MEANS IT'S BORING!
...I DUNNO. BLACK AND WHITE CAN GET PRETTY INTERESTING SOMETIMES.
DAAAAD!
FIX THE TRACKING!

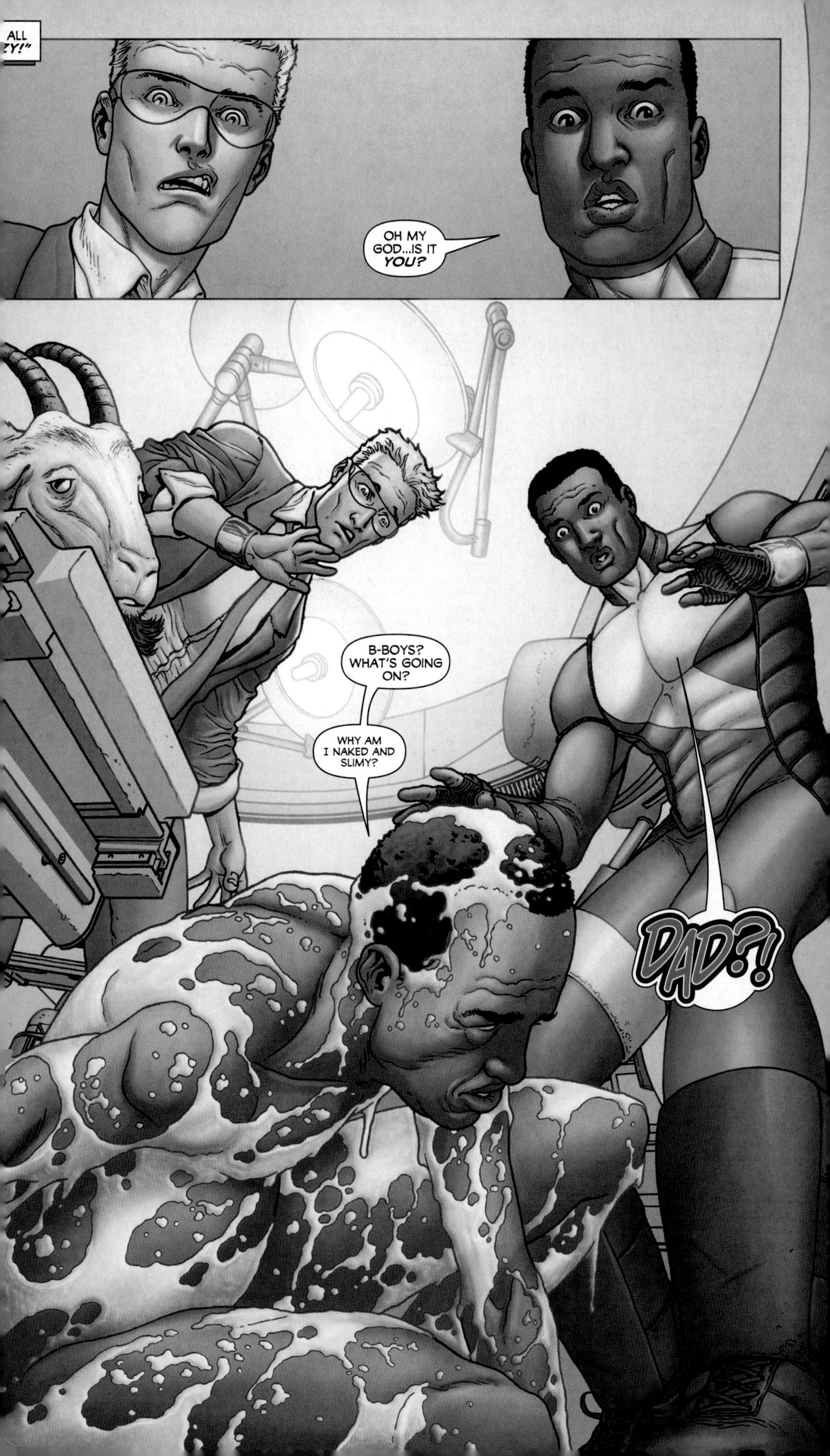
OH MY GOD...IS IT *YOU?*
B-BOYS? WHAT'S GOING ON?
WHY AM I NAKED AND SLIMY?
DAD?!

EVERYTHING'S A BLUR.

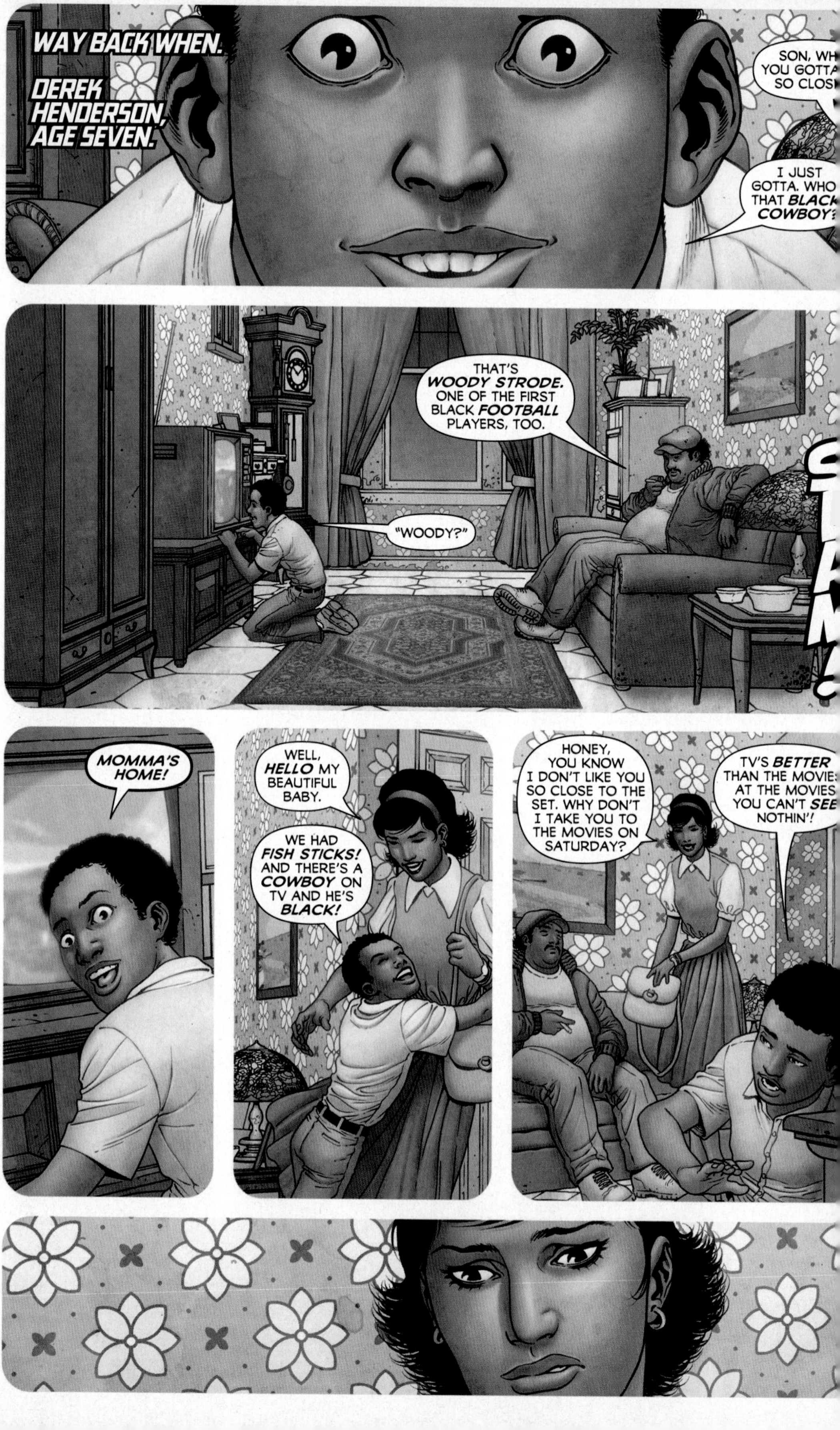

WAY BACK WHEN.
DEREK HENDERSON, AGE SEVEN.
SON, WH YOU GOTTA SO CLOS
I JUST GOTTA. WHO THAT BLACK COWBOY?
THAT'S WOODY STRODE. ONE OF THE FIRST BLACK FOOTBALL PLAYERS, TOO.
"WOODY?"
MOMMA'S HOME!
WELL, HELLO MY BEAUTIFUL BABY.
WE HAD FISH STICKS! AND THERE'S A COWBOY ON TV AND HE'S BLACK!
HONEY, YOU KNOW I DON'T LIKE YOU SO CLOSE TO THE SET. WHY DON'T I TAKE YOU TO THE MOVIES ON SATURDAY?
TV'S BETTER THAN THE MOVIES AT THE MOVIES YOU CAN'T SEE NOTHIN'!

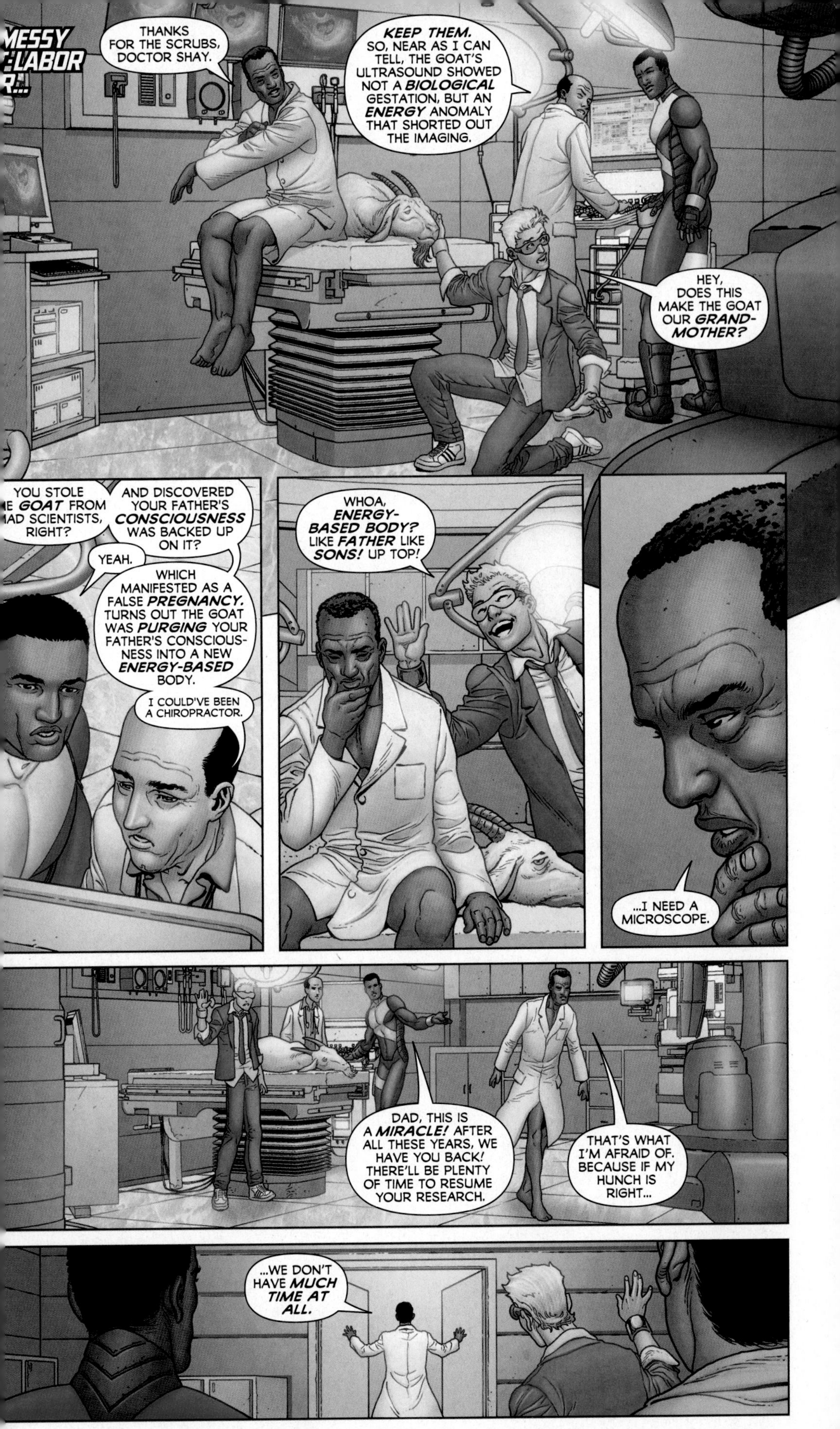
MESSY
LABOR
R...
THANKS FOR THE SCRUBS, DOCTOR SHAY.
KEEP THEM. SO, NEAR AS I CAN TELL, THE GOAT'S ULTRASOUND SHOWED NOT A BIOLOGICAL GESTATION, BUT AN ENERGY ANOMALY THAT SHORTED OUT THE IMAGING.
HEY, DOES THIS MAKE THE GOAT OUR GRAND-MOTHER?
YOU STOLE E GOAT FROM IAD SCIENTISTS, RIGHT?
AND DISCOVERED YOUR FATHER'S CONSCIOUSNESS WAS BACKED UP ON IT?
YEAH.
WHICH MANIFESTED AS A FALSE PREGNANCY. TURNS OUT THE GOAT WAS PURGING YOUR FATHER'S CONSCIOUS-NESS INTO A NEW ENERGY-BASED BODY.
I COULD'VE BEEN A CHIROPRACTOR.
WHOA, ENERGY-BASED BODY? LIKE FATHER LIKE SONS! UP TOP!
...I NEED A MICROSCOPE.
DAD, THIS IS A MIRACLE! AFTER ALL THESE YEARS, WE HAVE YOU BACK! THERE'LL BE PLENTY OF TIME TO RESUME YOUR RESEARCH.
THAT'S WHAT I'M AFRAID OF. BECAUSE IF MY HUNCH IS RIGHT...
...WE DON'T HAVE MUCH TIME AT ALL.

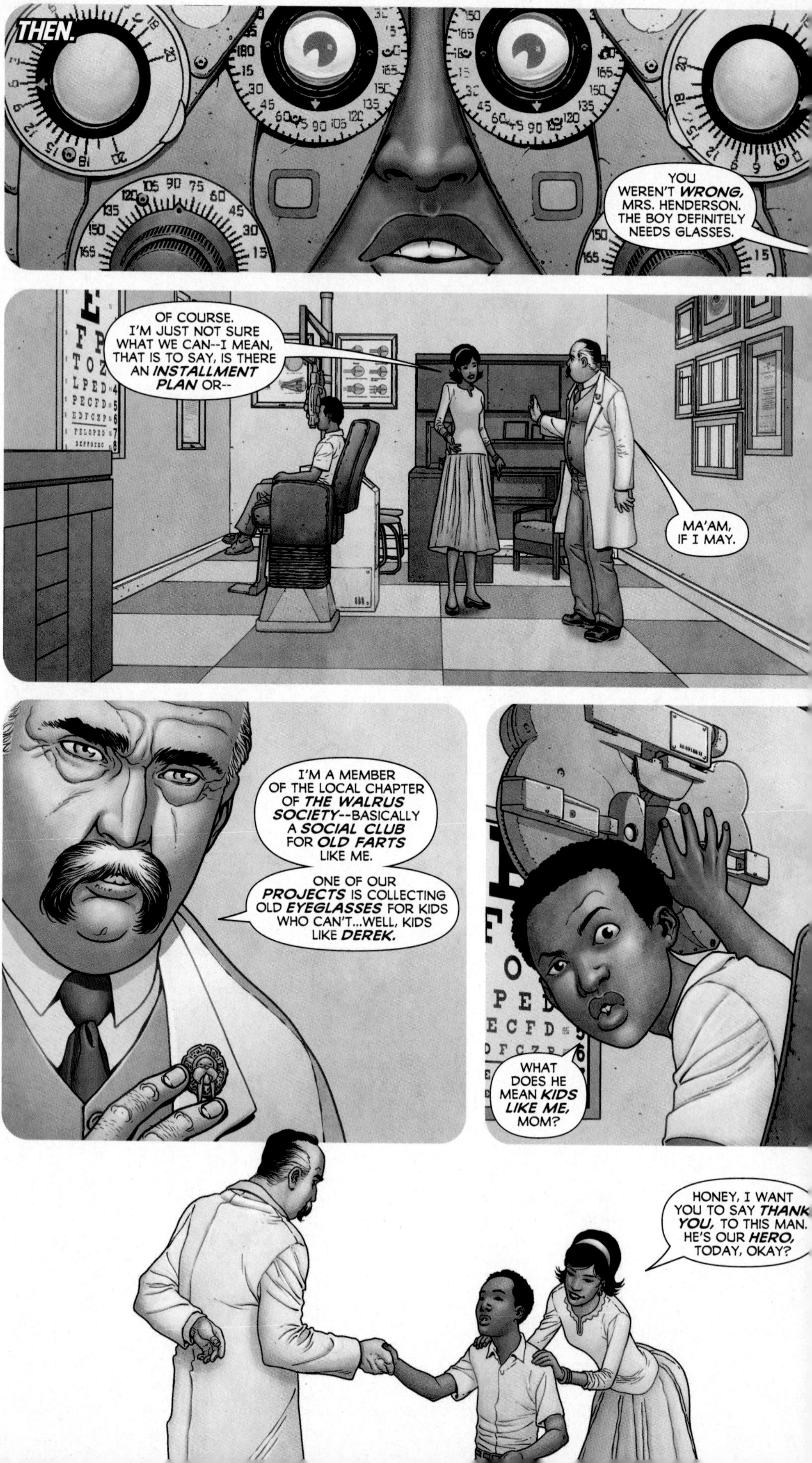
THEN.
YOU WEREN'T WRONG, MRS. HENDERSON. THE BOY DEFINITELY NEEDS GLASSES.
OF COURSE. I'M JUST NOT SURE WHAT WE CAN--I MEAN, THAT IS TO SAY, IS THERE AN INSTALLMENT PLAN OR--
MA'AM, IF I MAY.
I'M A MEMBER OF THE LOCAL CHAPTER OF THE WALRUS SOCIETY--BASICALLY A SOCIAL CLUB FOR OLD FARTS LIKE ME.
ONE OF OUR PROJECTS IS COLLECTING OLD EYEGLASSES FOR KIDS WHO CAN'T...WELL, KIDS LIKE DEREK.
WHAT DOES HE MEAN KIDS LIKE ME, MOM?
HONEY, I WANT YOU TO SAY THANK YOU, TO THIS MAN. HE'S OUR HERO, TODAY, OKAY?

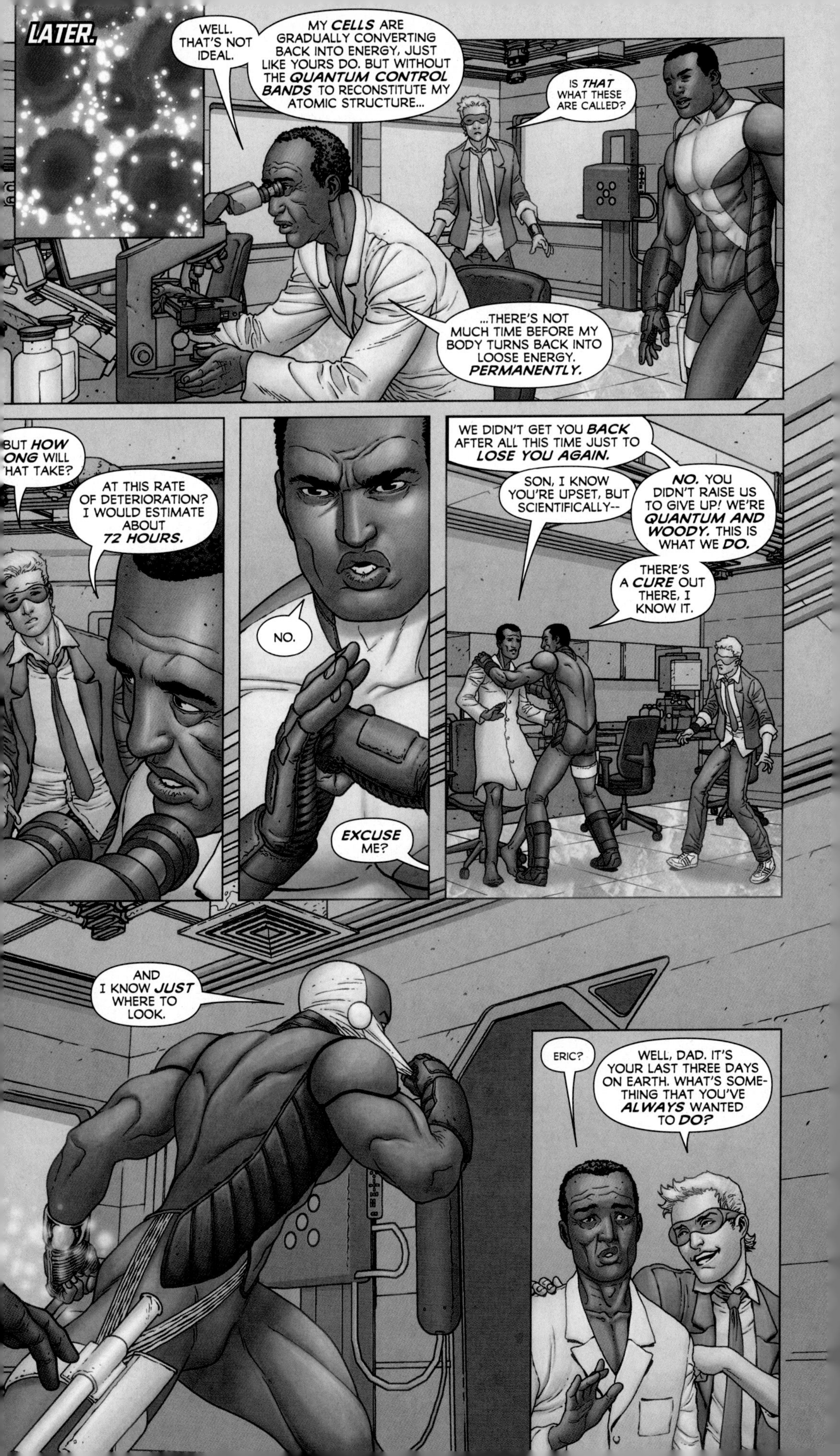
LATER.
WELL. THAT'S NOT IDEAL.
MY CELLS ARE GRADUALLY CONVERTING BACK INTO ENERGY, JUST LIKE YOURS DO. BUT WITHOUT THE QUANTUM CONTROL BANDS TO RECONSTITUTE MY ATOMIC STRUCTURE...
IS THAT WHAT THESE ARE CALLED?
...THERE'S NOT MUCH TIME BEFORE MY BODY TURNS BACK INTO LOOSE ENERGY. PERMANENTLY.
BUT HOW ONG WILL HAT TAKE?
AT THIS RATE OF DETERIORATION? I WOULD ESTIMATE ABOUT 72 HOURS.
NO.
EXCUSE ME?
WE DIDN'T GET YOU BACK AFTER ALL THIS TIME JUST TO LOSE YOU AGAIN.
SON, I KNOW YOU'RE UPSET, BUT SCIENTIFICALLY--
NO. YOU DIDN'T RAISE US TO GIVE UP! WE'RE QUANTUM AND WOODY. THIS IS WHAT WE DO.
THERE'S A CURE OUT THERE, I KNOW IT.
AND I KNOW JUST WHERE TO LOOK.
ERIC?
WELL, DAD. IT'S YOUR LAST THREE DAYS ON EARTH. WHAT'S SOMETHING THAT YOU'VE ALWAYS WANTED TO DO?

LET'S DO THE TIME WARP AGAIN.

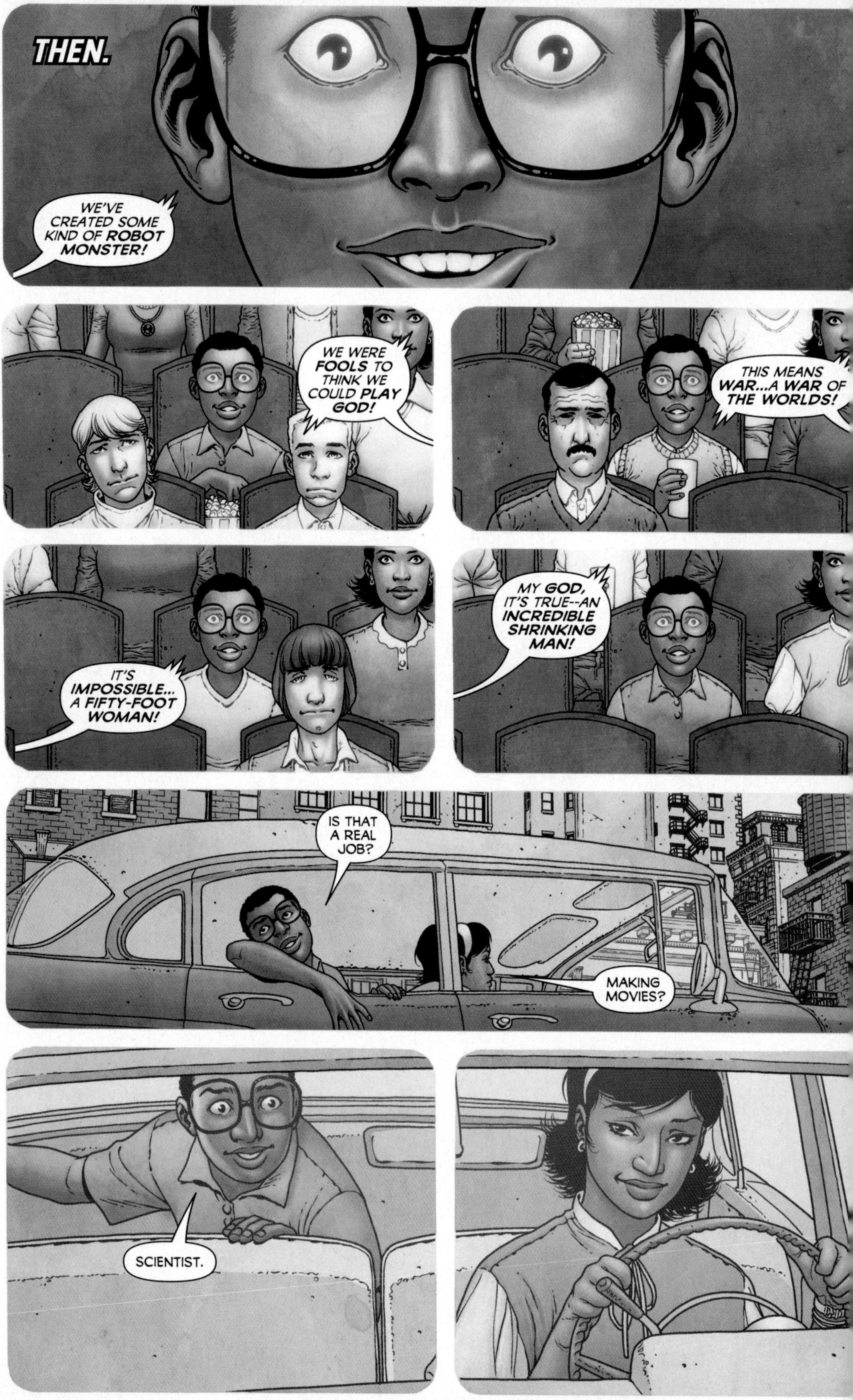
THEN.
WE'VE CREATED SOME KIND OF ROBOT MONSTER!
WE WERE FOOLS TO THINK WE COULD PLAY GOD!
THIS MEANS WAR...A WAR OF THE WORLDS!
IT'S IMPOSSIBLE... A FIFTY-FOOT WOMAN!
MY GOD, IT'S TRUE--AN INCREDIBLE SHRINKING MAN!
IS THAT A REAL JOB?
MAKING MOVIES?
SCIENTIST.

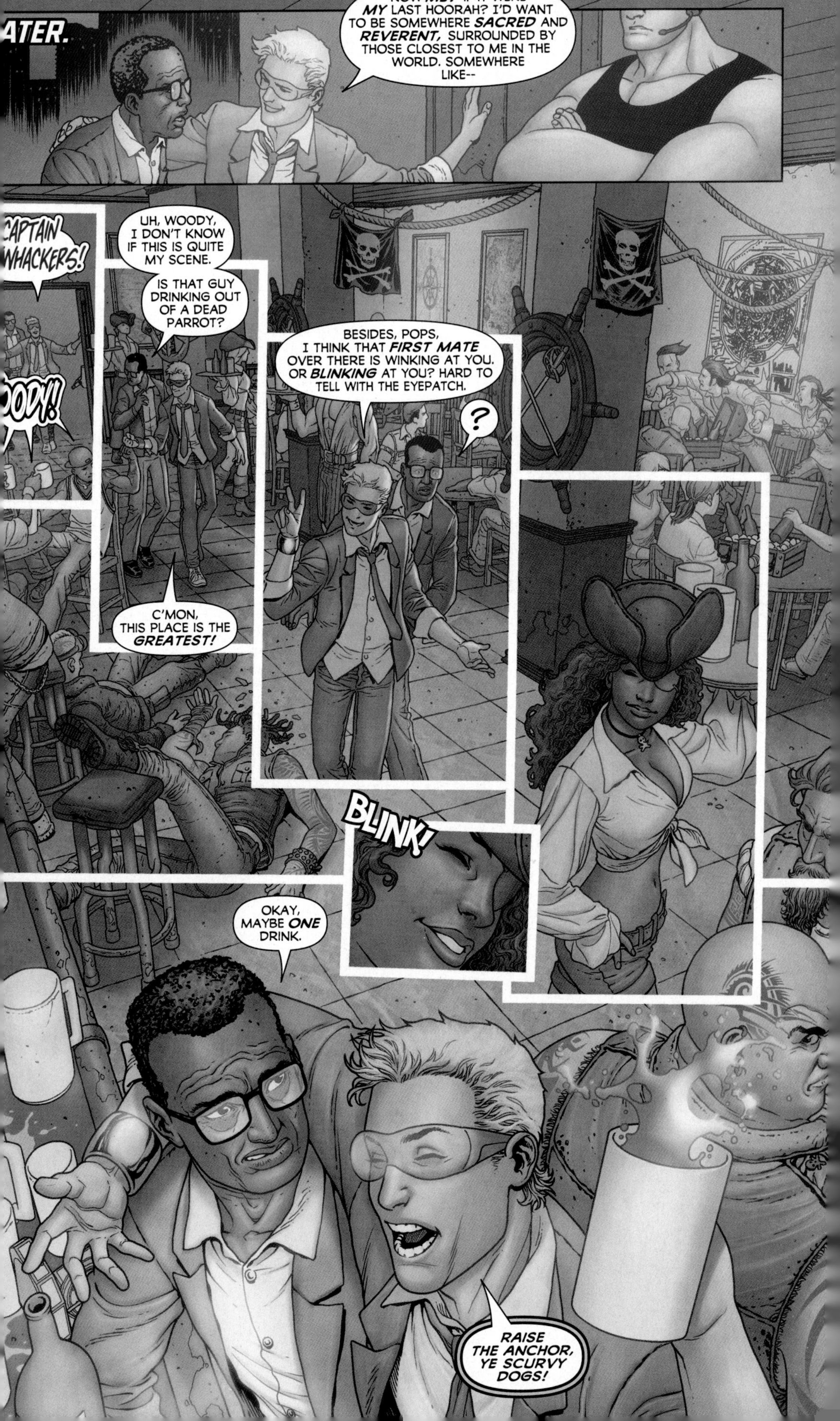
ATER.
NOW ME? IF IT WERE MY LAST HOORAH? I'D WANT TO BE SOMEWHERE SACRED AND REVERENT, SURROUNDED BY THOSE CLOSEST TO ME IN THE WORLD. SOMEWHERE LIKE--
CAPTAIN WHACKERS!
OODY!
UH, WOODY, I DON'T KNOW IF THIS IS QUITE MY SCENE.
IS THAT GUY DRINKING OUT OF A DEAD PARROT?
C'MON, THIS PLACE IS THE GREATEST!
BESIDES, POPS, I THINK THAT FIRST MATE OVER THERE IS WINKING AT YOU. OR BLINKING AT YOU? HARD TO TELL WITH THE EYEPATCH.
?
BLINK!
OKAY, MAYBE ONE DRINK.
RAISE THE ANCHOR, YE SCURVY DOGS!

LET'S SEE. THE EXPLOSION AT THE *SCIENCE CONFERENCE* WHERE DAD'S CONSCIOUSNESS WAS ACCIDENTALLY *UPLOADED INTO THE GOAT* MUST HAVE MADE THE *LOCAL* PAPERS.

SHH! NO MUMBLING!

IT'S ALL RIGHT, SIR. I'M ON A MISSION.

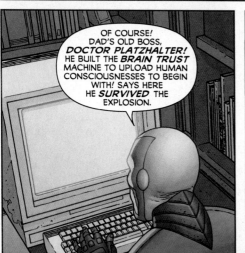

OF COURSE! DAD'S OLD BOSS, *DOCTOR PLATZHALTER!* HE BUILT THE *BRAIN TRUST* MACHINE TO UPLOAD HUMAN CONSCIOUSNESSES TO BEGIN WITH! SAYS HERE HE *SURVIVED* THE EXPLOSION.

IF HE EVER BU ANOTHER *BRA TRUST*, THEN J MAYBE WE CO *UPLOAD DA* AGAIN AND BI HIM SOME TIME!

YOU'RE STILL DOING IT!

JUST CRAZY ENOUGH TO WORK.

THEN.

WHICH IS WHY WE'D LIKE TO OFFER YOU A *FULL SCHOLARSHIP* TO THE *CHARLES PROTEUS STEINMETZ SCHOOL* FOR SCIENCE AND TECHNOLOGY.

AND ON A PERSONAL NOTE, DEREK--

I'M *HONORED* TO BE ADMITTING OUR FIRST *NEGRO* STUDENT.

THANK YOU, SIR.

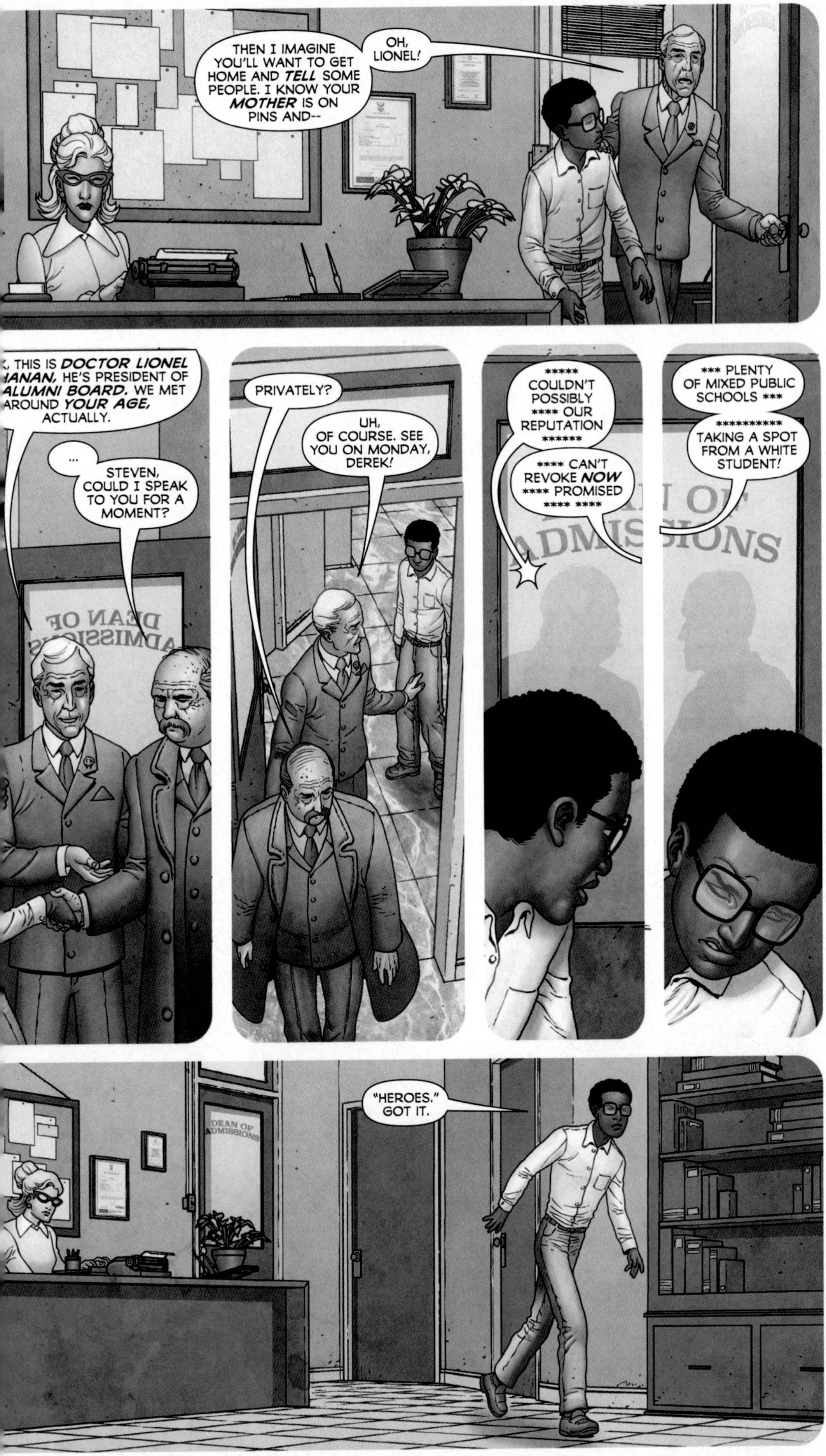
THEN I IMAGINE YOU'LL WANT TO GET HOME AND TELL SOME PEOPLE. I KNOW YOUR MOTHER IS ON PINS AND--
OH, LIONEL!
, THIS IS DOCTOR LIONEL HANAN, HE'S PRESIDENT OF ALUMNI BOARD. WE MET AROUND YOUR AGE, ACTUALLY.
...
STEVEN, COULD I SPEAK TO YOU FOR A MOMENT?
PRIVATELY?
UH, OF COURSE. SEE YOU ON MONDAY, DEREK!
DEAN OF ADMISSIONS
***** COULDN'T POSSIBLY **** OUR REPUTATION ******
**** CAN'T REVOKE NOW **** PROMISED **** ****
*** PLENTY OF MIXED PUBLIC SCHOOLS ***
********** TAKING A SPOT FROM A WHITE STUDENT!
DEAN OF ADMISSIONS
"HEROES." GOT IT.
DEAN OF ADMISSIONS

YOUNG, GIFTED, AND BLACK.

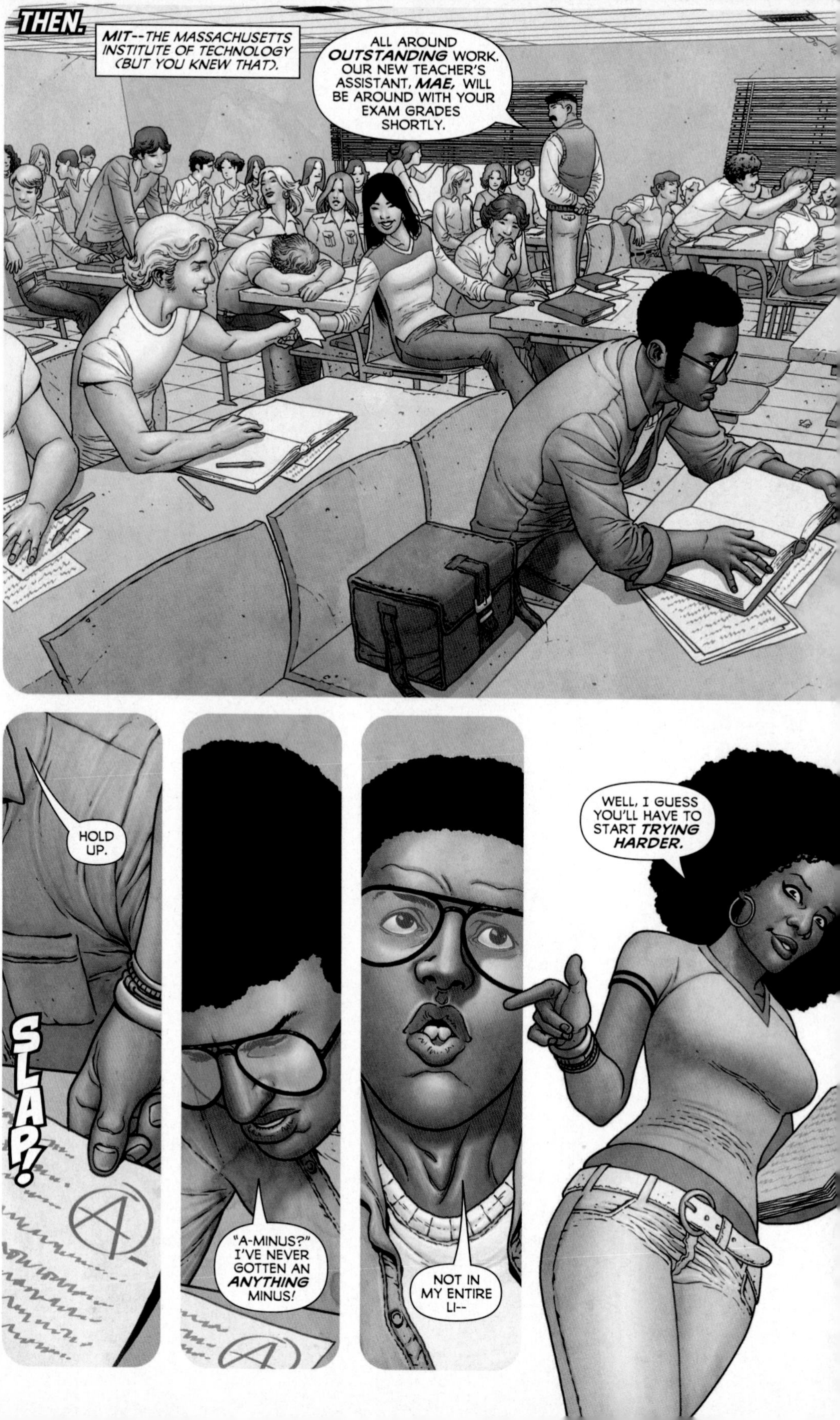
THEN.
MIT--THE MASSACHUSETTS INSTITUTE OF TECHNOLOGY (BUT YOU KNEW THAT).
ALL AROUND OUTSTANDING WORK. OUR NEW TEACHER'S ASSISTANT, MAE, WILL BE AROUND WITH YOUR EXAM GRADES SHORTLY.
HOLD UP.
SLAP!
"A-MINUS?" I'VE NEVER GOTTEN AN ANYTHING MINUS!
NOT IN MY ENTIRE LI--
WELL, I GUESS YOU'LL HAVE TO START TRYING HARDER.

LAP PARTNERS. I MEAN LAB! LAB!

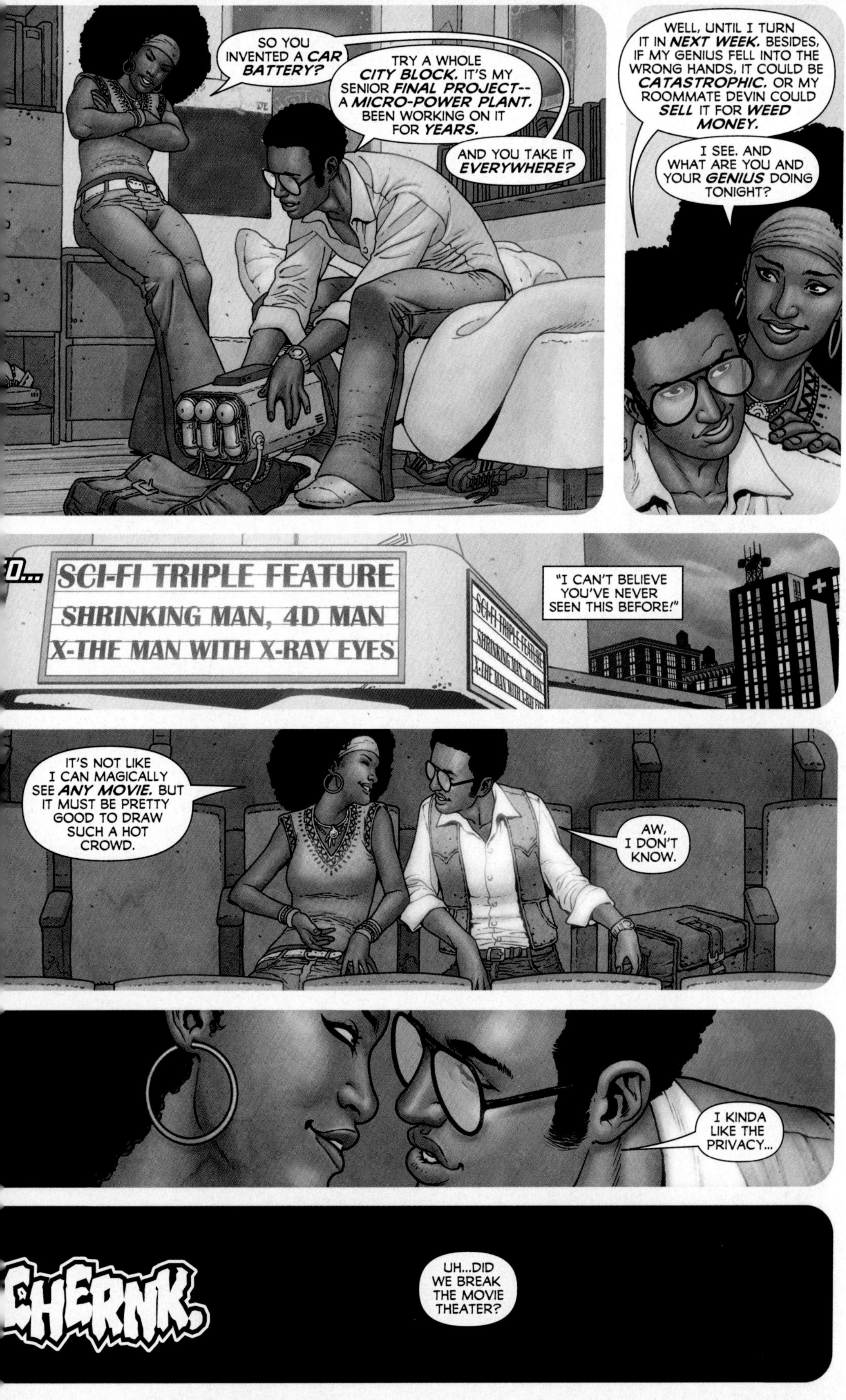
SO YOU INVENTED A CAR BATTERY?
TRY A WHOLE CITY BLOCK. IT'S MY SENIOR FINAL PROJECT-- A MICRO-POWER PLANT. BEEN WORKING ON IT FOR YEARS.
AND YOU TAKE IT EVERYWHERE?
WELL, UNTIL I TURN IT IN NEXT WEEK. BESIDES, IF MY GENIUS FELL INTO THE WRONG HANDS, IT COULD BE CATASTROPHIC. OR MY ROOMMATE DEVIN COULD SELL IT FOR WEED MONEY.
I SEE. AND WHAT ARE YOU AND YOUR GENIUS DOING TONIGHT?
SCI-FI TRIPLE FEATURE
SHRINKING MAN, 4D MAN
X-THE MAN WITH X-RAY EYES
"I CAN'T BELIEVE YOU'VE NEVER SEEN THIS BEFORE!"
IT'S NOT LIKE I CAN MAGICALLY SEE ANY MOVIE. BUT IT MUST BE PRETTY GOOD TO DRAW SUCH A HOT CROWD.
AW, I DON'T KNOW.
I KINDA LIKE THE PRIVACY...
CHERNK.
UH...DID WE BREAK THE MOVIE THEATER?

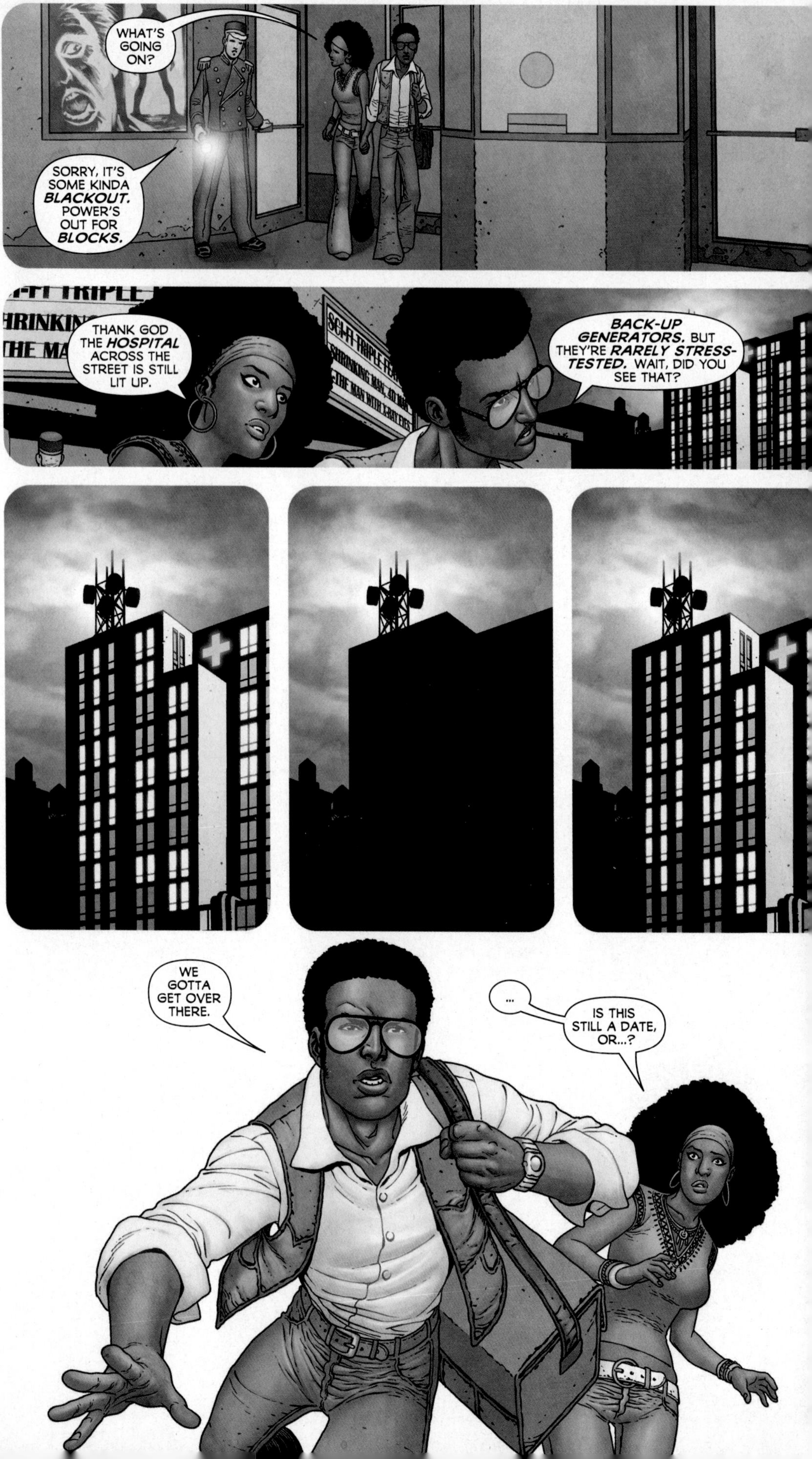
WHAT'S GOING ON?
SORRY, IT'S SOME KINDA BLACKOUT. POWER'S OUT FOR BLOCKS.
THANK GOD THE HOSPITAL ACROSS THE STREET IS STILL LIT UP.
BACK-UP GENERATORS. BUT THEY'RE RARELY STRESS-TESTED. WAIT, DID YOU SEE THAT?
WE GOTTA GET OVER THERE.
...
IS THIS STILL A DATE, OR...?

UGGGHH, I'M GONNA HAVE SUCH A HANGOVER.

DON'T YOU MEAN KLANG-OVER?

HAHAHA! I DON'T REMEMBER DAD BEING THIS FUNNY! OR THIS DRUNK!

SHHH, YOU'LL WAKE UP MY SON.

HE'S UP.

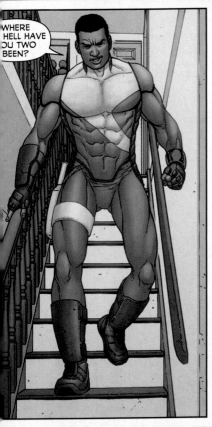

WHERE THE HELL HAVE YOU TWO BEEN?

US? WHERE THE HELL HAVE YOU BEEN?! WE'VE ONLY GOT A COUPLE DAYS LEFT WITH DAD AND YOU SPENT IT OFF PLAYING SUPERHERO!

I SPENT IT LOOKING FOR LEADS! I THINK WE CAN SAVE DAD BY RECREATING THE PROCESS THAT BACKED-UP HIS CONSCIOUSNESS TO BEGIN WITH.

...UH, SON, I AIN'T GOIN' BACK IN NO GOAT.

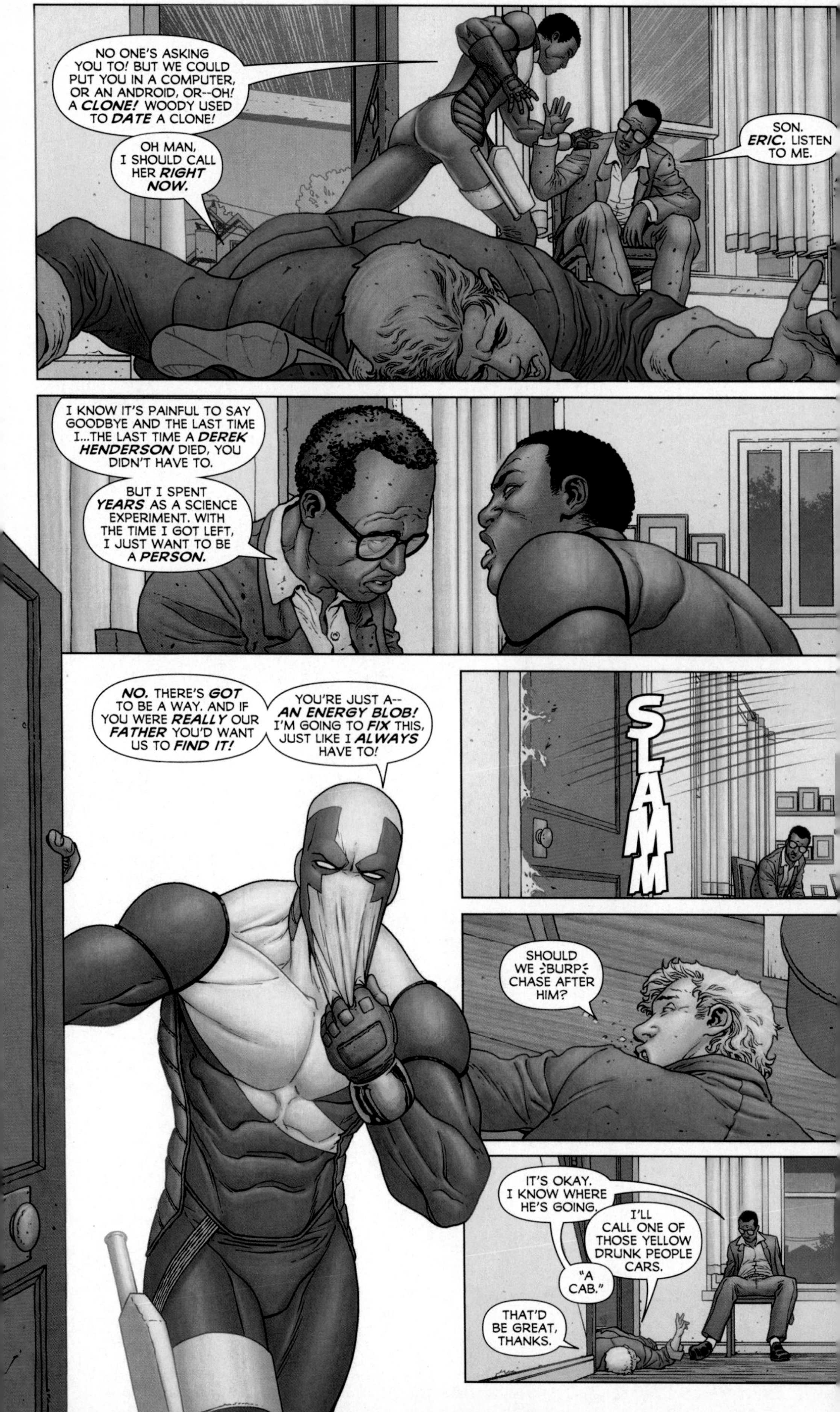
NO ONE'S ASKING YOU TO! BUT WE COULD PUT YOU IN A COMPUTER, OR AN ANDROID, OR--OH! A CLONE! WOODY USED TO DATE A CLONE!
OH MAN, I SHOULD CALL HER RIGHT NOW.
SON. ERIC. LISTEN TO ME.
I KNOW IT'S PAINFUL TO SAY GOODBYE AND THE LAST TIME I...THE LAST TIME A DEREK HENDERSON DIED, YOU DIDN'T HAVE TO.
BUT I SPENT YEARS AS A SCIENCE EXPERIMENT. WITH THE TIME I GOT LEFT, I JUST WANT TO BE A PERSON.
NO. THERE'S GOT TO BE A WAY. AND IF YOU WERE REALLY OUR FATHER YOU'D WANT US TO FIND IT!
YOU'RE JUST A-- AN ENERGY BLOB! I'M GOING TO FIX THIS, JUST LIKE I ALWAYS HAVE TO!
SLAMM
SHOULD WE BURP CHASE AFTER HIM?
IT'S OKAY. I KNOW WHERE HE'S GOING.
I'LL CALL ONE OF THOSE YELLOW DRUNK PEOPLE CARS.
"A CAB."
THAT'D BE GREAT, THANKS.

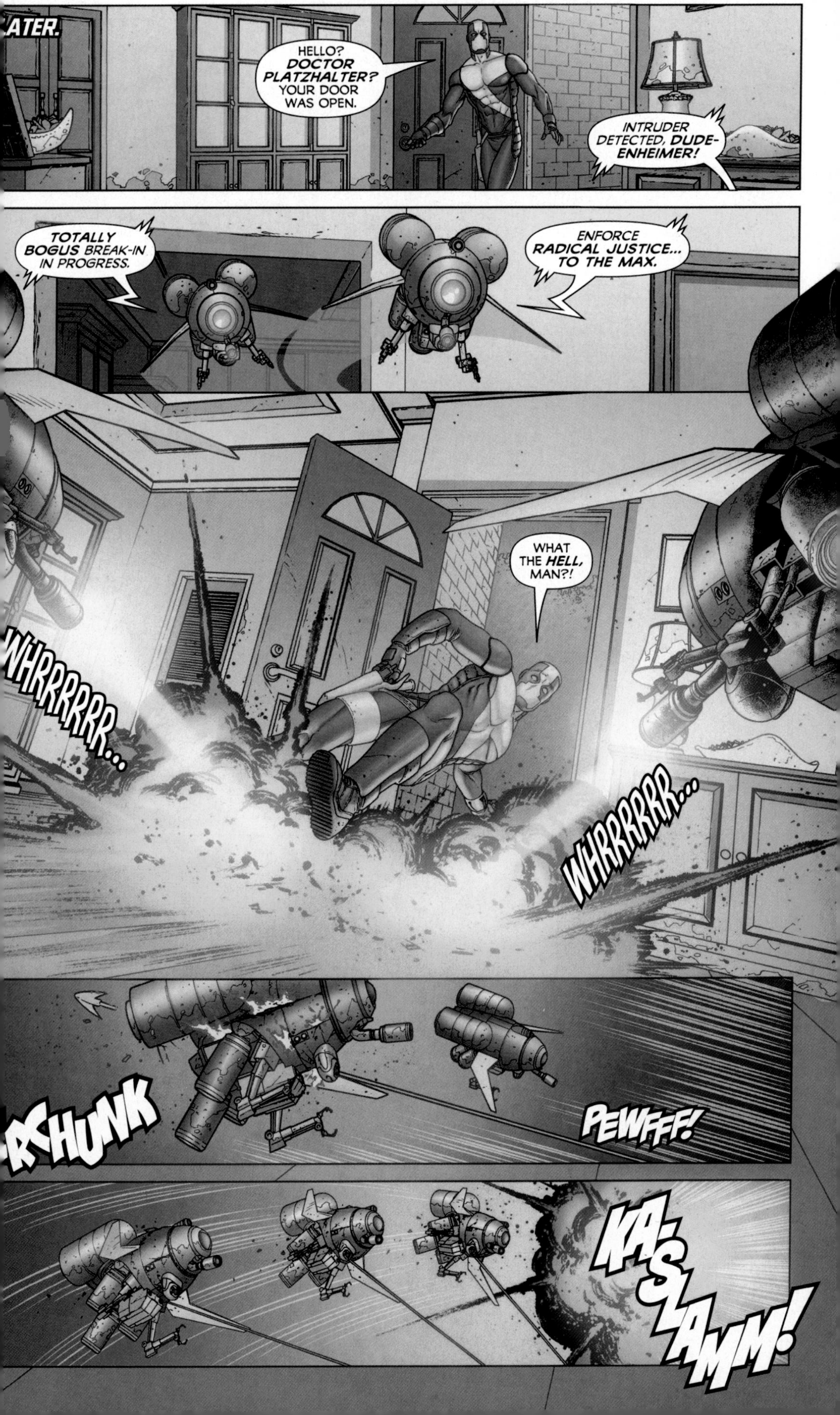

LATER.
HELLO? DOCTOR PLATZHALTER? YOUR DOOR WAS OPEN.
INTRUDER DETECTED, DUDE-ENHEIMER!
TOTALLY BOGUS BREAK-IN IN PROGRESS.
ENFORCE RADICAL JUSTICE... TO THE MAX.
WHAT THE HELL, MAN?!
WHRRRRRR...
WHRRRRRR...
RCHUNK
PEWFFF!
KA-SLAMM!

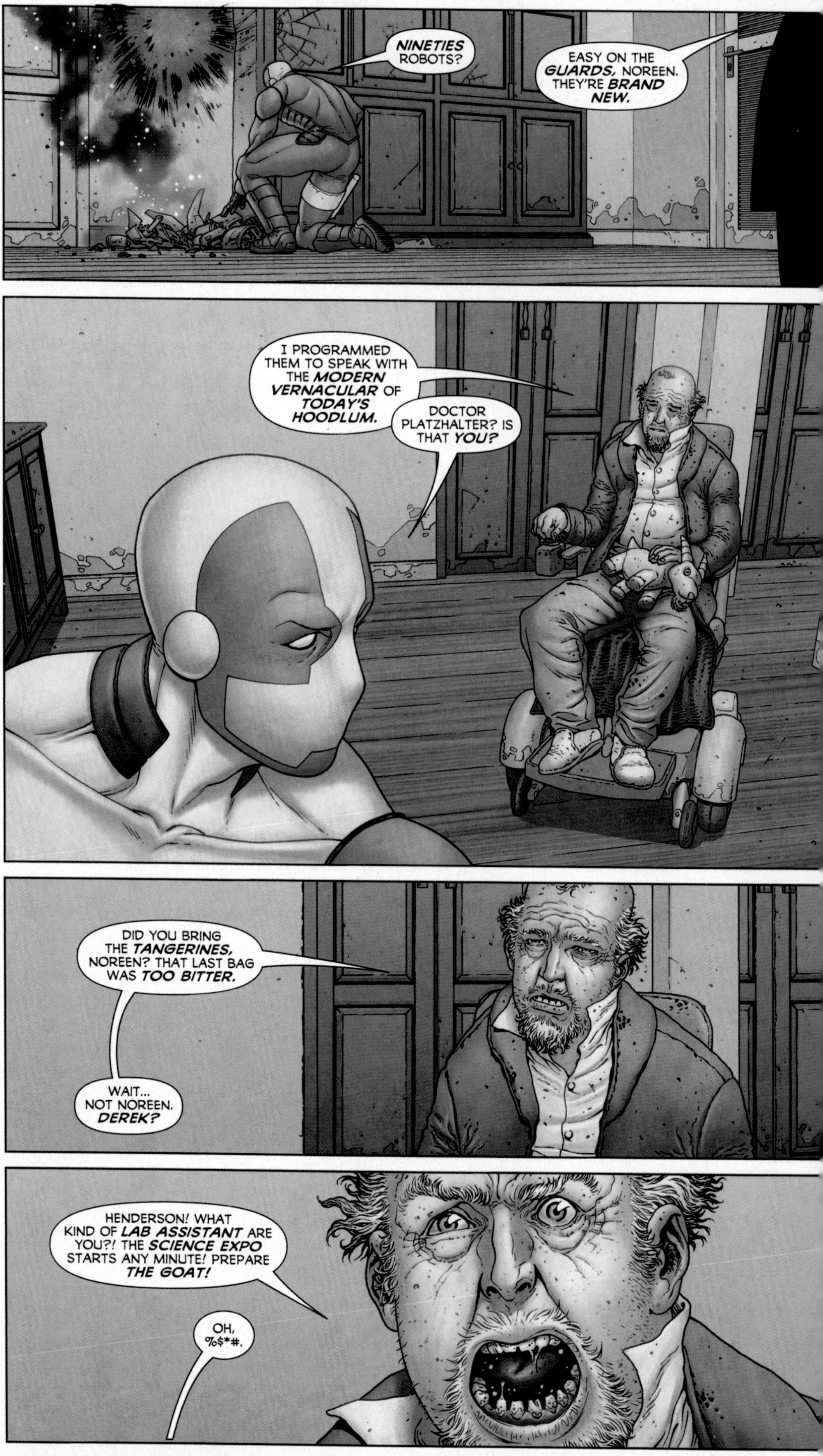
NINETIES ROBOTS?
EASY ON THE GUARDS, NOREEN. THEY'RE BRAND NEW.
I PROGRAMMED THEM TO SPEAK WITH THE MODERN VERNACULAR OF TODAY'S HOODLUM.
DOCTOR PLATZHALTER? IS THAT YOU?
DID YOU BRING THE TANGERINES, NOREEN? THAT LAST BAG WAS TOO BITTER.
WAIT... NOT NOREEN. DEREK?
HENDERSON! WHAT KIND OF LAB ASSISTANT ARE YOU?! THE SCIENCE EXPO STARTS ANY MINUTE! PREPARE THE GOAT!
OH, %$*#.

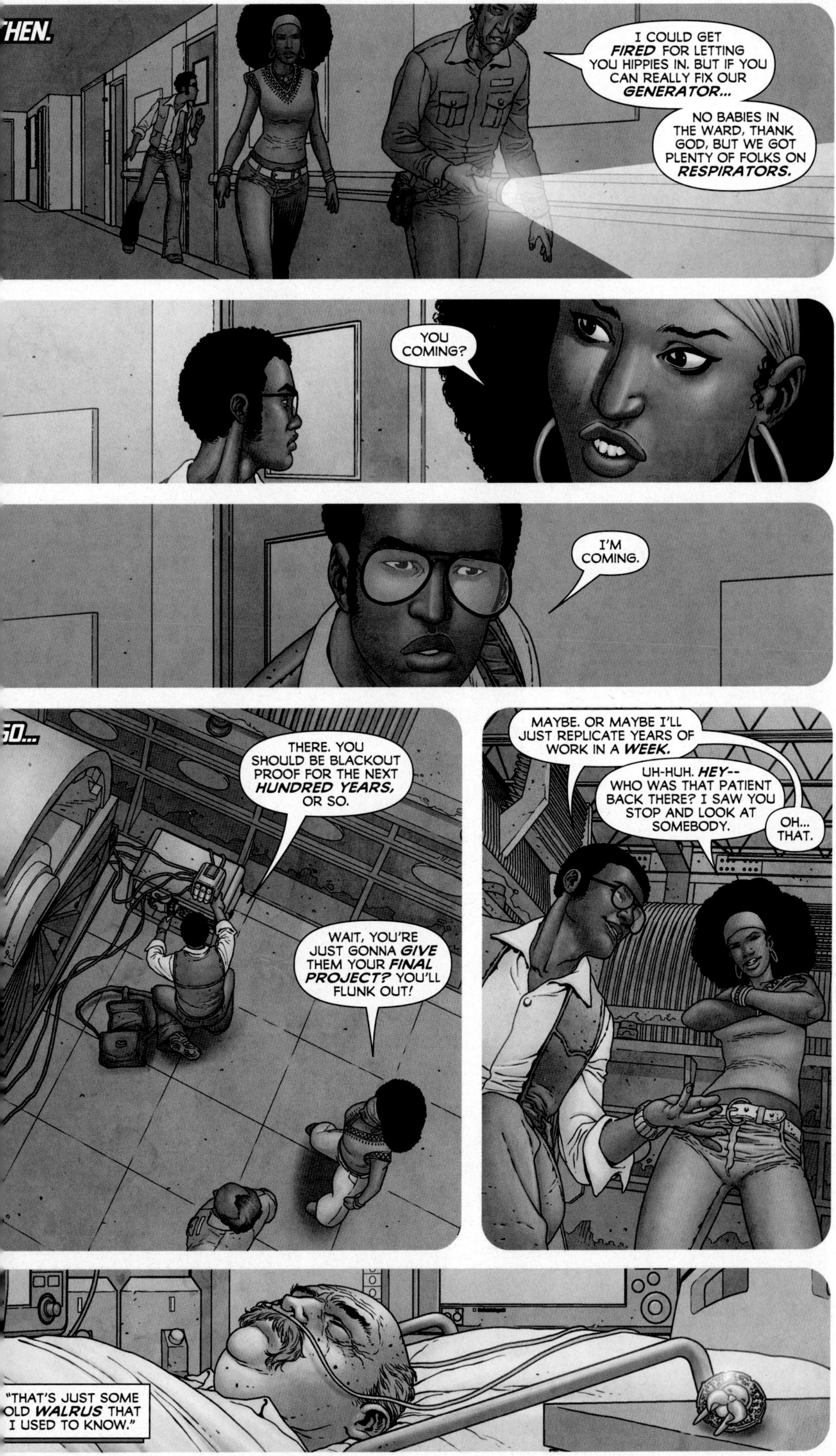
THEN.
I COULD GET FIRED FOR LETTING YOU HIPPIES IN. BUT IF YOU CAN REALLY FIX OUR GENERATOR...
NO BABIES IN THE WARD, THANK GOD, BUT WE GOT PLENTY OF FOLKS ON RESPIRATORS.
YOU COMING?
I'M COMING.
SO...
THERE. YOU SHOULD BE BLACKOUT PROOF FOR THE NEXT HUNDRED YEARS, OR SO.
WAIT, YOU'RE JUST GONNA GIVE THEM YOUR FINAL PROJECT? YOU'LL FLUNK OUT!
MAYBE. OR MAYBE I'LL JUST REPLICATE YEARS OF WORK IN A WEEK.
UH-HUH. HEY-- WHO WAS THAT PATIENT BACK THERE? I SAW YOU STOP AND LOOK AT SOMEBODY.
OH... THAT.
"THAT'S JUST SOME OLD WALRUS THAT I USED TO KNOW."

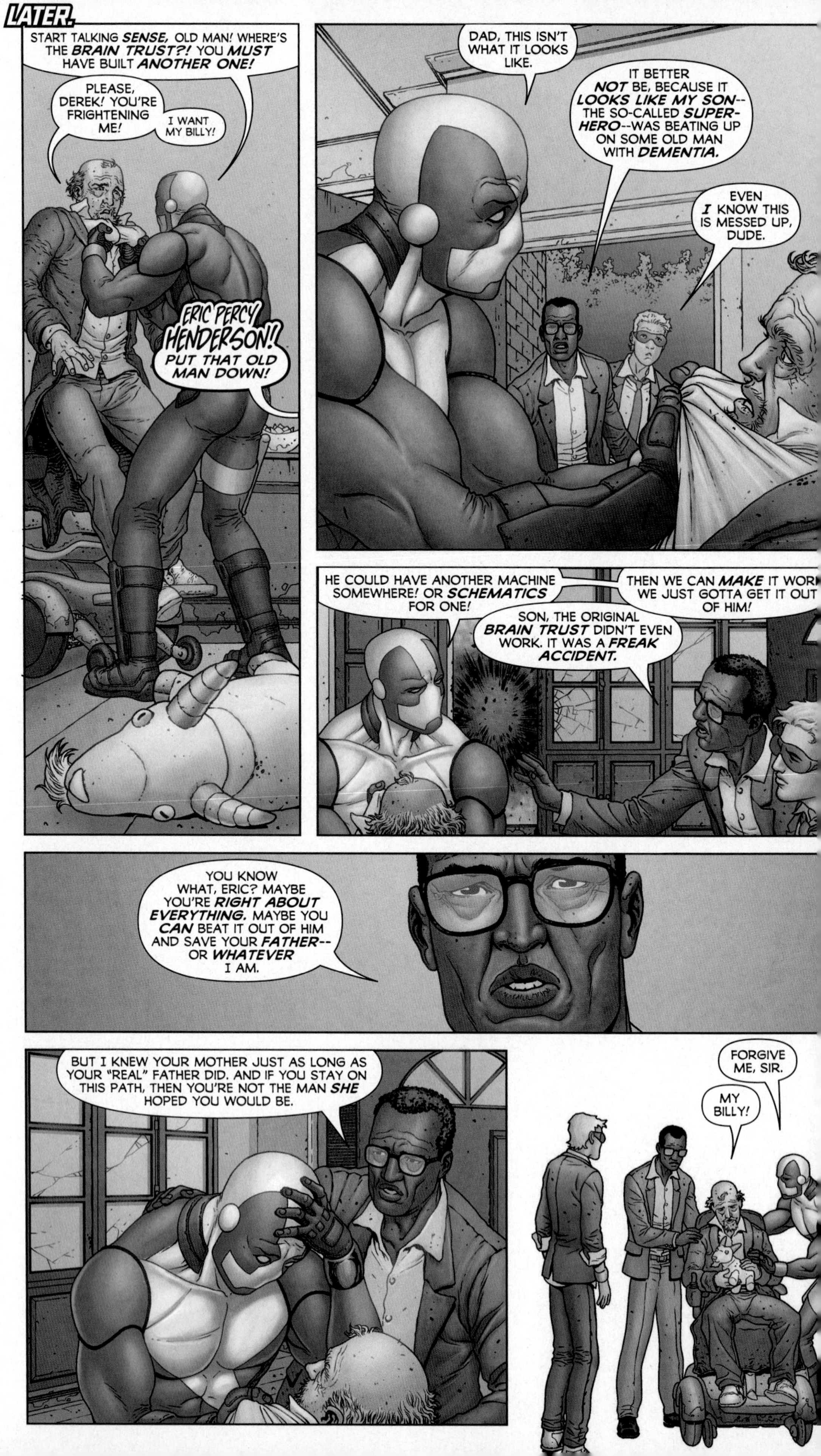
LATER.
START TALKING SENSE, OLD MAN! WHERE'S THE BRAIN TRUST?! YOU MUST HAVE BUILT ANOTHER ONE!
PLEASE, DEREK! YOU'RE FRIGHTENING ME!
I WANT MY BILLY!
ERIC PERCY HENDERSON!! PUT THAT OLD MAN DOWN!
DAD, THIS ISN'T WHAT IT LOOKS LIKE.
IT BETTER NOT BE, BECAUSE IT LOOKS LIKE MY SON-- THE SO-CALLED SUPER-HERO--WAS BEATING UP ON SOME OLD MAN WITH DEMENTIA.
EVEN I KNOW THIS IS MESSED UP, DUDE.
HE COULD HAVE ANOTHER MACHINE SOMEWHERE! OR SCHEMATICS FOR ONE!
THEN WE CAN MAKE IT WOR WE JUST GOTTA GET IT OUT OF HIM!
SON, THE ORIGINAL BRAIN TRUST DIDN'T EVEN WORK. IT WAS A FREAK ACCIDENT.
YOU KNOW WHAT, ERIC? MAYBE YOU'RE RIGHT ABOUT EVERYTHING. MAYBE YOU CAN BEAT IT OUT OF HIM AND SAVE YOUR FATHER-- OR WHATEVER I AM.
BUT I KNEW YOUR MOTHER JUST AS LONG AS YOUR "REAL" FATHER DID. AND IF YOU STAY ON THIS PATH, THEN YOU'RE NOT THE MAN SHE HOPED YOU WOULD BE.
FORGIVE ME, SIR.
MY BILLY!

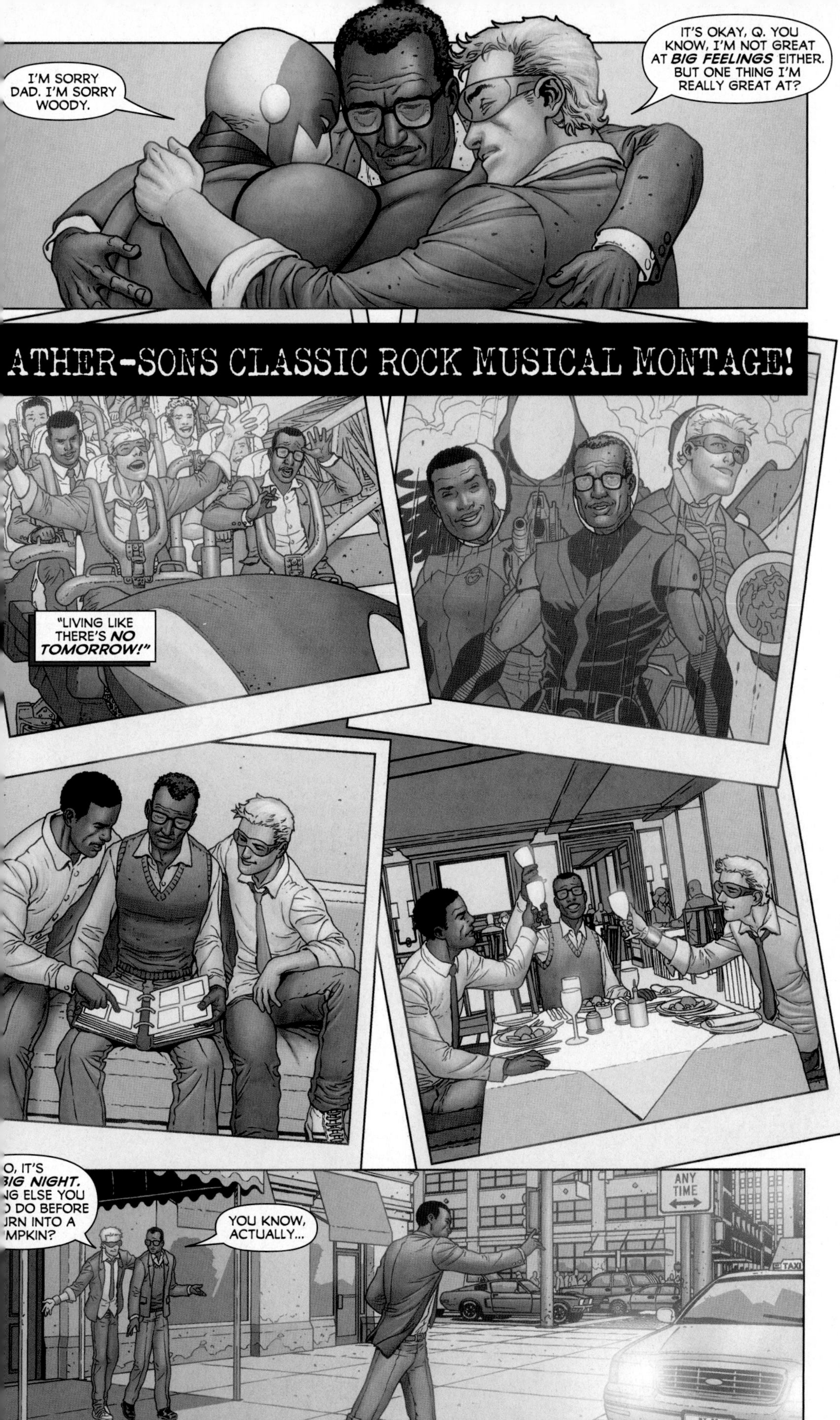
I'M SORRY DAD. I'M SORRY WOODY.
IT'S OKAY, Q. YOU KNOW, I'M NOT GREAT AT BIG FEELINGS EITHER. BUT ONE THING I'M REALLY GREAT AT?
ATHER-SONS CLASSIC ROCK MUSICAL MONTAGE!
"LIVING LIKE THERE'S NO TOMORROW!"
O, IT'S BIG NIGHT. NG ELSE YOU) DO BEFORE URN INTO A MPKIN?
YOU KNOW, ACTUALLY...
ANY TIME
TAXI

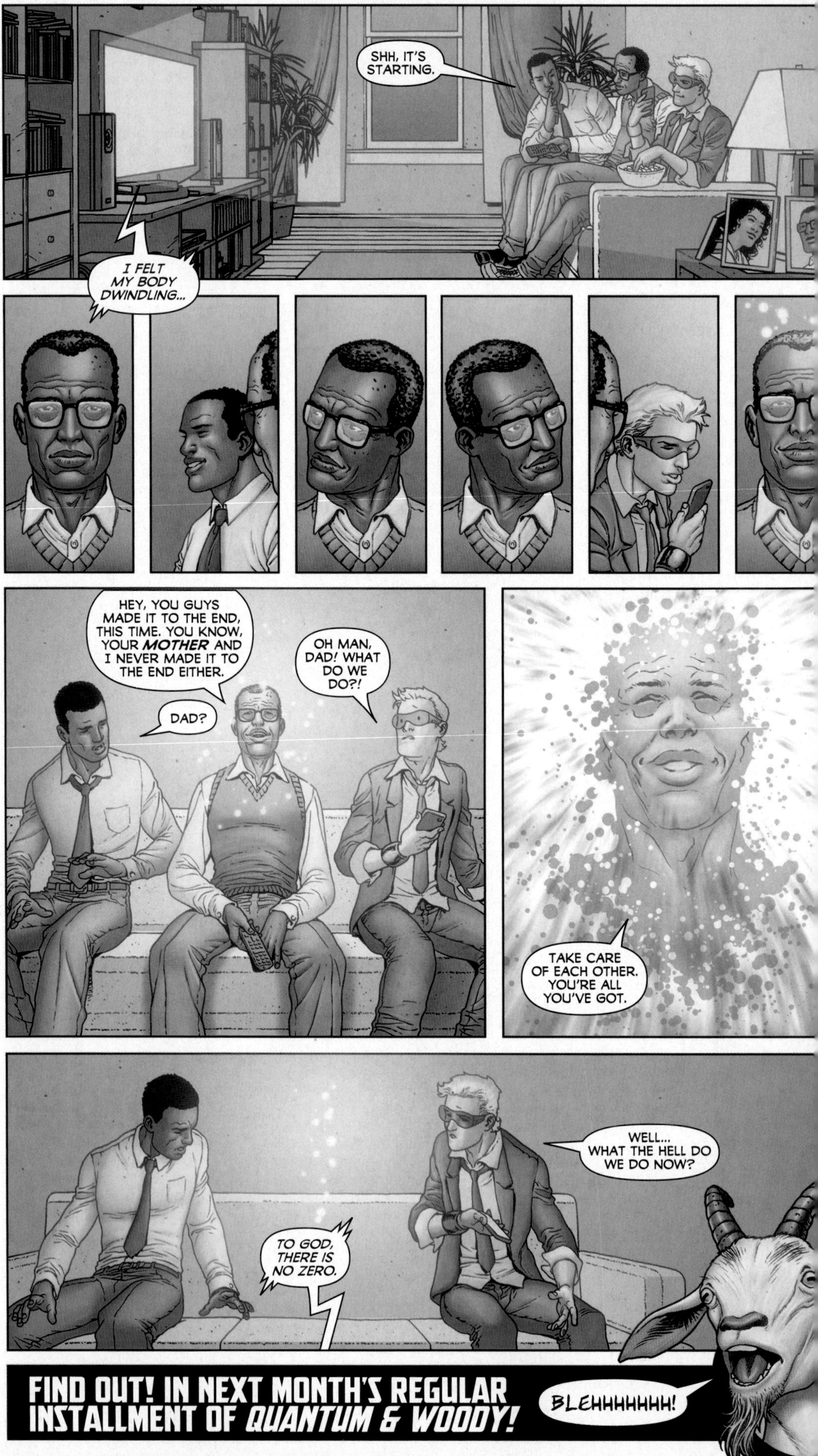

SHH, IT'S STARTING.
I FELT MY BODY DWINDLING...
HEY, YOU GUYS MADE IT TO THE END, THIS TIME. YOU KNOW, YOUR MOTHER AND I NEVER MADE IT TO THE END EITHER.
DAD?
OH MAN, DAD! WHAT DO WE DO?!
TAKE CARE OF EACH OTHER. YOU'RE ALL YOU'VE GOT.
WELL... WHAT THE HELL DO WE DO NOW?
TO GOD, THERE IS NO ZERO.
FIND OUT! IN NEXT MONTH'S REGULAR INSTALLMENT OF QUANTUM & WOODY!
BLEHHHHHHH!

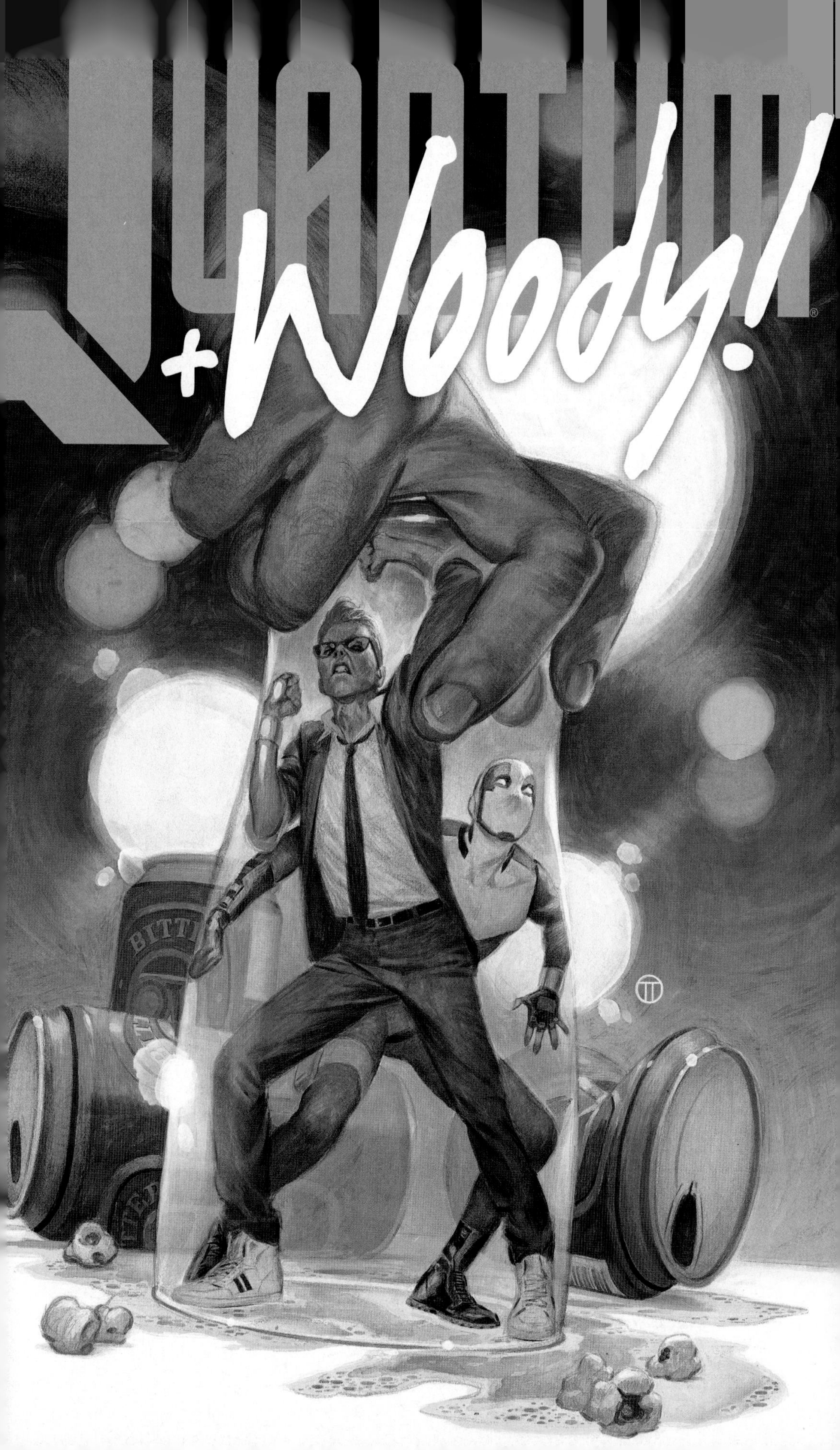
QUANTUM
+Woody!

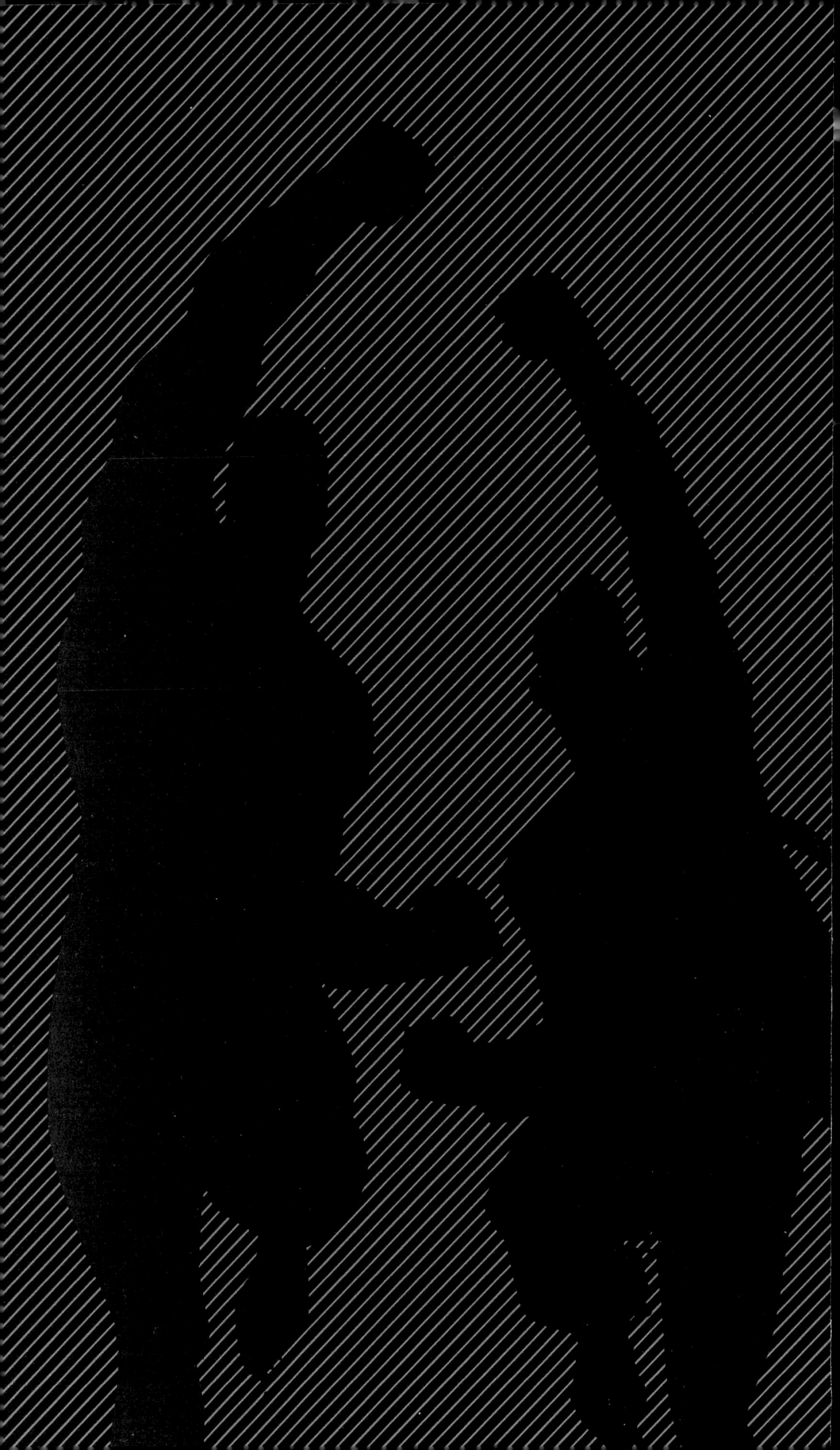

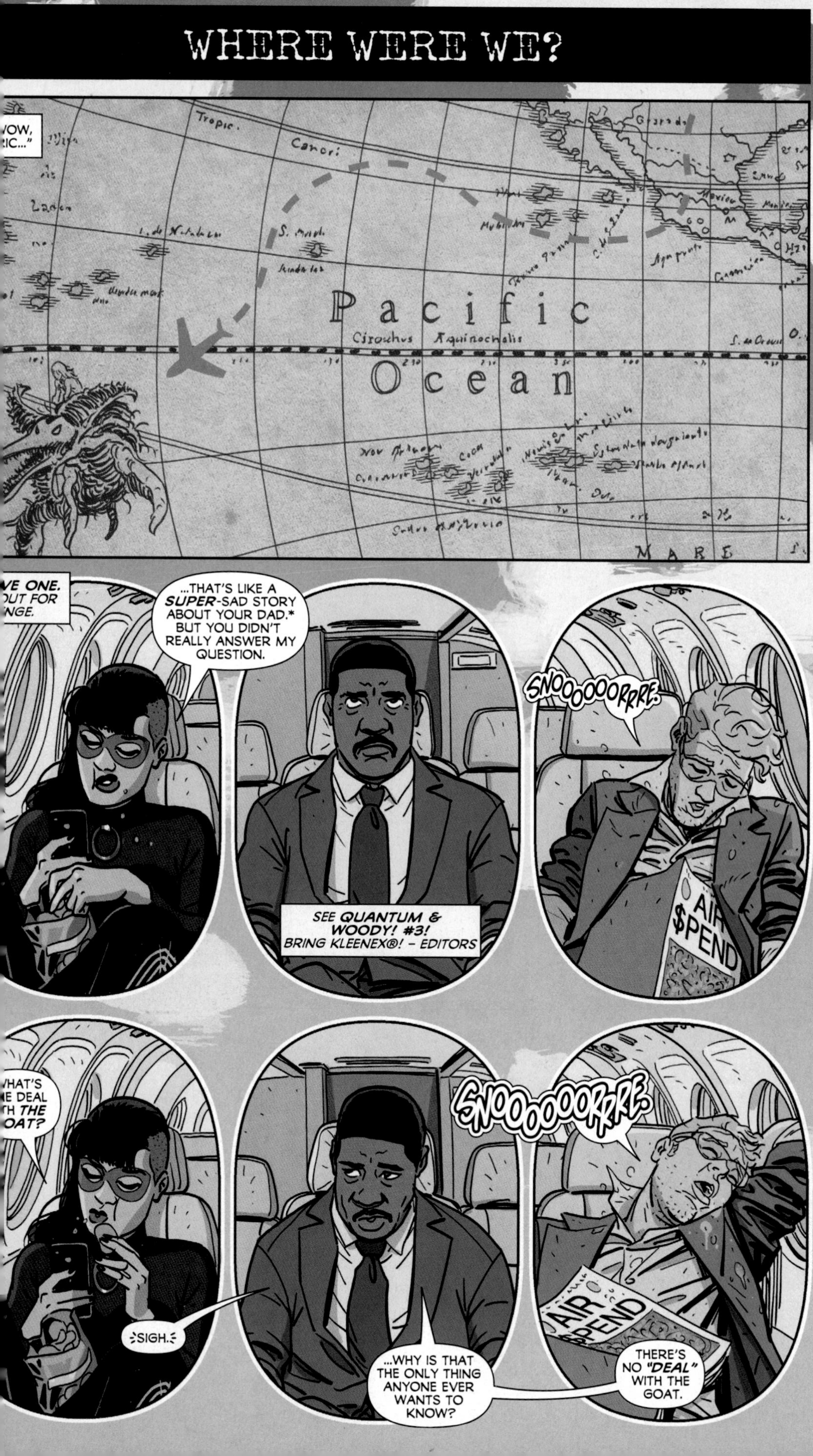

WHERE WERE WE?
WOW, ...RIC..."
Tropic. Cancri
Pacific
Ocean
...VE ONE. ...OUT FOR ...NGE.
...THAT'S LIKE A SUPER-SAD STORY ABOUT YOUR DAD.* BUT YOU DIDN'T REALLY ANSWER MY QUESTION.
SEE QUANTUM & WOODY! #3! BRING KLEENEX®! – EDITORS
SNOOOOOORRRE.
AIR $PEND
...WHAT'S ...E DEAL ...TH THE ...OAT?
SNOOOOOORRRE.
SIGH.
...WHY IS THAT THE ONLY THING ANYONE EVER WANTS TO KNOW?
THERE'S NO "DEAL" WITH THE GOAT.
AIR $PEND

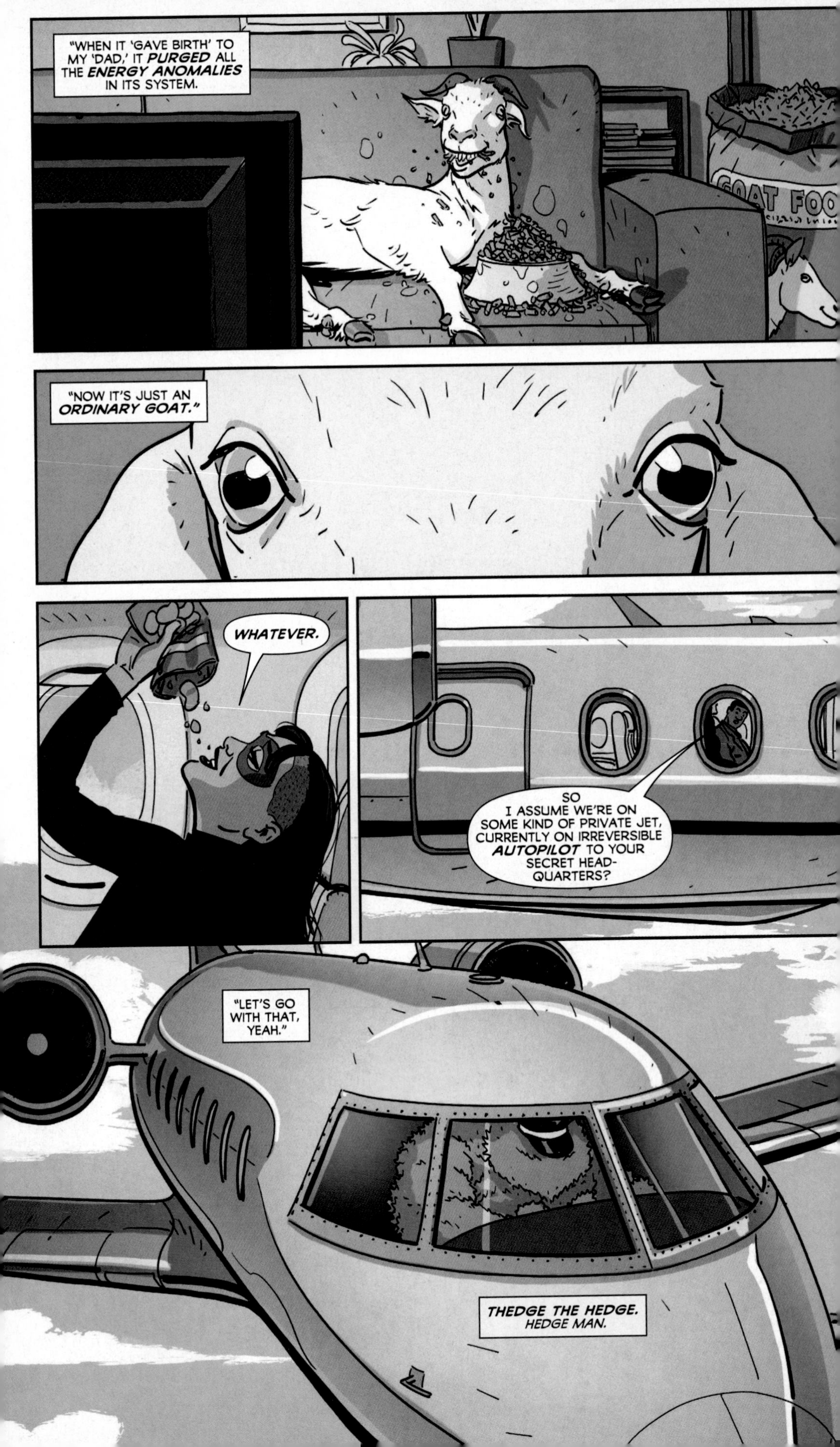
"WHEN IT 'GAVE BIRTH' TO MY 'DAD,' IT PURGED ALL THE ENERGY ANOMALIES IN ITS SYSTEM.
GOAT FOO
"NOW IT'S JUST AN ORDINARY GOAT."
WHATEVER.
SO I ASSUME WE'RE ON SOME KIND OF PRIVATE JET, CURRENTLY ON IRREVERSIBLE AUTOPILOT TO YOUR SECRET HEAD-QUARTERS?
"LET'S GO WITH THAT, YEAH."
THEDGE THE HEDGE.
HEDGE MAN.

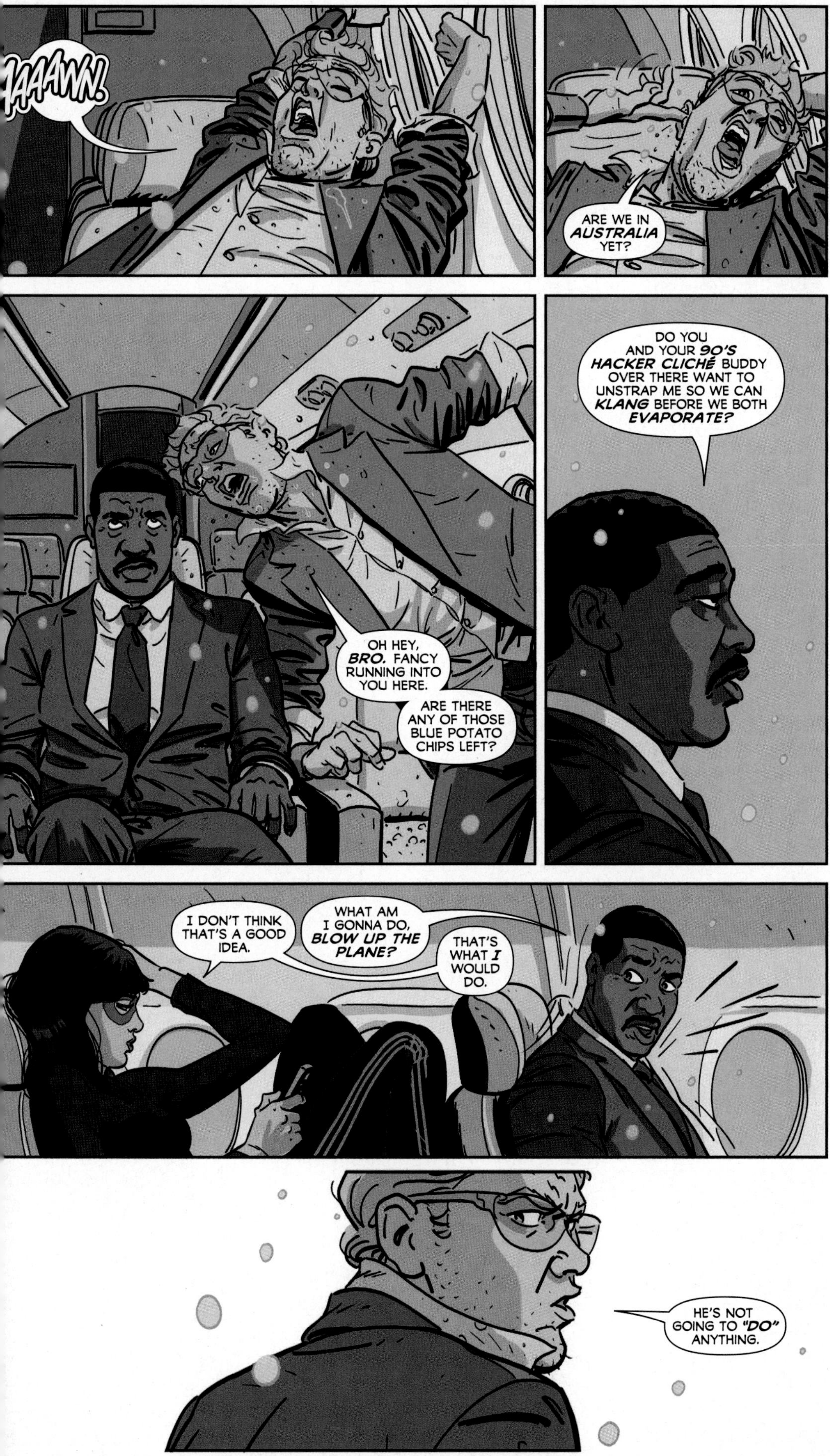

YAAAWN!
ARE WE IN AUSTRALIA YET?
OH HEY, BRO. FANCY RUNNING INTO YOU HERE.
ARE THERE ANY OF THOSE BLUE POTATO CHIPS LEFT?
DO YOU AND YOUR 90'S HACKER CLICHÉ BUDDY OVER THERE WANT TO UNSTRAP ME SO WE CAN KLANG BEFORE WE BOTH EVAPORATE?
I DON'T THINK THAT'S A GOOD IDEA.
WHAT AM I GONNA DO, BLOW UP THE PLANE?
THAT'S WHAT I WOULD DO.
HE'S NOT GOING TO "DO" ANYTHING.

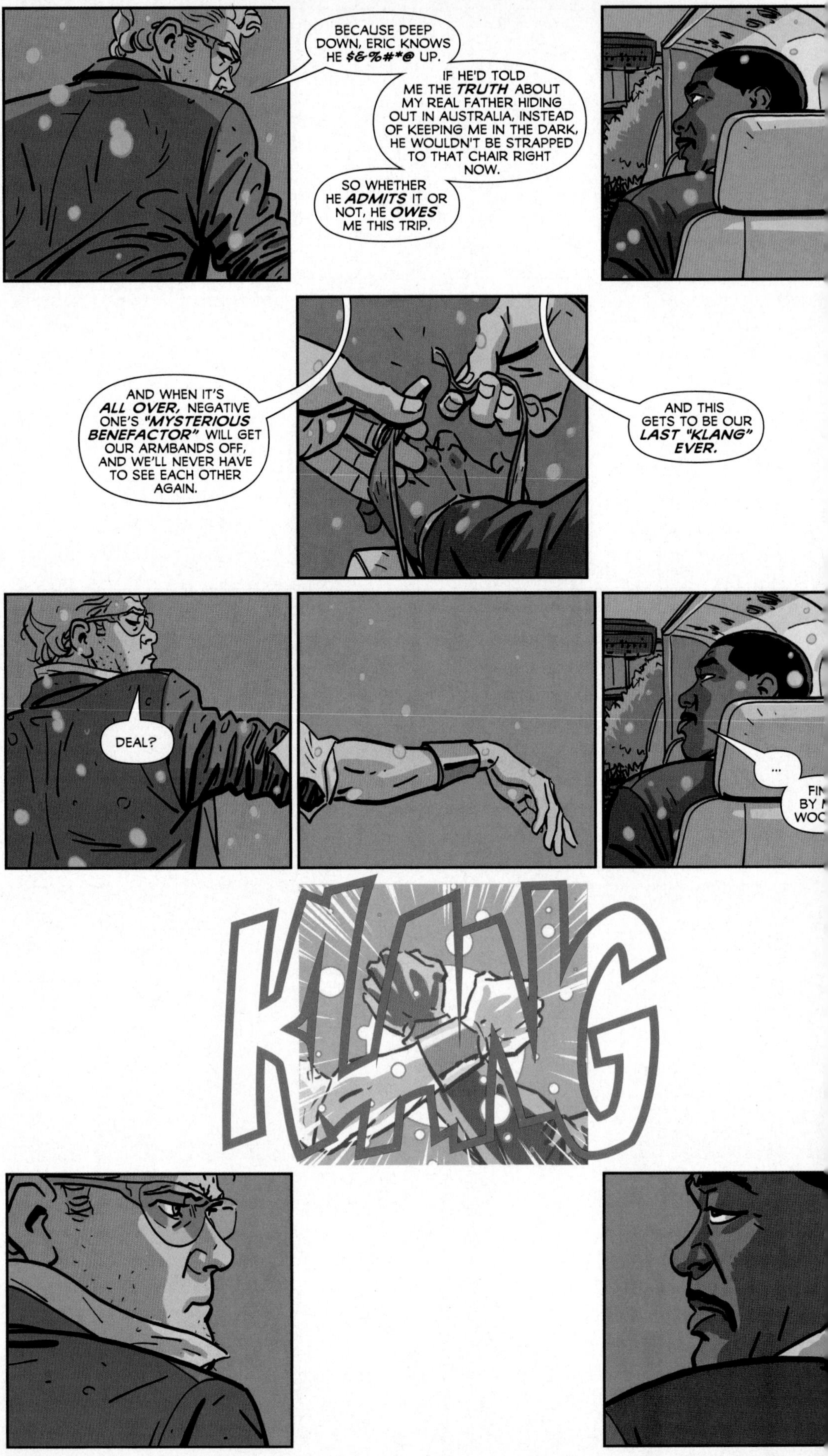
BECAUSE DEEP DOWN, ERIC KNOWS HE $&%#*@ UP.
IF HE'D TOLD ME THE *TRUTH* ABOUT MY REAL FATHER HIDING OUT IN AUSTRALIA, INSTEAD OF KEEPING ME IN THE DARK, HE WOULDN'T BE STRAPPED TO THAT CHAIR RIGHT NOW.
SO WHETHER HE *ADMITS* IT OR NOT, HE *OWES* ME THIS TRIP.
AND WHEN IT'S ***ALL OVER,*** NEGATIVE ONE'S ***"MYSTERIOUS BENEFACTOR"*** WILL GET OUR ARMBANDS OFF, AND WE'LL NEVER HAVE TO SEE EACH OTHER AGAIN.
AND THIS GETS TO BE OUR ***LAST "KLANG" EVER.***
DEAL?
...
KLANG

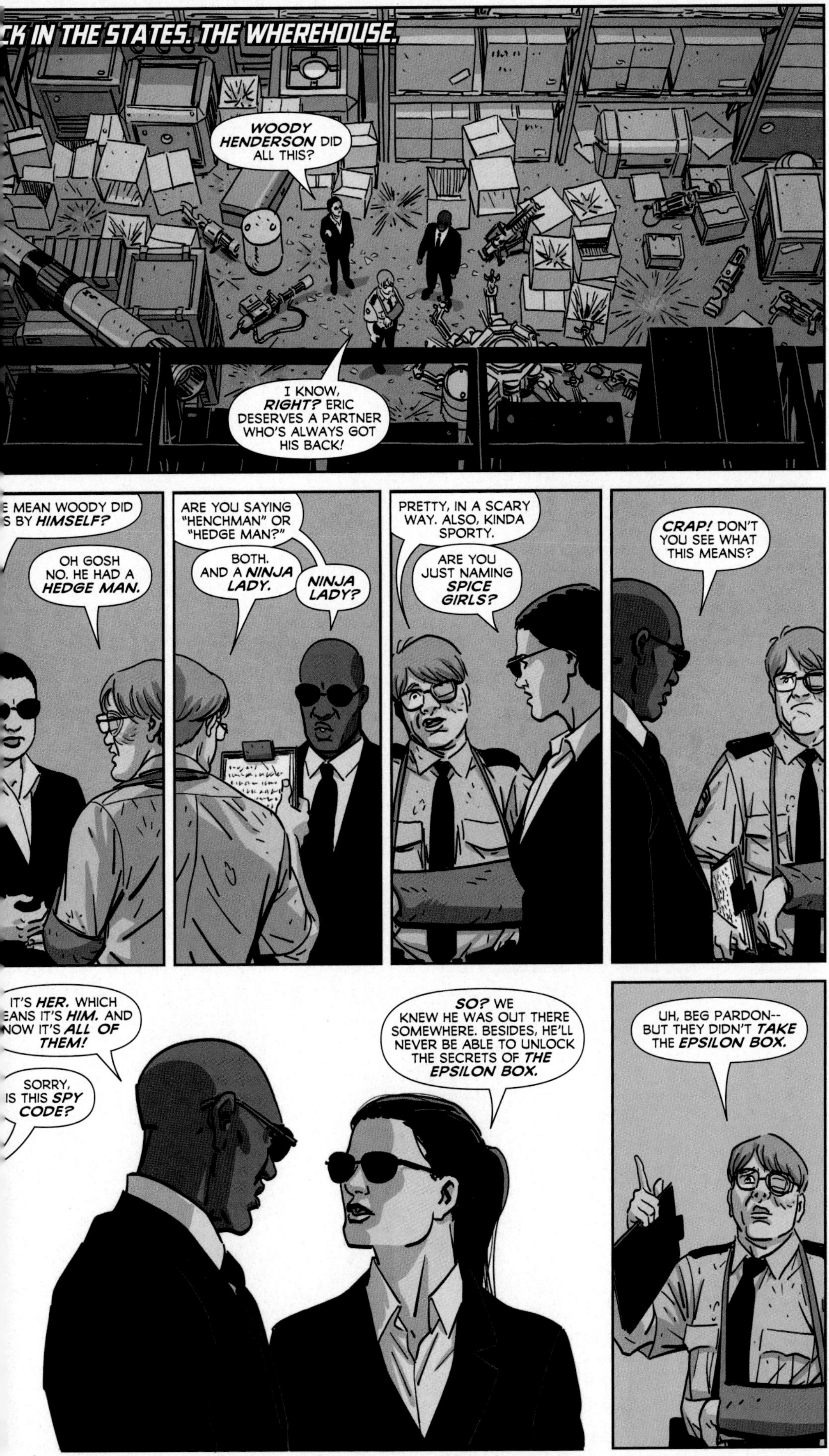
CK IN THE STATES. THE WHEREHOUSE.
WOODY HENDERSON DID ALL THIS?
I KNOW, RIGHT? ERIC DESERVES A PARTNER WHO'S ALWAYS GOT HIS BACK!
E MEAN WOODY DID S BY HIMSELF?
OH GOSH NO. HE HAD A HEDGE MAN.
ARE YOU SAYING "HENCHMAN" OR "HEDGE MAN?"
BOTH. AND A NINJA LADY.
NINJA LADY?
PRETTY, IN A SCARY WAY. ALSO, KINDA SPORTY.
ARE YOU JUST NAMING SPICE GIRLS?
CRAP! DON'T YOU SEE WHAT THIS MEANS?
IT'S HER. WHICH EANS IT'S HIM. AND NOW IT'S ALL OF THEM!
SORRY, IS THIS SPY CODE?
SO? WE KNEW HE WAS OUT THERE SOMEWHERE. BESIDES, HE'LL NEVER BE ABLE TO UNLOCK THE SECRETS OF THE EPSILON BOX.
UH, BEG PARDON-- BUT THEY DIDN'T TAKE THE EPSILON BOX.

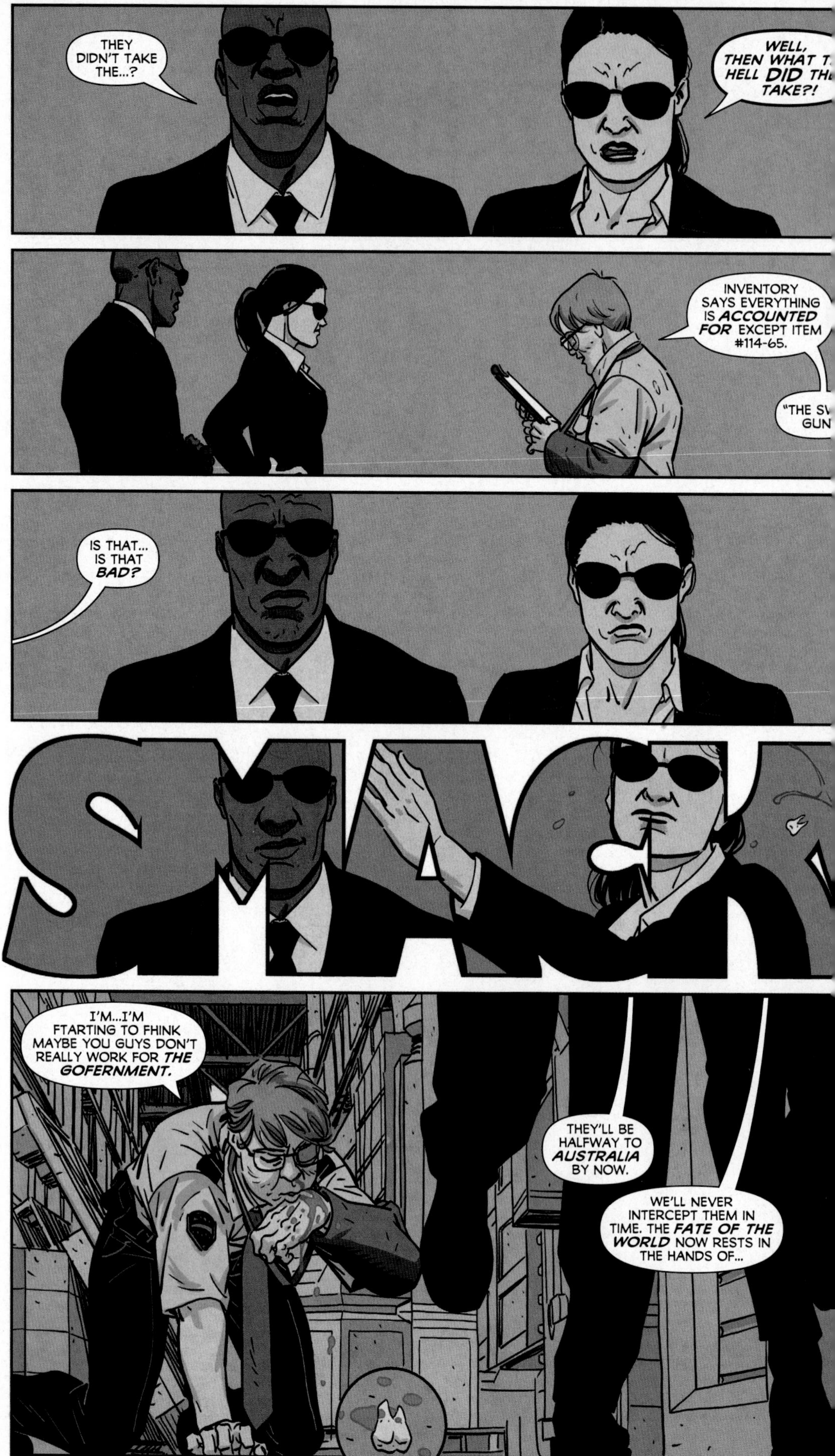
THEY DIDN'T TAKE THE...?
WELL, THEN WHAT
HELL DID
TAKE?!
INVENTORY SAYS EVERYTHING IS ACCOUNTED FOR EXCEPT ITEM #114-65.
IS THAT... IS THAT BAD?
I'M...I'M FTARTING TO FHINK MAYBE YOU GUYS DON'T REALLY WORK FOR THE GOFERNMENT.
THEY'LL BE HALFWAY TO AUSTRALIA BY NOW.
WE'LL NEVER INTERCEPT THEM IN TIME. THE FATE OF THE WORLD NOW RESTS IN THE HANDS OF...

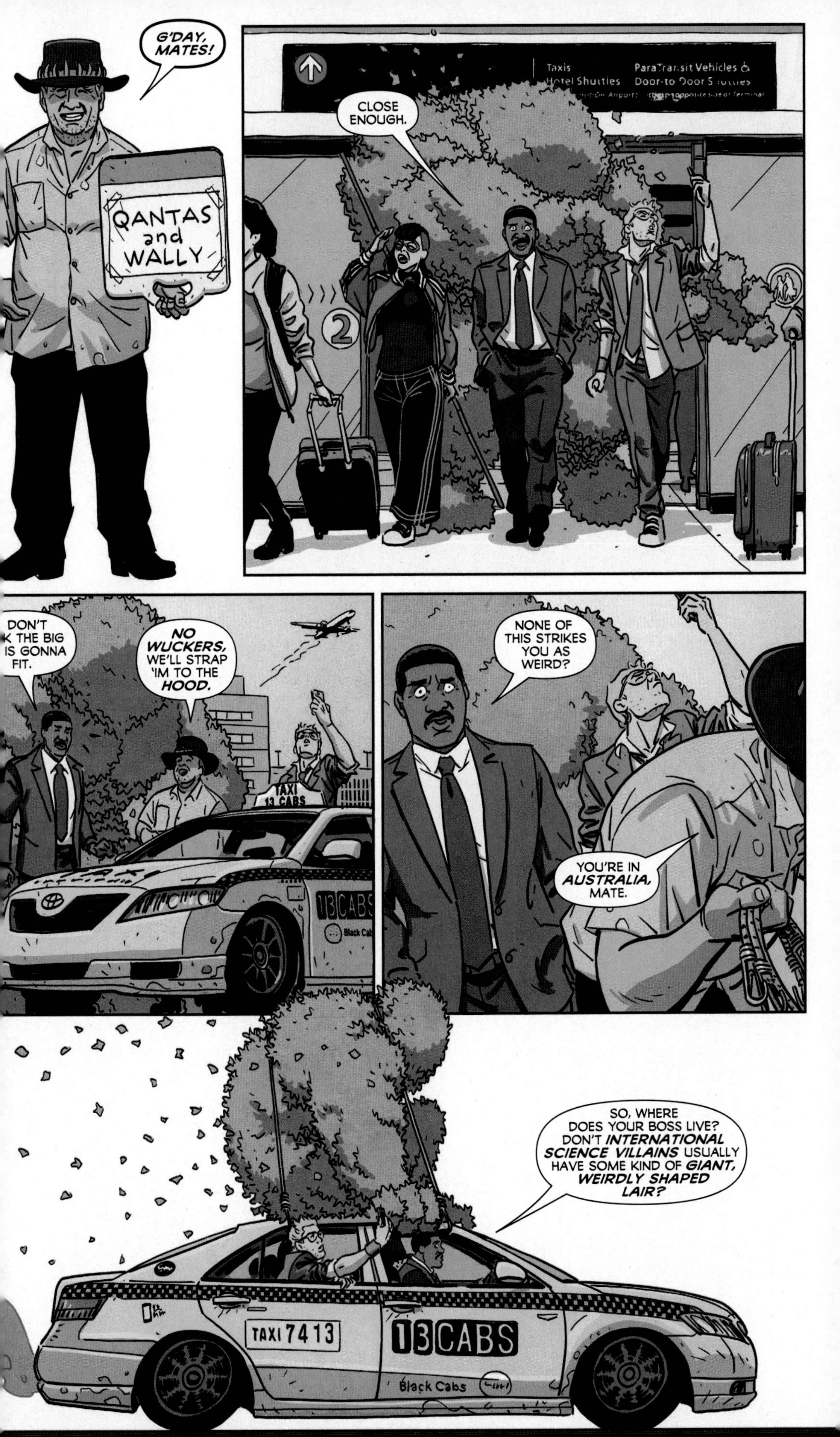

G'DAY, MATES!
QANTAS and WALLY
Taxis
Hotel Shuttles
ParaTransit Vehicles
CLOSE ENOUGH.
DON'T
K THE BIG
IS GONNA
FIT.
NO WUCKERS, WE'LL STRAP 'IM TO THE HOOD.
TAXI 13 CABS
13CABS
Black Cabs
NONE OF THIS STRIKES YOU AS WEIRD?
YOU'RE IN AUSTRALIA, MATE.
SO, WHERE DOES YOUR BOSS LIVE? DON'T INTERNATIONAL SCIENCE VILLAINS USUALLY HAVE SOME KIND OF GIANT, WEIRDLY SHAPED LAIR?
TAXI 7413
13CABS
Black Cabs

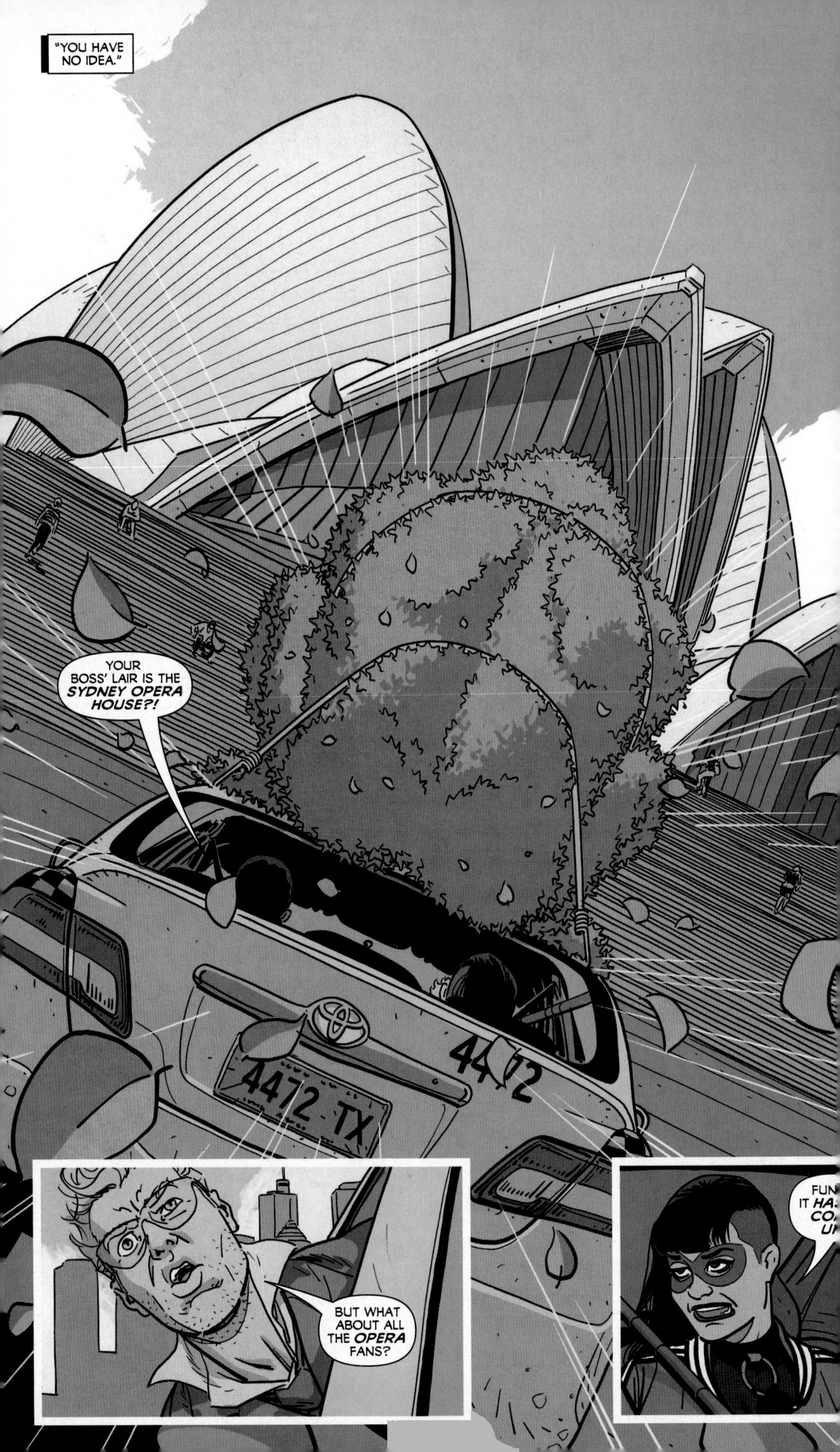
"YOU HAVE NO IDEA."
YOUR BOSS' LAIR IS THE *SYDNEY OPERA HOUSE?!*
4472 TX
BUT WHAT ABOUT ALL THE *OPERA* FANS?

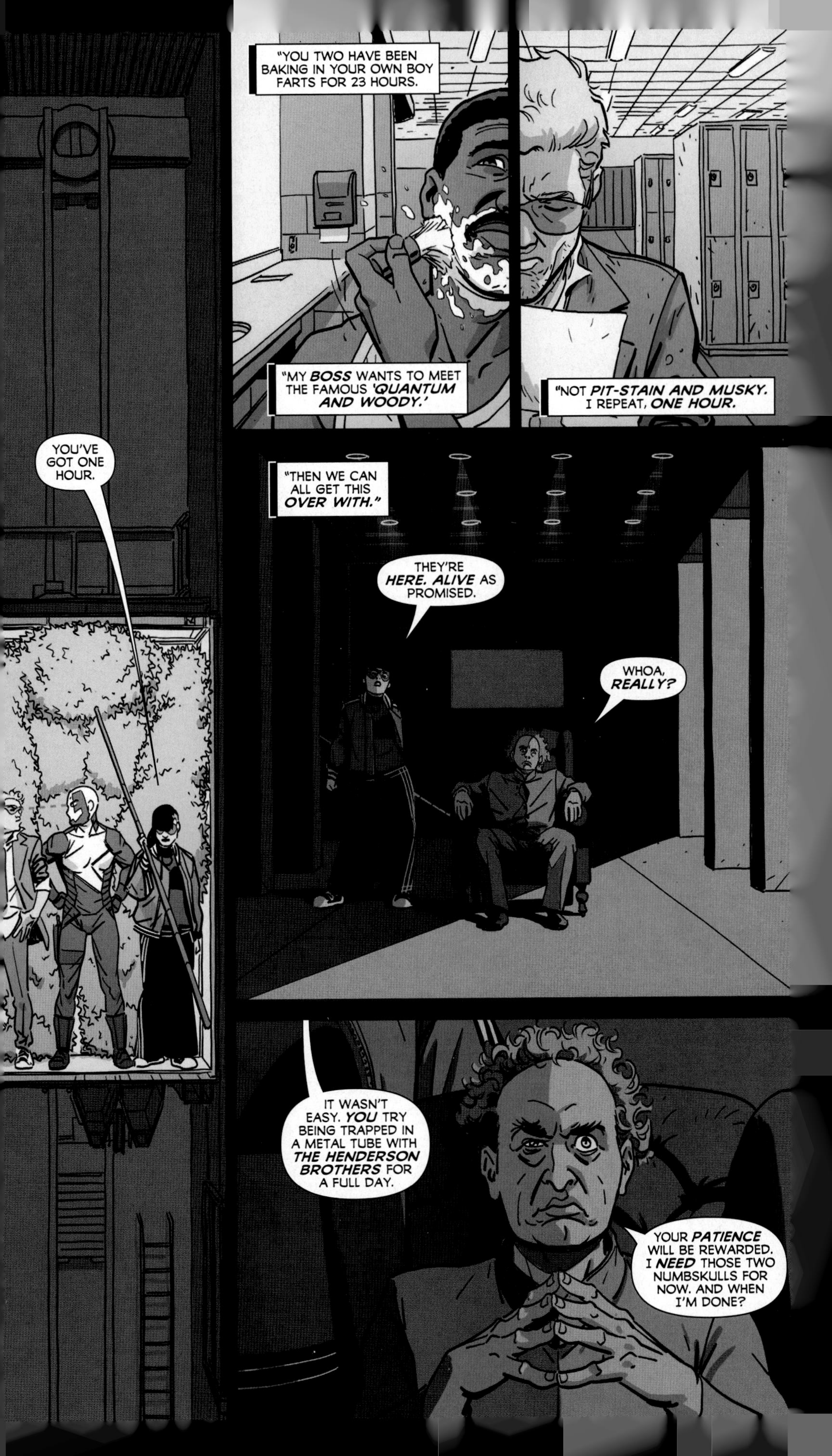
"YOU TWO HAVE BEEN BAKING IN YOUR OWN BOY FARTS FOR 23 HOURS.
"MY BOSS WANTS TO MEET THE FAMOUS 'QUANTUM AND WOODY.'
"NOT PIT-STAIN AND MUSKY. I REPEAT, ONE HOUR.
YOU'VE GOT ONE HOUR.
"THEN WE CAN ALL GET THIS OVER WITH."
THEY'RE HERE. ALIVE AS PROMISED.
WHOA, REALLY?
IT WASN'T EASY. YOU TRY BEING TRAPPED IN A METAL TUBE WITH THE HENDERSON BROTHERS FOR A FULL DAY.
YOUR PATIENCE WILL BE REWARDED. I NEED THOSE TWO NUMBSKULLS FOR NOW. AND WHEN I'M DONE?

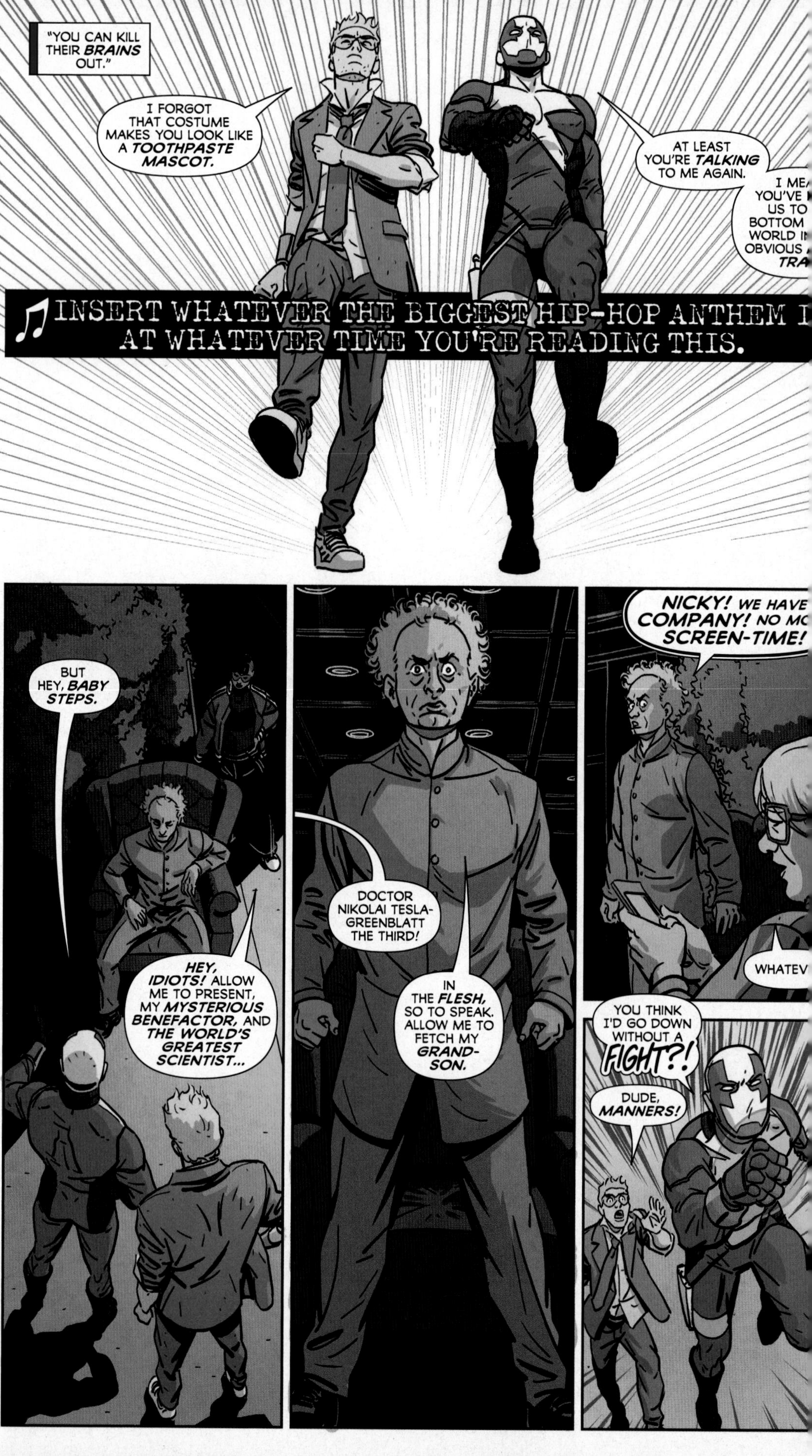

"YOU CAN KILL THEIR BRAINS OUT."
I FORGOT THAT COSTUME MAKES YOU LOOK LIKE A TOOTHPASTE MASCOT.
AT LEAST YOU'RE TALKING TO ME AGAIN.
I ME YOU'VE US TO BOTTOM WORLD I OBVIOUS TRA
INSERT WHATEVER THE BIGGEST HIP-HOP ANTHEM I AT WHATEVER TIME YOU'RE READING THIS.
BUT HEY, BABY STEPS.
HEY, IDIOTS! ALLOW ME TO PRESENT, MY MYSTERIOUS BENEFACTOR, AND THE WORLD'S GREATEST SCIENTIST...
DOCTOR NIKOLAI TESLA-GREENBLATT THE THIRD!
IN THE FLESH, SO TO SPEAK. ALLOW ME TO FETCH MY GRAND-SON.
NICKY! WE HAVE COMPANY! NO MO SCREEN-TIME!
WHATEV
YOU THINK I'D GO DOWN WITHOUT A FIGHT?!
DUDE, MANNERS!

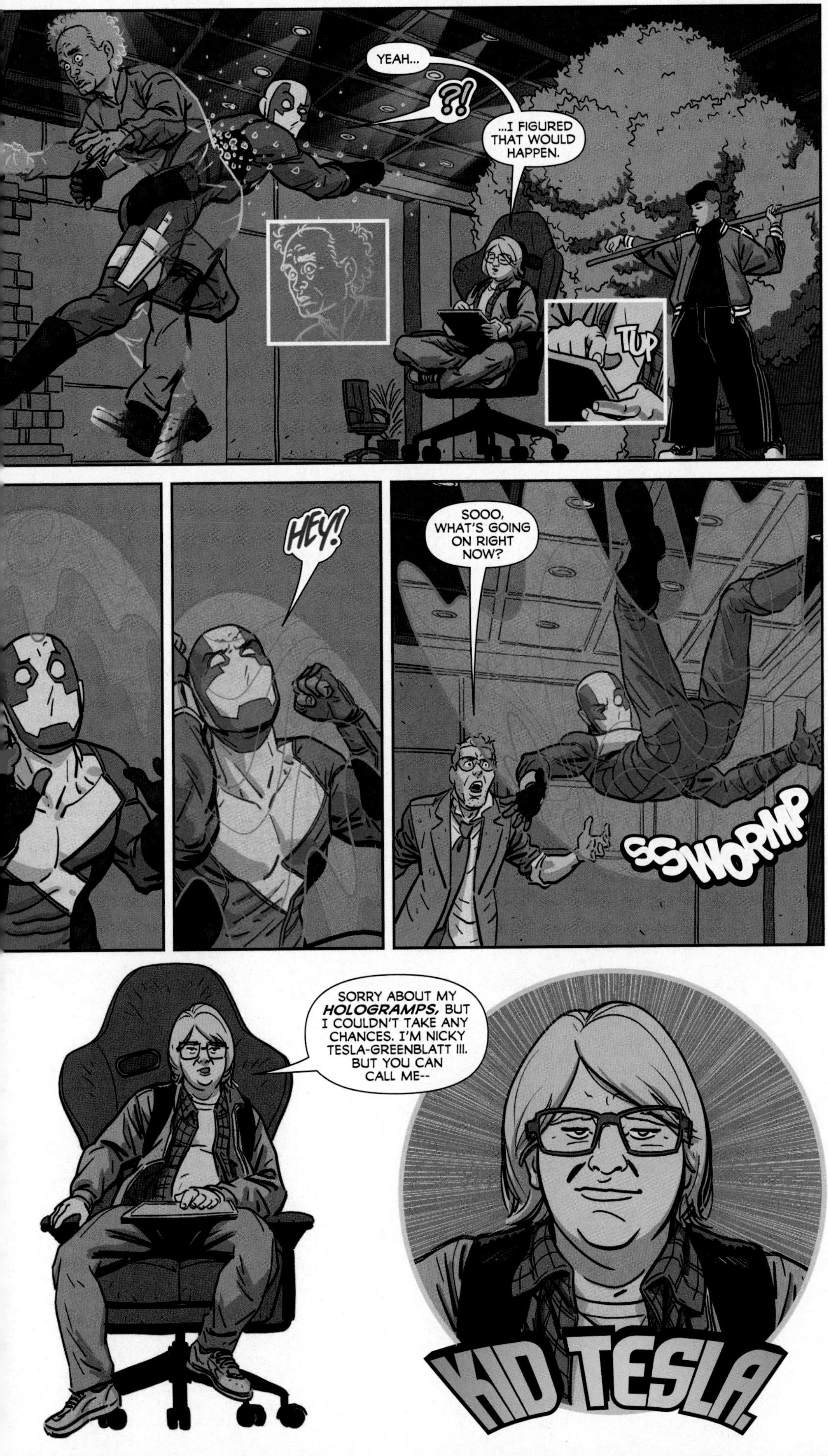
YEAH...
?!
...I FIGURED THAT WOULD HAPPEN.
TUP
HEY!
SOOO, WHAT'S GOING ON RIGHT NOW?
SSWORMP
SORRY ABOUT MY ***HOLOGRAMPS,*** BUT I COULDN'T TAKE ANY CHANCES. I'M NICKY TESLA-GREENBLATT III. BUT YOU CAN CALL ME--
KID TESLA.

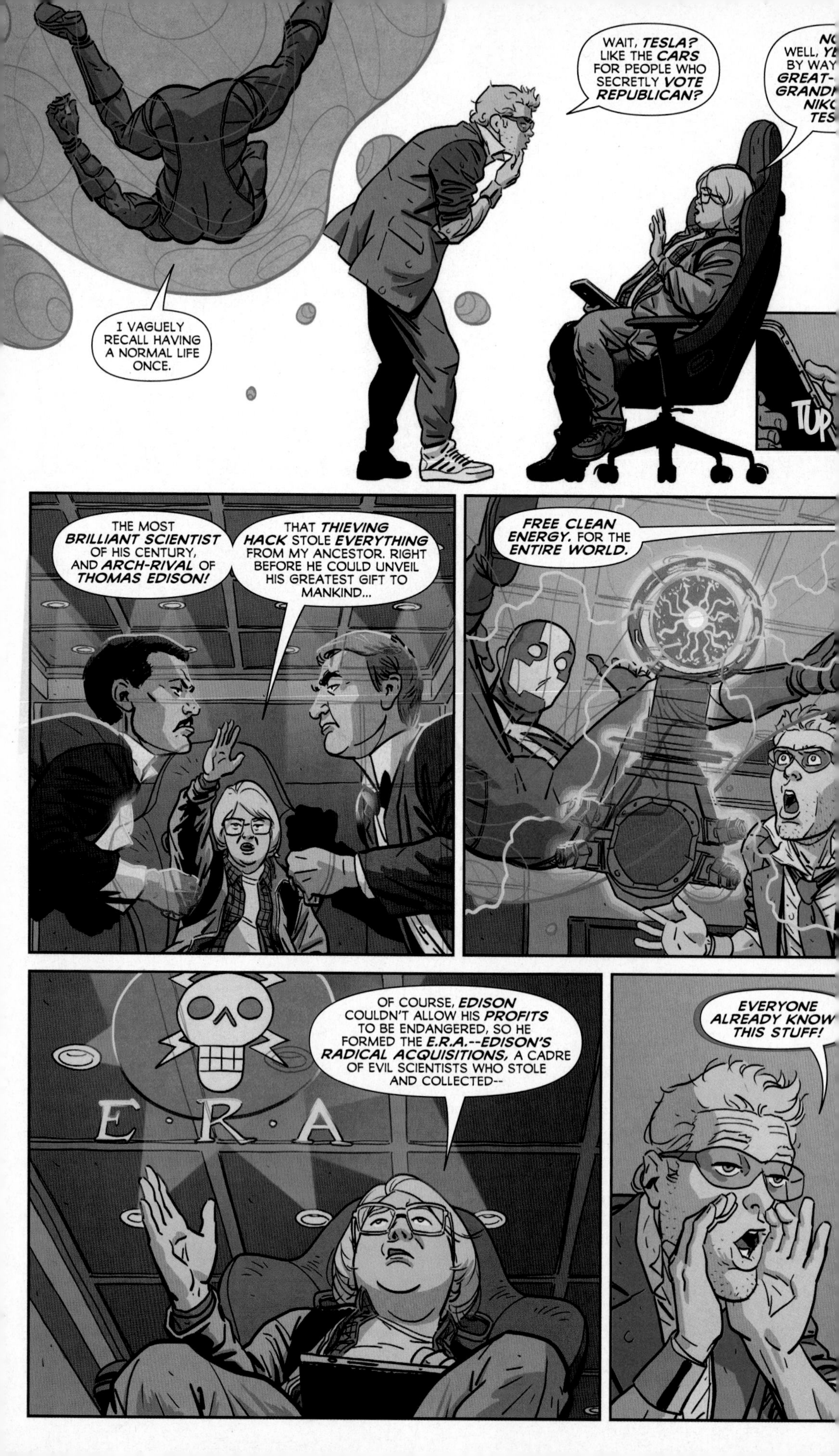

I VAGUELY RECALL HAVING A NORMAL LIFE ONCE.
WAIT, *TESLA?* LIKE THE *CARS* FOR PEOPLE WHO SECRETLY *VOTE REPUBLICAN?*
NO WELL, YE BY WAY GREAT- GRANDI NIKO TES
TUP
THE MOST *BRILLIANT SCIENTIST* OF HIS CENTURY, AND *ARCH-RIVAL* OF *THOMAS EDISON!*
THAT *THIEVING HACK* STOLE *EVERYTHING* FROM MY ANCESTOR. RIGHT BEFORE HE COULD UNVEIL HIS GREATEST GIFT TO MANKIND...
FREE CLEAN ENERGY. FOR THE *ENTIRE WORLD.*
E.R.A
OF COURSE, *EDISON* COULDN'T ALLOW HIS *PROFITS* TO BE ENDANGERED, SO HE FORMED THE *E.R.A.--EDISON'S RADICAL ACQUISITIONS,* A CADRE OF EVIL SCIENTISTS WHO STOLE AND COLLECTED--
EVERYONE ALREADY KNOW THIS STUFF!

PES, WE *CARE* OF CLOWNS! V STYLE!

HEY! I'M...I'M NERATION Y!

DID YOU, *OLD MAN?*

YOU PUT A *DENT* IN THE E.R.A.'S RANKS, BUT THEY WENT *INCOGNITO* TO REBUILD.

ERIC, YOU KNOW THEM AS YOUR BOSSES-- *THE COMPANY MEN.*

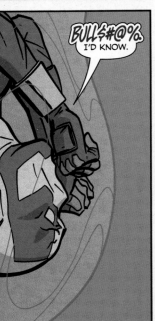

BULL$#@%. I'D KNOW.

WOULD YOU? OR WOULD YOU BE SO *GRATEFUL* FOR THE APPROVAL FROM *AUTHORITY FIGURES* THAT YOU'D GO ALONG WITH ANYTHING?

OH SNAP, HE'S GOT YOU THERE, DUDE.

TO GET *REVENGE* FOR *MY FAMILY,* I NEEDED TO STEAL METHING *BACK* FROM EDISON AND HIS CRONIES. LUCKILY, I HAD AN INSIDE MAN.

WHO? THAT *KEITH* GUY?

ARE YOU SERIOUS? IT WAS *YOU,* DUMMY! *YOU'RE THE INSIDE MAN!*

"**I'M** THE ONE WHO HIRED **DOCTOR UNFATHOMA** IDIOT TO ROB THE WHEREH

"OF COURSE, I COULDN **TRUST** HIM TO BRING MY **REAL QUARRY,** I SENT HIM ON A WILD G CHASE--THE EPSILON B

"AND **I'M** THE ONE WHO PLANTED THE ANONYMOUS TIP THAT SENT YOU CHASING AFTER HIM--KNOWING **THE E.R.A.** WOULD GET THERE BEFORE THE POLICE.

#HotTip: Dr. U is robbing govt warehouse RN!!! #TeamWoody #WoodyRulez

New message

"JUST LIK I KNEW T COULD NE RESIST ADD YOU TO T **COLLECTI** QUANTUM WOODY THE **GREAT INVENTION** DEREK **HENDERSO**

DON'T YOU **DARE** SAY HIS NAME!

DAMN, ERIC. **DADDY ISSUES** MUCH?

THA YO

I DON'T GET IT.

THERE'S A SHOCKER.

HOW COULD ERIC BE YOUR INSIDE MAN IF HE DIDN'T EVEN **KNOW** HE WAS WORKING FOR THE BAD GUYS?

UH, NO OFFENSE.

BECAUSE OF **YOU.**

"YOU MAKE A **BIG SHOW** OF FIGHTING EACH OTHER, BUT WHEN IT COMES TO **YOU,** WOODY, HE PULLS HIS PUNCHES.

"EVERY TIME."

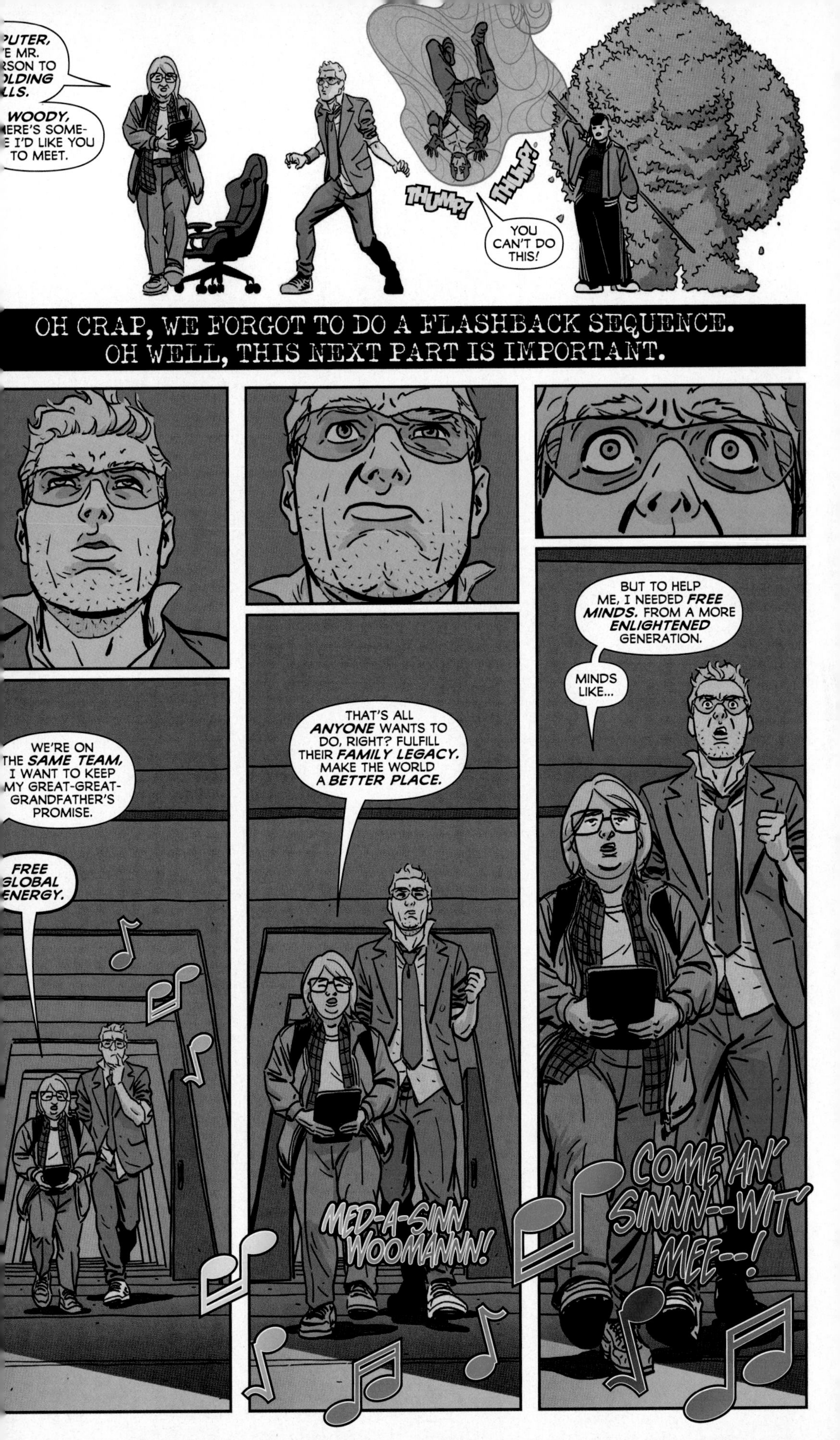
WOODY,
I'D LIKE YOU
TO MEET.
THUMP!
THUMP!
YOU CAN'T DO THIS!
OH CRAP, WE FORGOT TO DO A FLASHBACK SEQUENCE. OH WELL, THIS NEXT PART IS IMPORTANT.
WE'RE ON THE SAME TEAM, I WANT TO KEEP MY GREAT-GREAT-GRANDFATHER'S PROMISE.
FREE GLOBAL ENERGY.
THAT'S ALL ANYONE WANTS TO DO, RIGHT? FULFILL THEIR FAMILY LEGACY. MAKE THE WORLD A BETTER PLACE.
MED-A-SINN WOOMANNN!
BUT TO HELP ME, I NEEDED FREE MINDS. FROM A MORE ENLIGHTENED GENERATION.
MINDS LIKE...
COME AN' SINNN--WIT' MEE--!

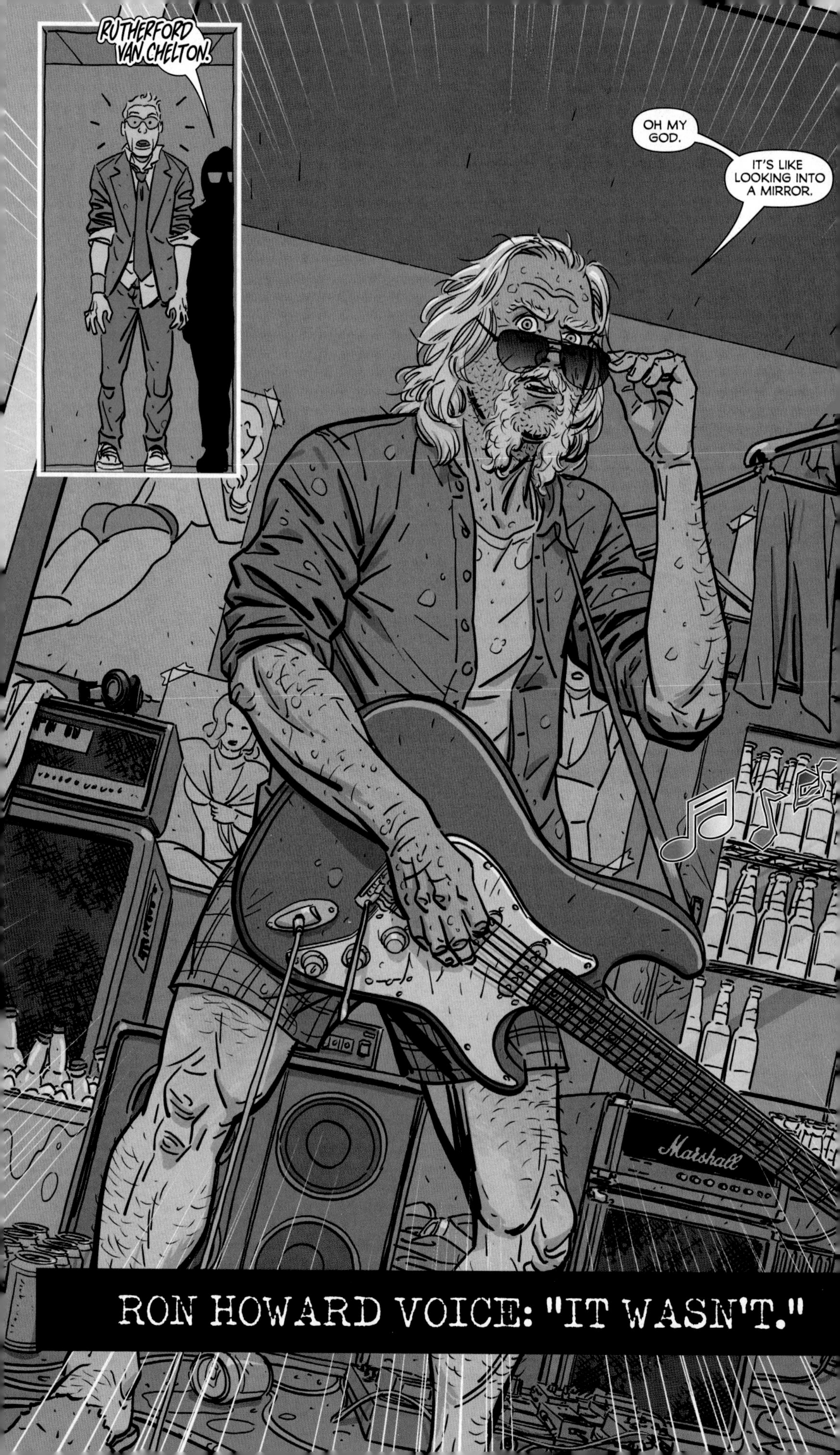
RUTHERFORD VAN CHELTON!
OH MY GOD.
IT'S LIKE LOOKING INTO A MIRROR.
RON HOWARD VOICE: "IT WASN'T."
Marshall

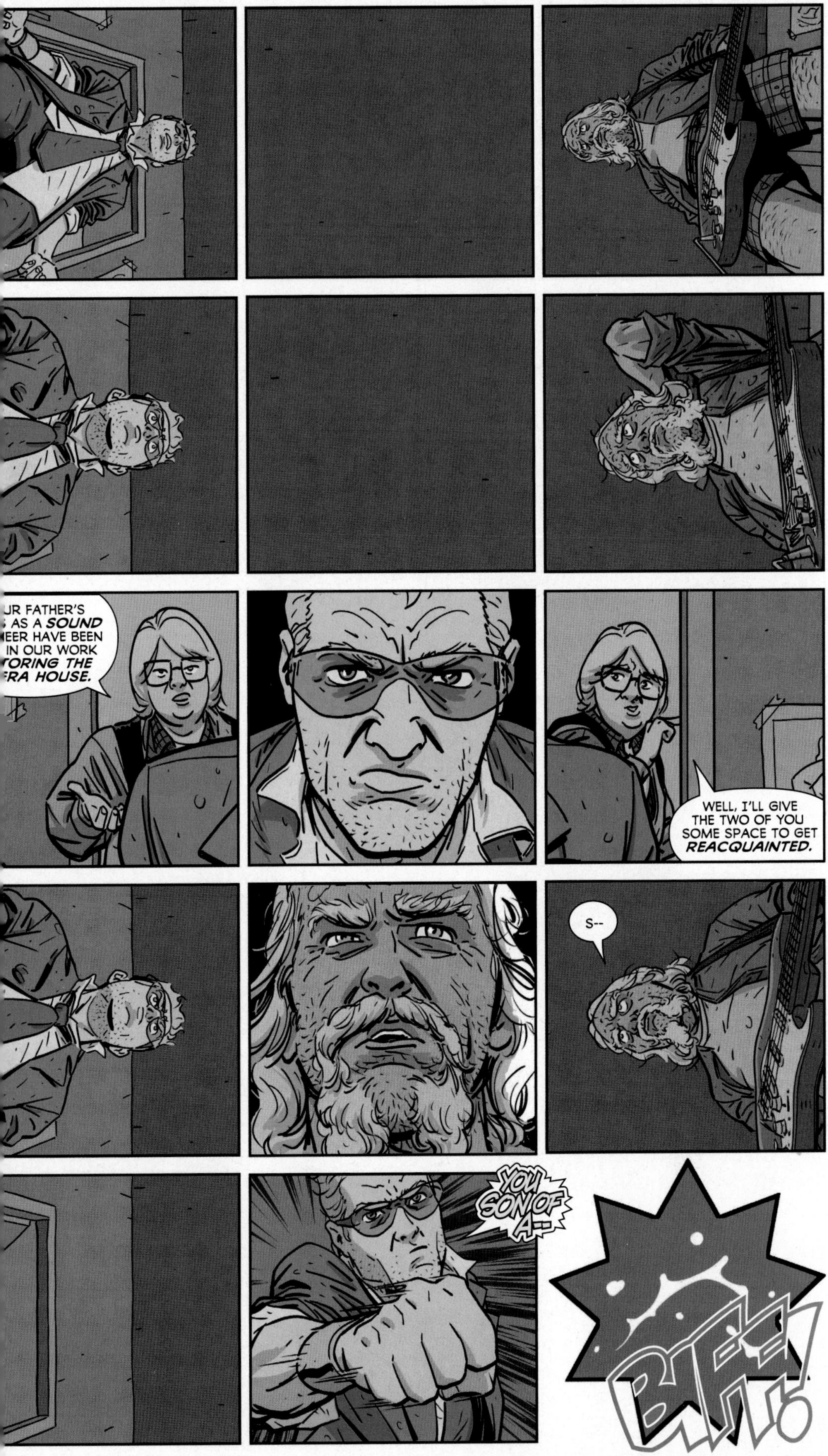

...UR FATHER'S ...S AS A *SOUND* ...EER HAVE BEEN ... IN OUR WORK ...*TORING THE* ...*ERA HOUSE.*
WELL, I'LL GIVE THE TWO OF YOU SOME SPACE TO GET *REACQUAINTED.*
S--
YOU SON OF A--

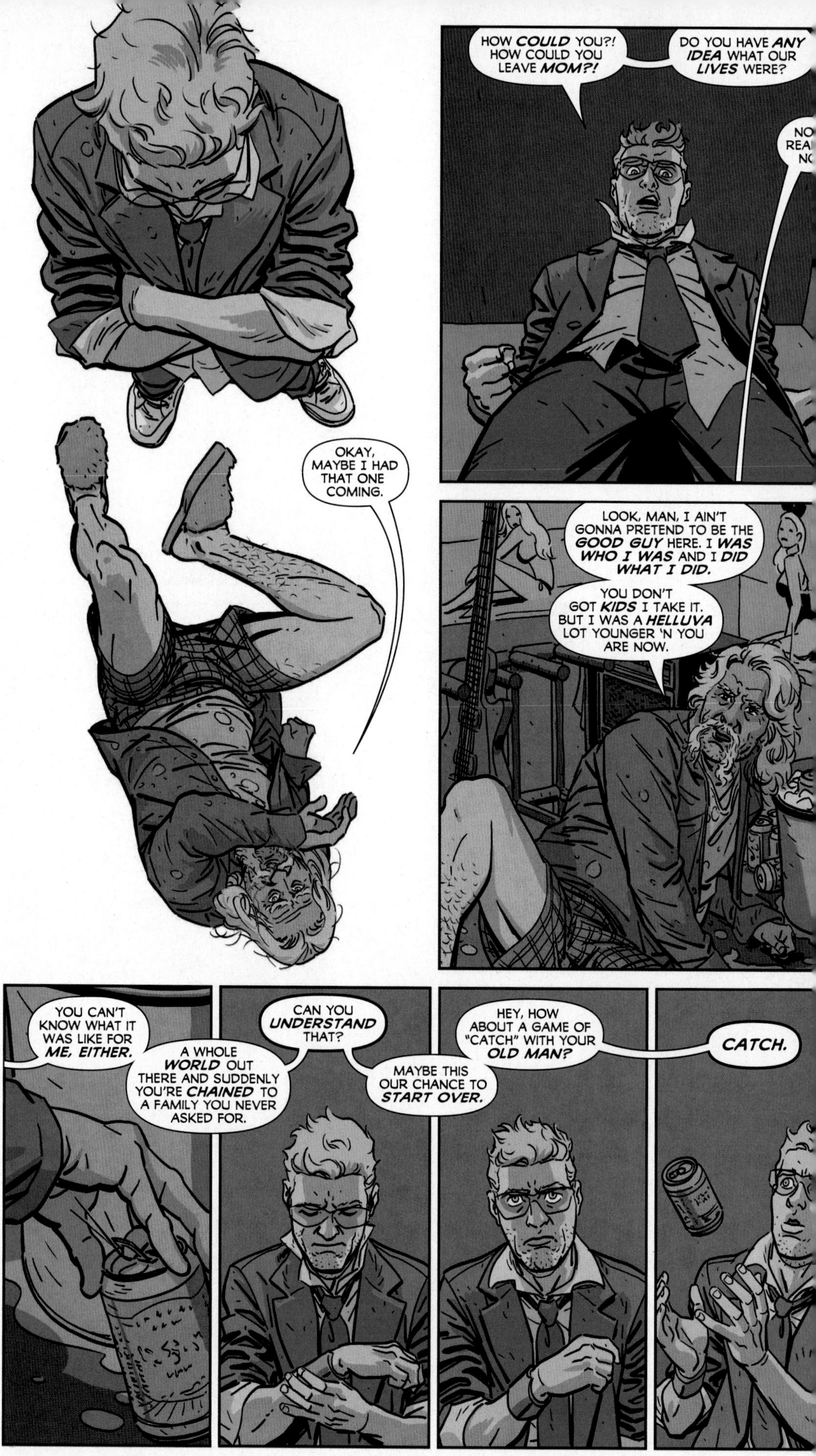
OKAY, MAYBE I HAD THAT ONE COMING.
HOW COULD YOU?! HOW COULD YOU LEAVE MOM?!
DO YOU HAVE ANY IDEA WHAT OUR LIVES WERE?
LOOK, MAN, I AIN'T GONNA PRETEND TO BE THE GOOD GUY HERE. I WAS WHO I WAS AND I DID WHAT I DID.
YOU DON'T GOT KIDS I TAKE IT. BUT I WAS A HELLUVA LOT YOUNGER 'N YOU ARE NOW.
YOU CAN'T KNOW WHAT IT WAS LIKE FOR ME, EITHER.
A WHOLE WORLD OUT THERE AND SUDDENLY YOU'RE CHAINED TO A FAMILY YOU NEVER ASKED FOR.
CAN YOU UNDERSTAND THAT?
MAYBE THIS OUR CHANCE TO START OVER.
HEY, HOW ABOUT A GAME OF "CATCH" WITH YOUR OLD MAN?
CATCH.

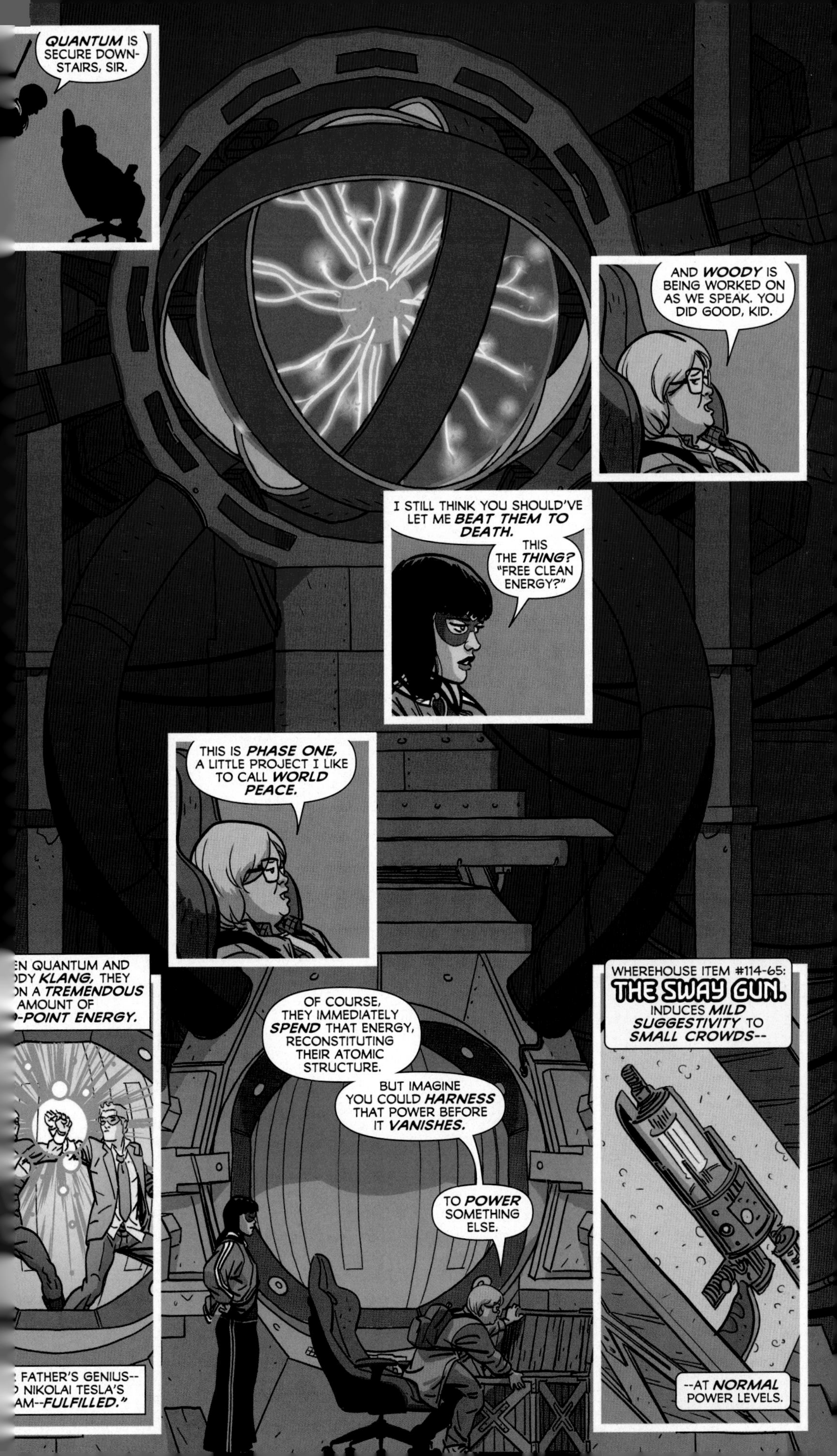

QUANTUM IS SECURE DOWN-STAIRS, SIR.
AND WOODY IS BEING WORKED ON AS WE SPEAK. YOU DID GOOD, KID.
I STILL THINK YOU SHOULD'VE LET ME BEAT THEM TO DEATH.
THIS THE THING? "FREE CLEAN ENERGY?"
THIS IS PHASE ONE, A LITTLE PROJECT I LIKE TO CALL WORLD PEACE.
EN QUANTUM AND ODY KLANG, THEY ON A TREMENDOUS AMOUNT OF -POINT ENERGY.
OF COURSE, THEY IMMEDIATELY SPEND THAT ENERGY, RECONSTITUTING THEIR ATOMIC STRUCTURE.
BUT IMAGINE YOU COULD HARNESS THAT POWER BEFORE IT VANISHES.
TO POWER SOMETHING ELSE.
FATHER'S GENIUS-- NIKOLAI TESLA'S AM--FULFILLED."
WHEREHOUSE ITEM #114-65:
THE SWAY GUN.
INDUCES MILD SUGGESTIVITY TO SMALL CROWDS--
--AT NORMAL POWER LEVELS.

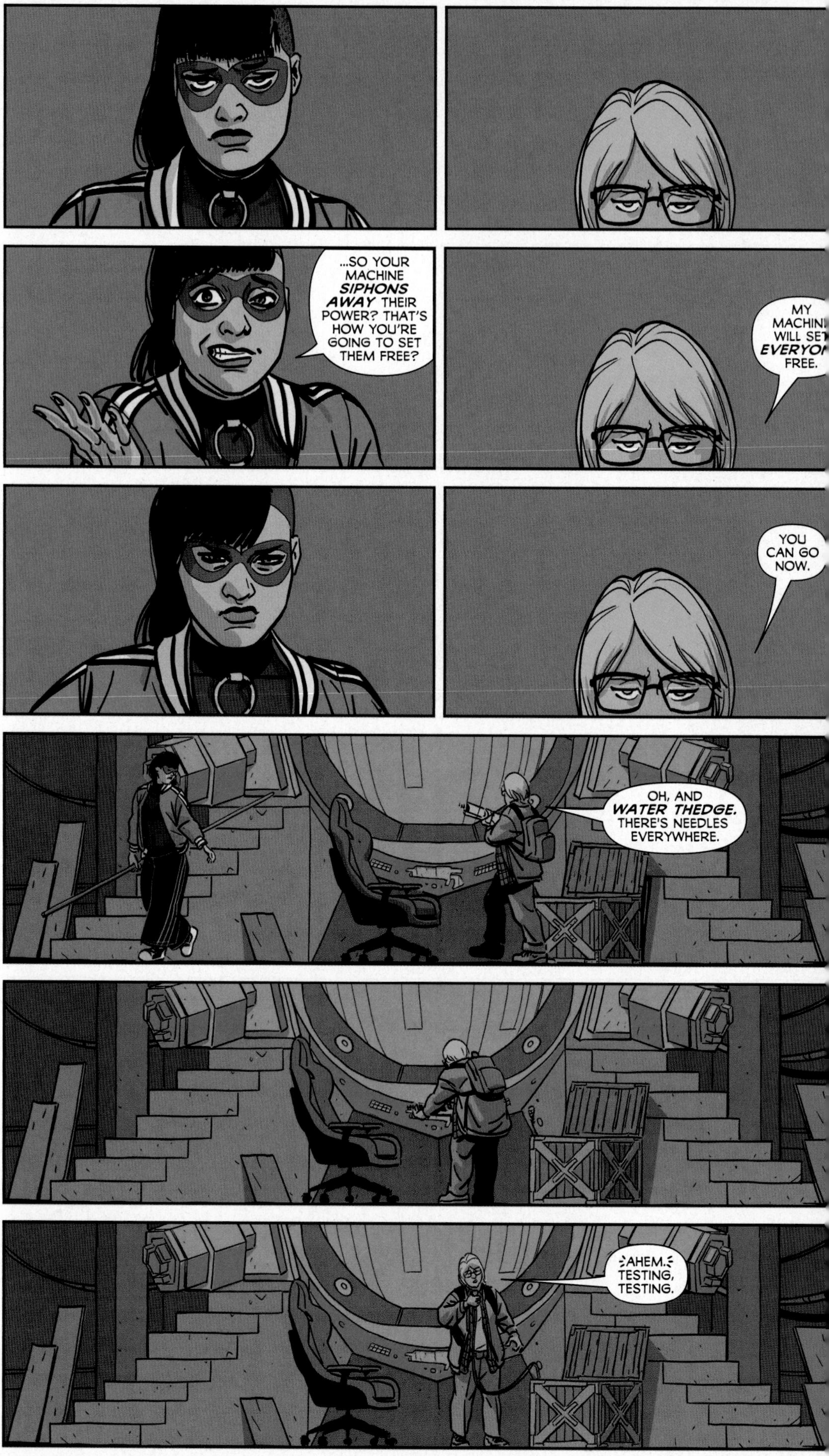
...SO YOUR MACHINE SIPHONS AWAY THEIR POWER? THAT'S HOW YOU'RE GOING TO SET THEM FREE?
MY MACHIN WILL SET EVERYO FREE.
YOU CAN GO NOW.
OH, AND WATER THEDGE. THERE'S NEEDLES EVERYWHERE.
AHEM. TESTING, TESTING.

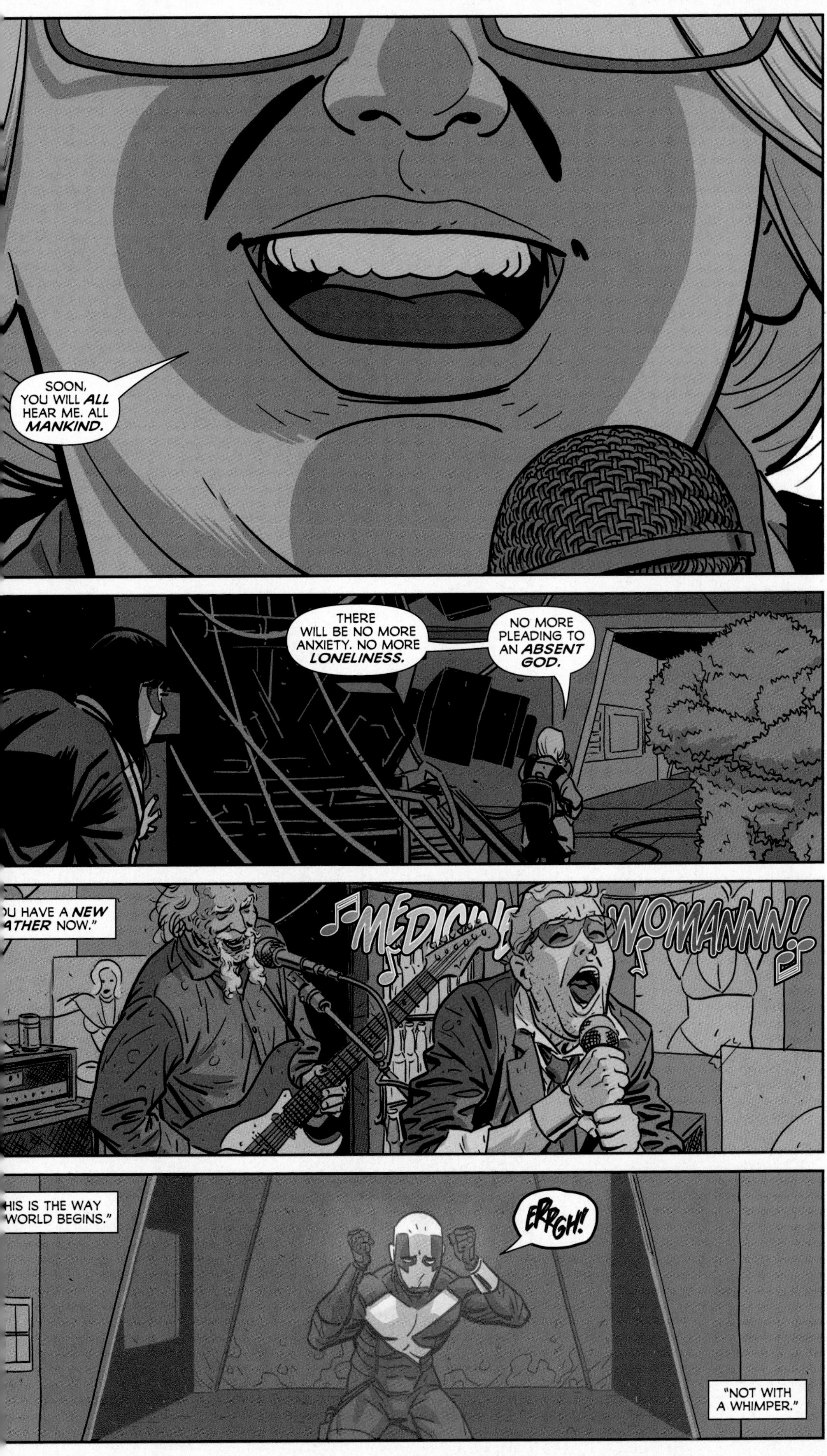
SOON, YOU WILL ALL HEAR ME. ALL MANKIND.
THERE WILL BE NO MORE ANXIETY. NO MORE LONELINESS.
NO MORE PLEADING TO AN ABSENT GOD.
OU HAVE A NEW ATHER NOW."
MEDICINE WOMANNN!
HIS IS THE WAY WORLD BEGINS."
ERRGH!
"NOT WITH A WHIMPER."

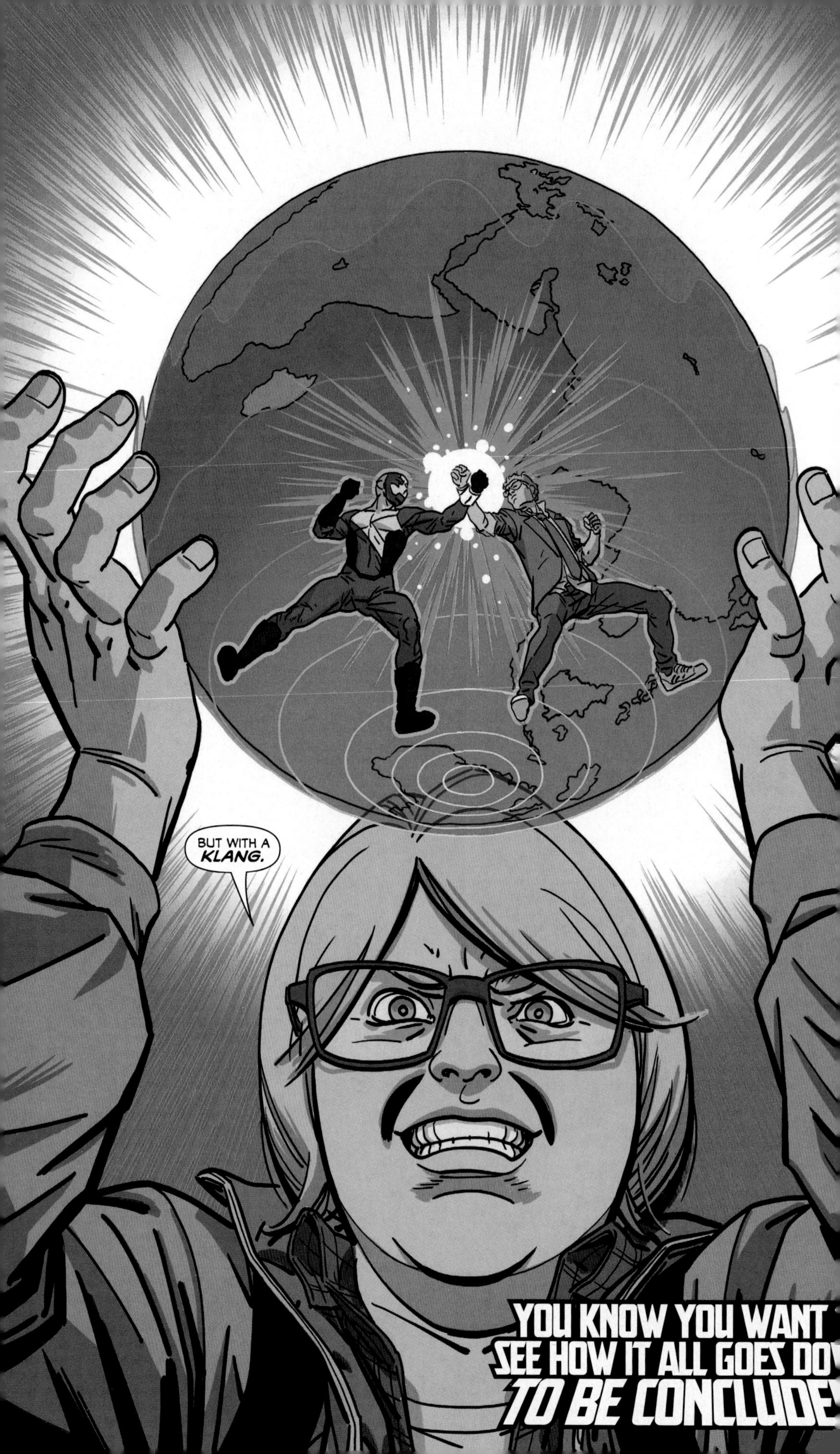
BUT WITH A KLANG.
YOU KNOW YOU WANT
SEE HOW IT ALL GOES DO
TO BE CONCLUDE

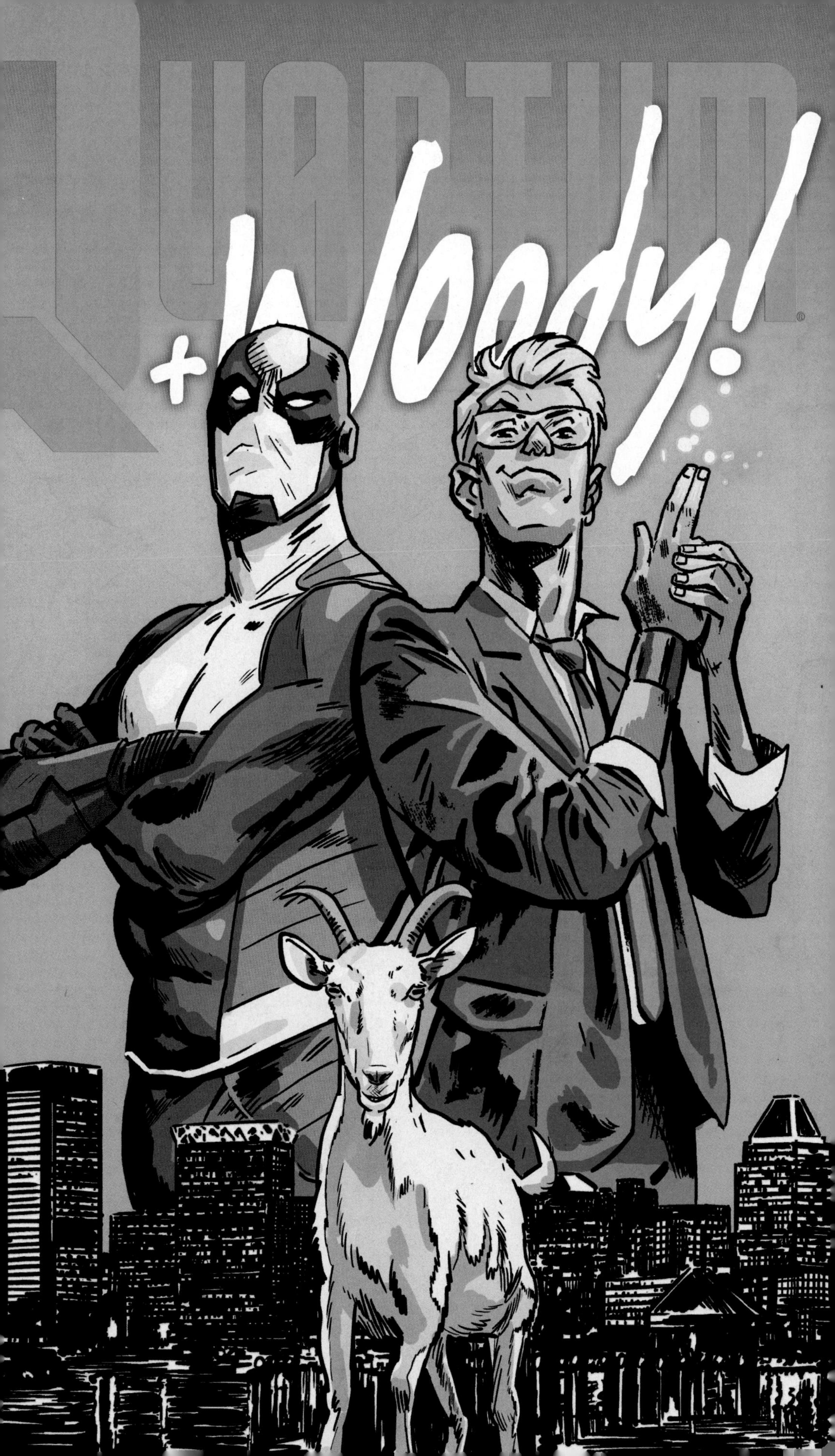
+Woody!

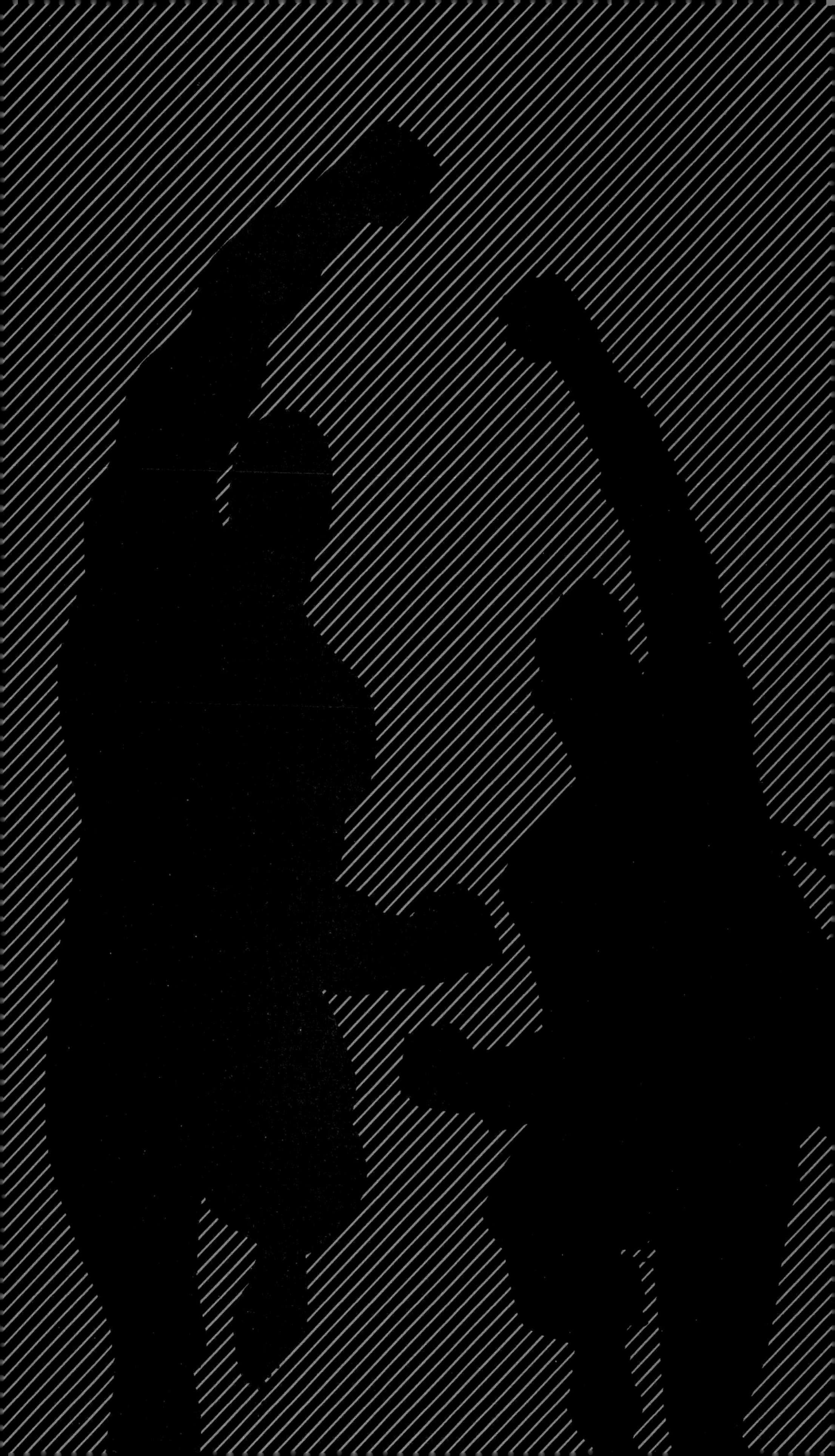

"Having lots of siblings is like having built-in best friends." --KIM KARDASHIAN

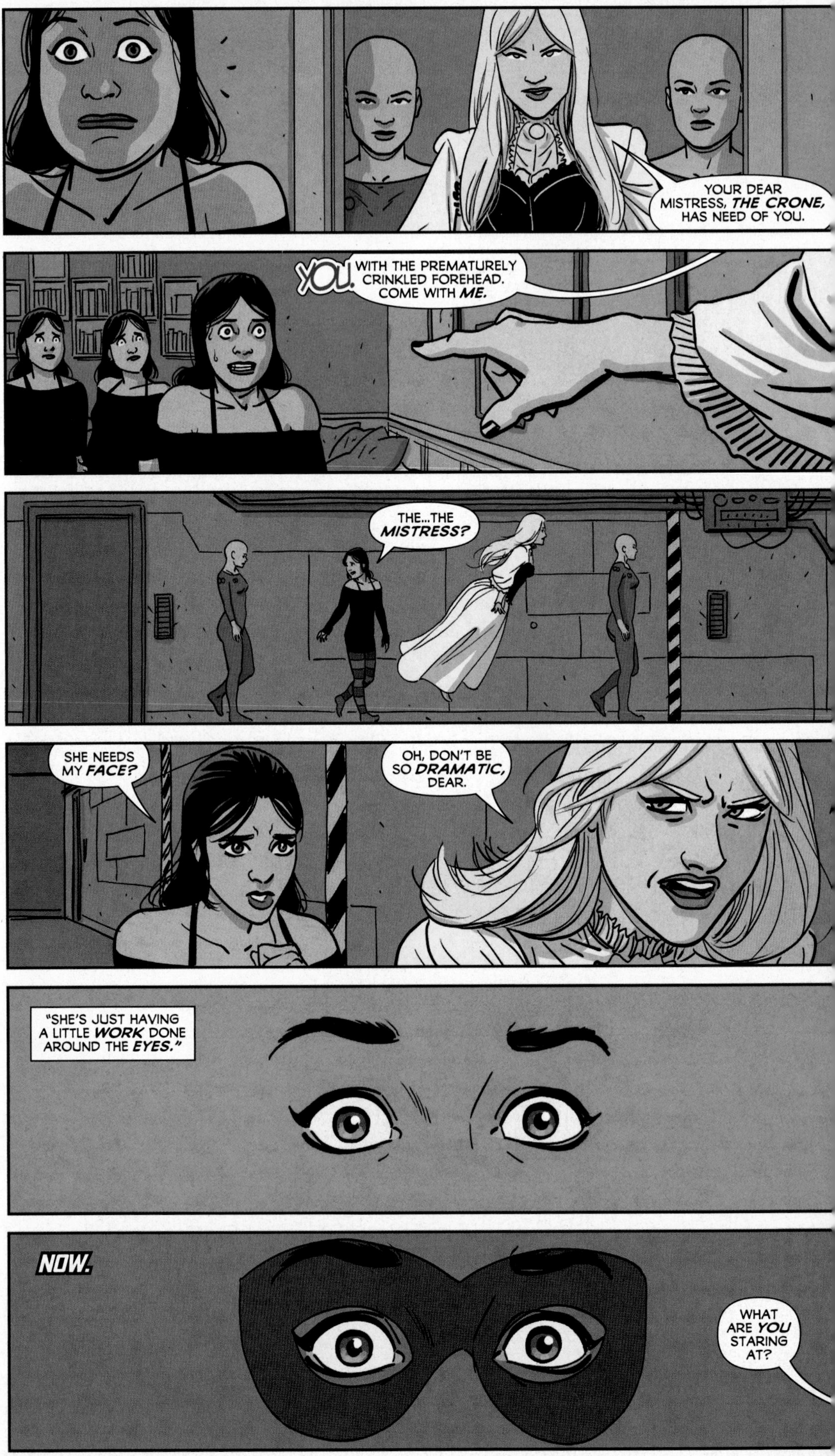
YOUR DEAR MISTRESS, THE CRONE, HAS NEED OF YOU.
YOU.
WITH THE PREMATURELY CRINKLED FOREHEAD. COME WITH ME.
THE...THE MISTRESS?
SHE NEEDS MY FACE?
OH, DON'T BE SO DRAMATIC, DEAR.
"SHE'S JUST HAVING A LITTLE WORK DONE AROUND THE EYES."
NOW.
WHAT ARE YOU STARING AT?

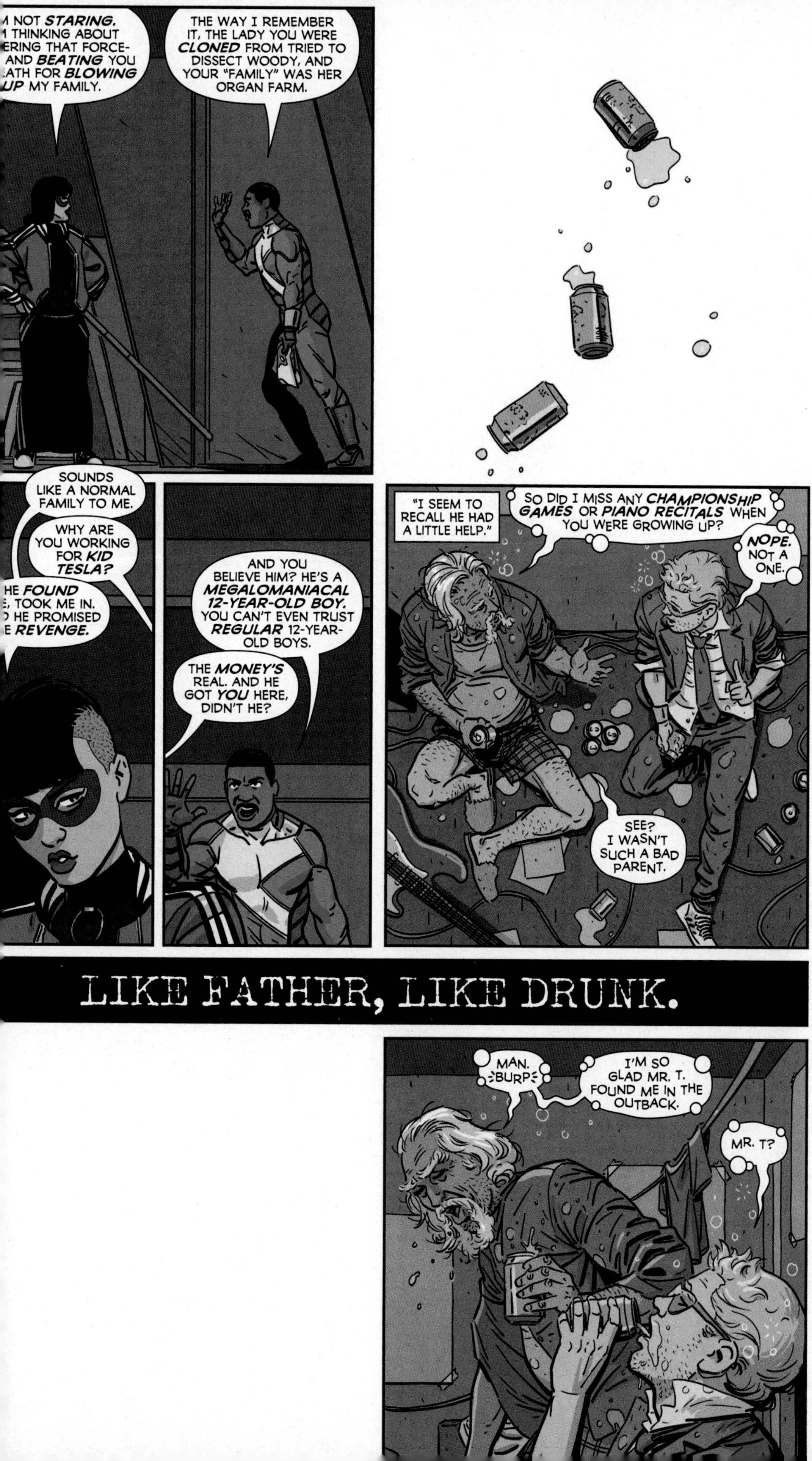

M NOT STARING. M THINKING ABOUT ERING THAT FORCE- AND BEATING YOU EATH FOR BLOWING UP MY FAMILY.
THE WAY I REMEMBER IT, THE LADY YOU WERE CLONED FROM TRIED TO DISSECT WOODY, AND YOUR "FAMILY" WAS HER ORGAN FARM.
SOUNDS LIKE A NORMAL FAMILY TO ME.
WHY ARE YOU WORKING FOR KID TESLA?
HE FOUND E, TOOK ME IN. D HE PROMISED E REVENGE.
AND YOU BELIEVE HIM? HE'S A MEGALOMANIACAL 12-YEAR-OLD BOY. YOU CAN'T EVEN TRUST REGULAR 12-YEAR-OLD BOYS.
THE MONEY'S REAL. AND HE GOT YOU HERE, DIDN'T HE?
"I SEEM TO RECALL HE HAD A LITTLE HELP."
SO DID I MISS ANY CHAMPIONSHIP GAMES OR PIANO RECITALS WHEN YOU WERE GROWING UP?
NOPE. NOT A ONE.
SEE? I WASN'T SUCH A BAD PARENT.
LIKE FATHER, LIKE DRUNK.
MAN. *BURP*
I'M SO GLAD MR. T. FOUND ME IN THE OUTBACK.
MR. T?

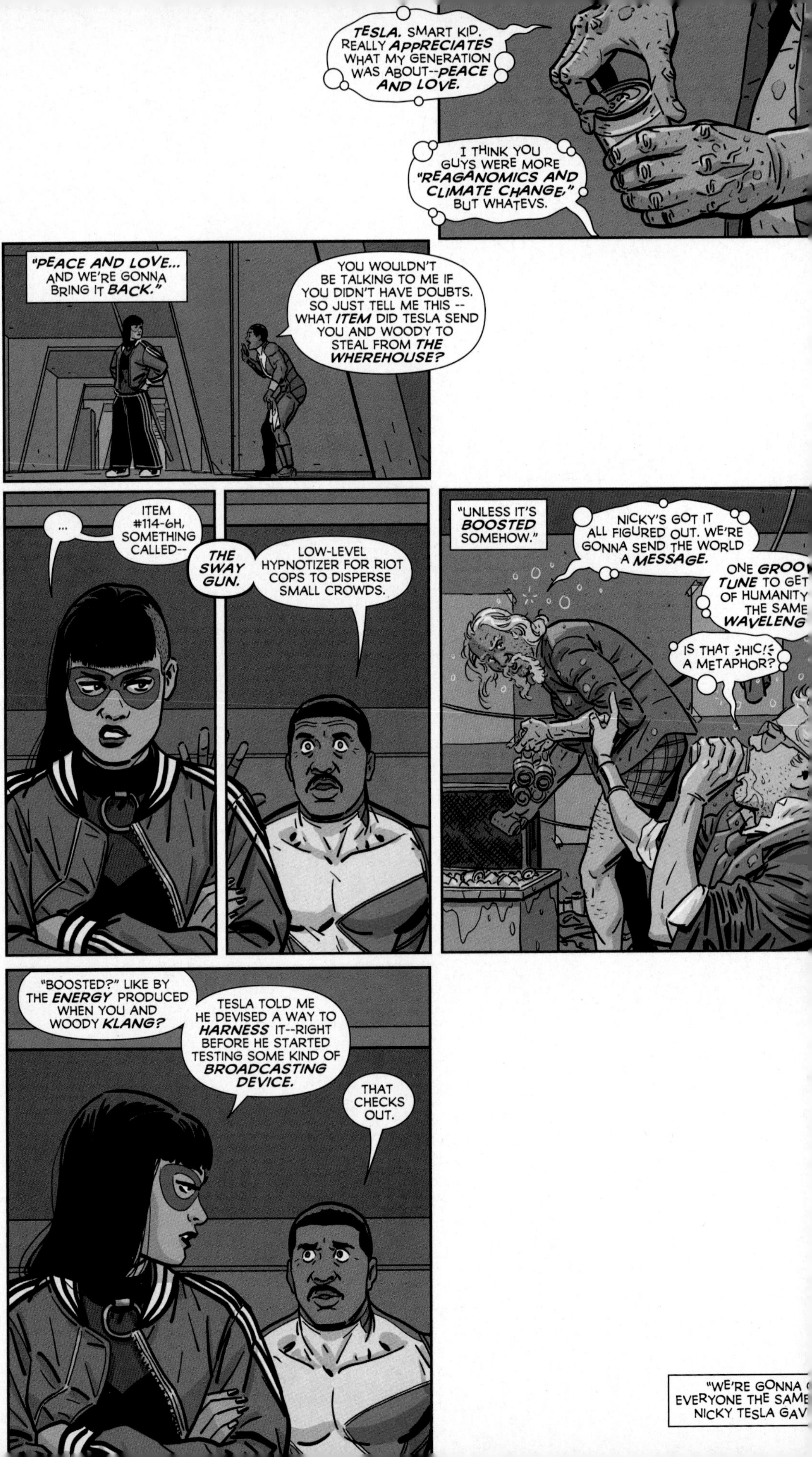
TESLA. SMART KID. REALLY APPRECIATES WHAT MY GENERATION WAS ABOUT--PEACE AND LOVE.
I THINK YOU GUYS WERE MORE "REAGANOMICS AND CLIMATE CHANGE," BUT WHATEVS.
"PEACE AND LOVE... AND WE'RE GONNA BRING IT BACK."
YOU WOULDN'T BE TALKING TO ME IF YOU DIDN'T HAVE DOUBTS. SO JUST TELL ME THIS -- WHAT ITEM DID TESLA SEND YOU AND WOODY TO STEAL FROM THE WHEREHOUSE?
...
ITEM #114-6H, SOMETHING CALLED--
THE SWAY GUN.
LOW-LEVEL HYPNOTIZER FOR RIOT COPS TO DISPERSE SMALL CROWDS.
"UNLESS IT'S BOOSTED SOMEHOW."
NICKY'S GOT IT ALL FIGURED OUT. WE'RE GONNA SEND THE WORLD A MESSAGE.
ONE GROO TUNE TO GET OF HUMANITY THE SAME WAVELENG
IS THAT HIC! A METAPHOR?
"BOOSTED?" LIKE BY THE ENERGY PRODUCED WHEN YOU AND WOODY KLANG?
TESLA TOLD ME HE DEVISED A WAY TO HARNESS IT--RIGHT BEFORE HE STARTED TESTING SOME KIND OF BROADCASTING DEVICE.
THAT CHECKS OUT.
"WE'RE GONNA EVERYONE THE SAME NICKY TESLA GAV

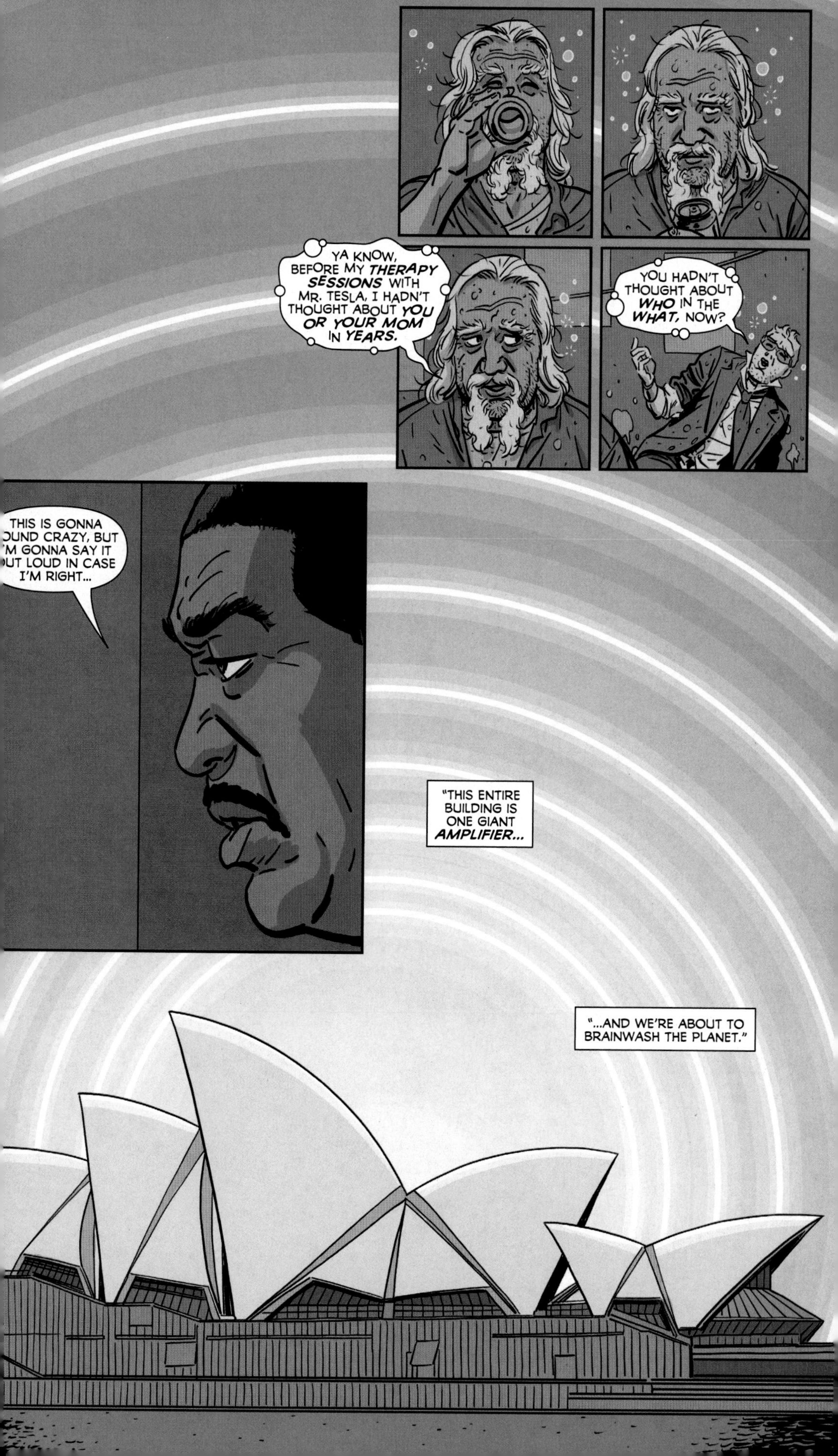
YA KNOW, BEFORE MY THERAPY SESSIONS WITH MR. TESLA, I HADN'T THOUGHT ABOUT YOU OR YOUR MOM IN YEARS.
YOU HADN'T THOUGHT ABOUT WHO IN THE WHAT, NOW?
THIS IS GONNA OUND CRAZY, BUT 'M GONNA SAY IT UT LOUD IN CASE I'M RIGHT...
"THIS ENTIRE BUILDING IS ONE GIANT AMPLIFIER...
"...AND WE'RE ABOUT TO BRAINWASH THE PLANET."

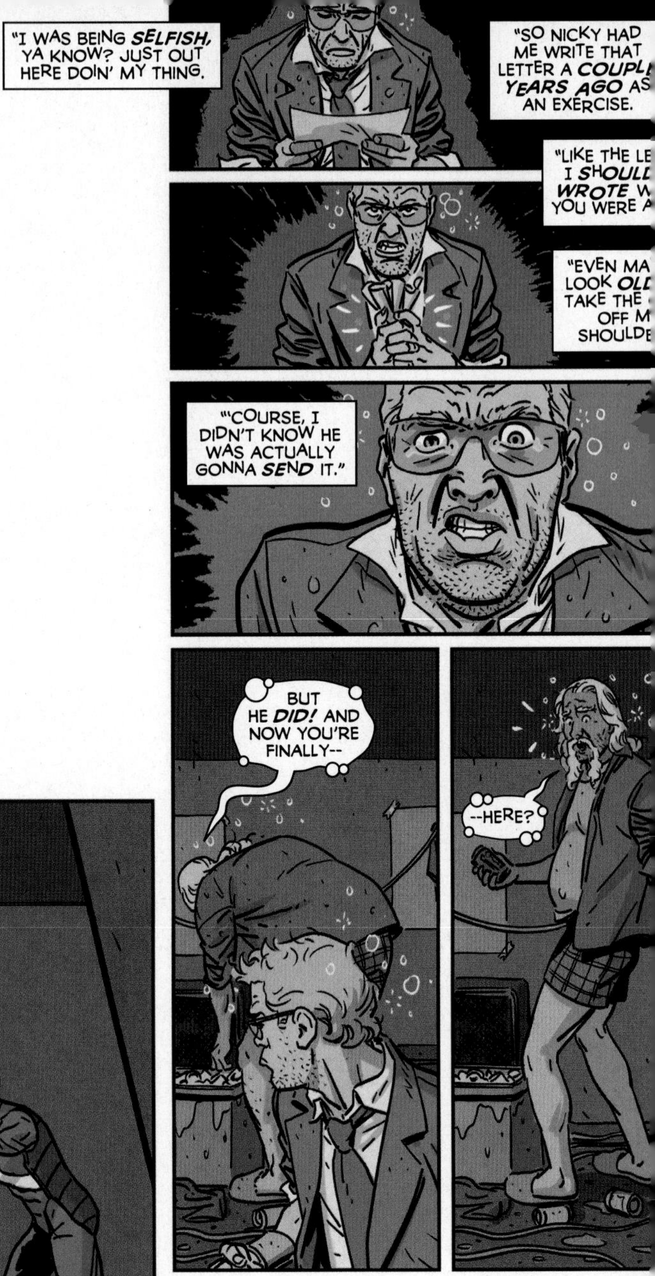
"I WAS BEING SELFISH, YA KNOW? JUST OUT HERE DOIN' MY THING.
"SO NICKY HAD ME WRITE THAT LETTER A COUPL YEARS AGO AS AN EXERCISE.
"LIKE THE LE I SHOULL WROTE W YOU WERE A
"EVEN MA LOOK OLL TAKE THE OFF M SHOULDE
"'COURSE, I DIDN'T KNOW HE WAS ACTUALLY GONNA SEND IT."
BUT HE DID! AND NOW YOU'RE FINALLY--
--HERE?

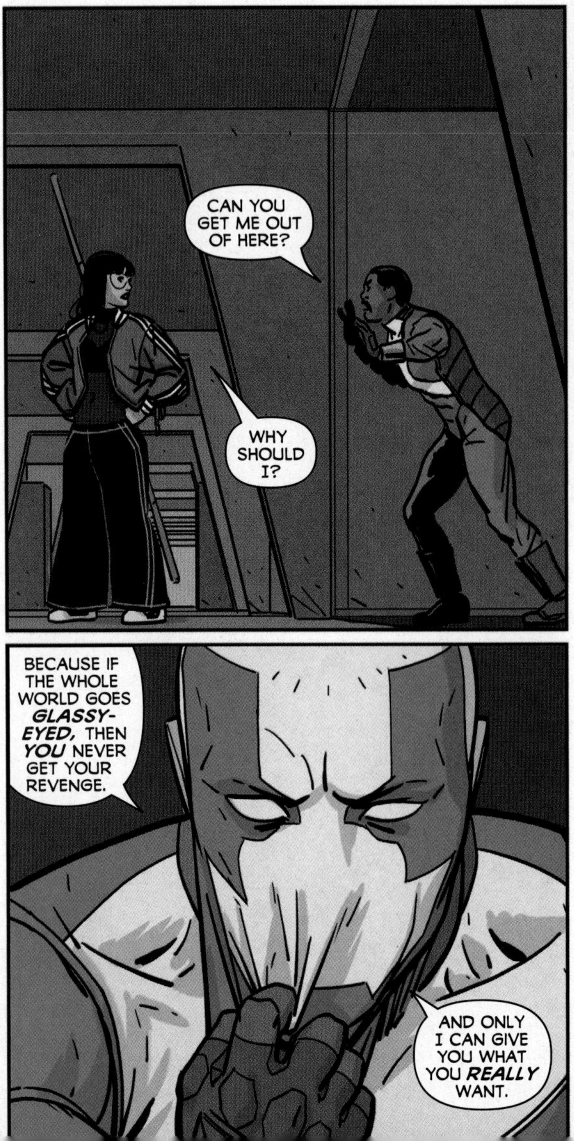
CAN YOU GET ME OUT OF HERE?
WHY SHOULD I?
BECAUSE IF THE WHOLE WORLD GOES GLASSY-EYED, THEN YOU NEVER GET YOUR REVENGE.
AND ONLY I CAN GIVE YOU WHAT YOU REALLY WANT.

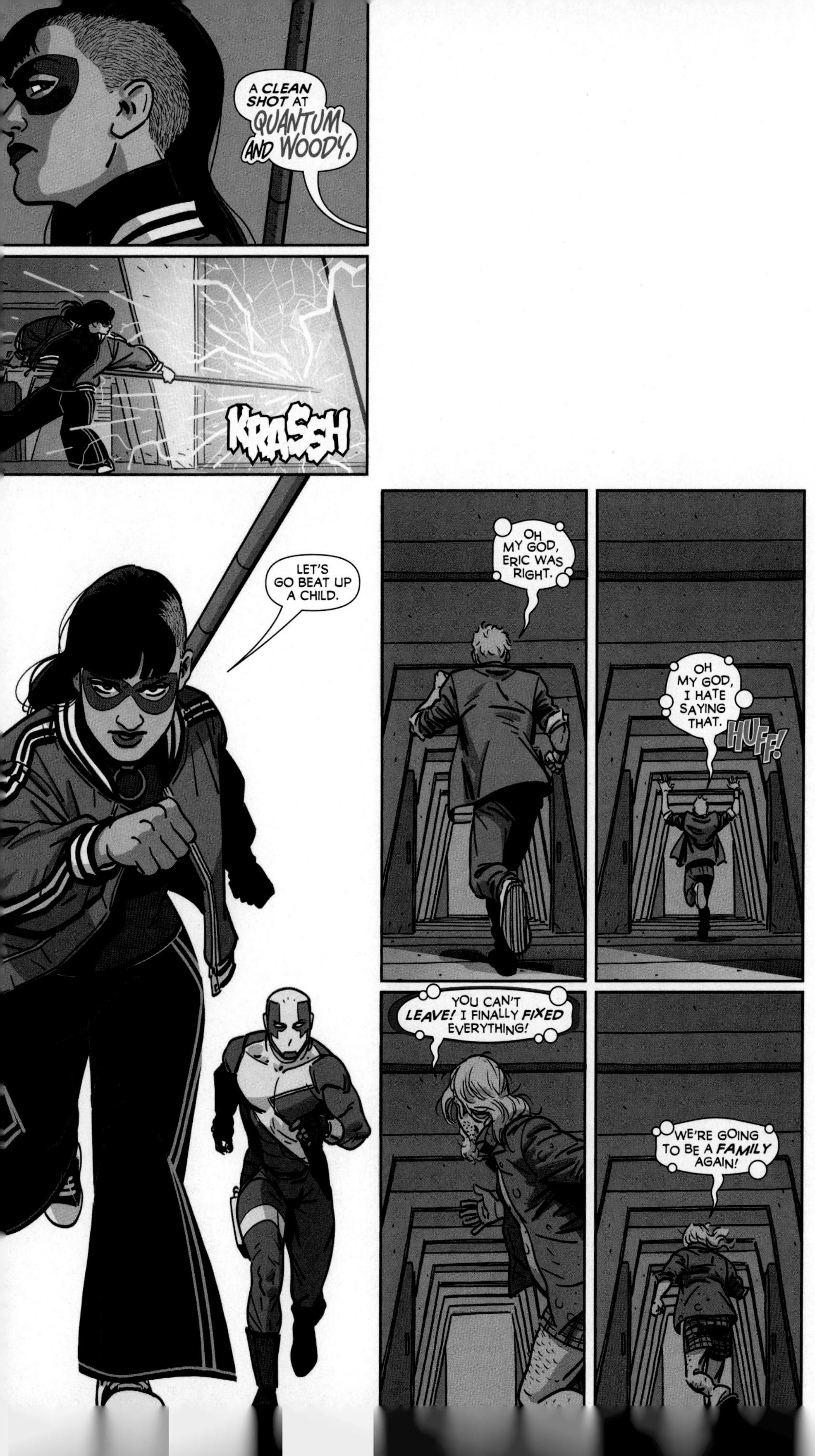
A CLEAN SHOT AT QUANTUM AND WOODY.
KRASSH
LET'S GO BEAT UP A CHILD.
OH MY GOD, ERIC WAS RIGHT.
OH MY GOD, I HATE SAYING THAT.
HUFF!
YOU CAN'T LEAVE! I FINALLY FIXED EVERYTHING!
WE'RE GOING TO BE A FAMILY AGAIN!

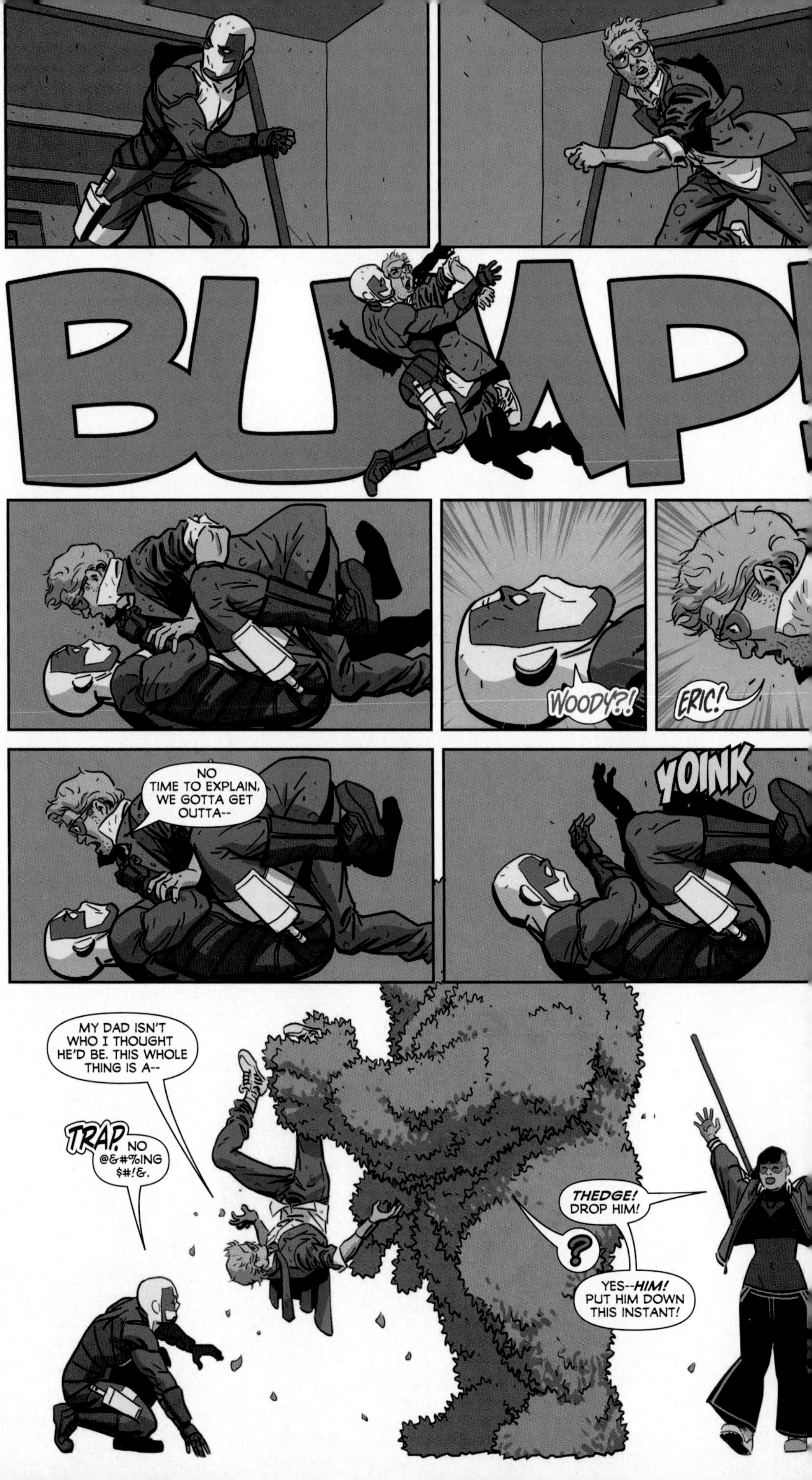
BUMP!
WOODY?!
ERIC!
NO TIME TO EXPLAIN, WE GOTTA GET OUTTA--
YOINK
MY DAD ISN'T WHO I THOUGHT HE'D BE. THIS WHOLE THING IS A--
TRAP. NO @&#%ING $#!&.
THEDGE! DROP HIM!
?
YES--HIM! PUT HIM DOWN THIS INSTANT!

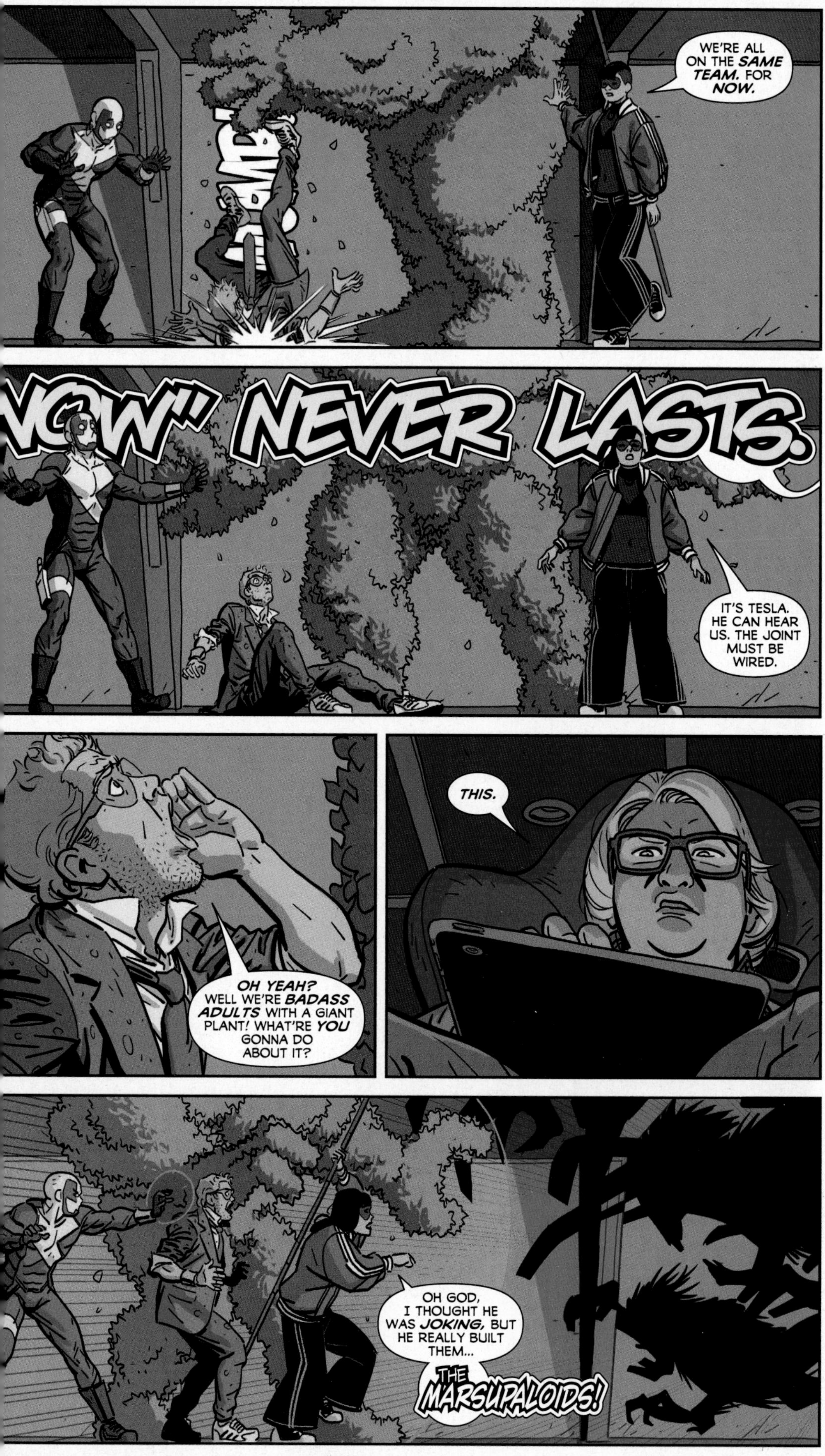
WE'RE ALL ON THE SAME TEAM. FOR NOW.
"NOW" NEVER LASTS.
IT'S TESLA. HE CAN HEAR US. THE JOINT MUST BE WIRED.
OH YEAH? WELL WE'RE BADASS ADULTS WITH A GIANT PLANT! WHAT'RE YOU GONNA DO ABOUT IT?
THIS.
OH GOD, I THOUGHT HE WAS JOKING, BUT HE REALLY BUILT THEM...
THE MARSUPALOIDS!

 FYOOSSH

OKAY, IT'S OFFICIAL. *I HATE AUSTRALIA!*

 I'M *HURT,* YOU GUYS!

 NOT AS HURT AS YOU'RE *GONNA BE,* VIRGIN!

 I WAS GOING TO GIVE YOU *FREEDOM...*

 OF COURSE, THE PROCESS IS GOING TO KILL YOU.

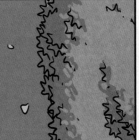

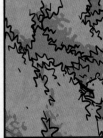

 KEEP BLASTING, WOODY! WE'RE ALMOST THROUGH THEM!

 THIS ALMOST FEELS LIKE WE'RE BACK TO *NORMAL.*

THIS IS MY *NORMAL?* GOD, THAT'S SAD.

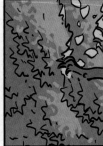

 WOODY! *MECHA-KOALA* AT 12 O'CLOCK!

 I HAVEN'T SEEN THIS MANY POUCHES SINCE THE *90'S!*

 ERIC, IF WE DON'T GET THROUGH THIS...LOOK, I KNOW I MESSED UP.

YEAH. YOU REALLY DID.

 YOU GUYS ARE DOING THIS *NOW?*

 BUT, I MESSED UP *FIRST.*

 IF I D[...] GET A C[...] TO SA[...]

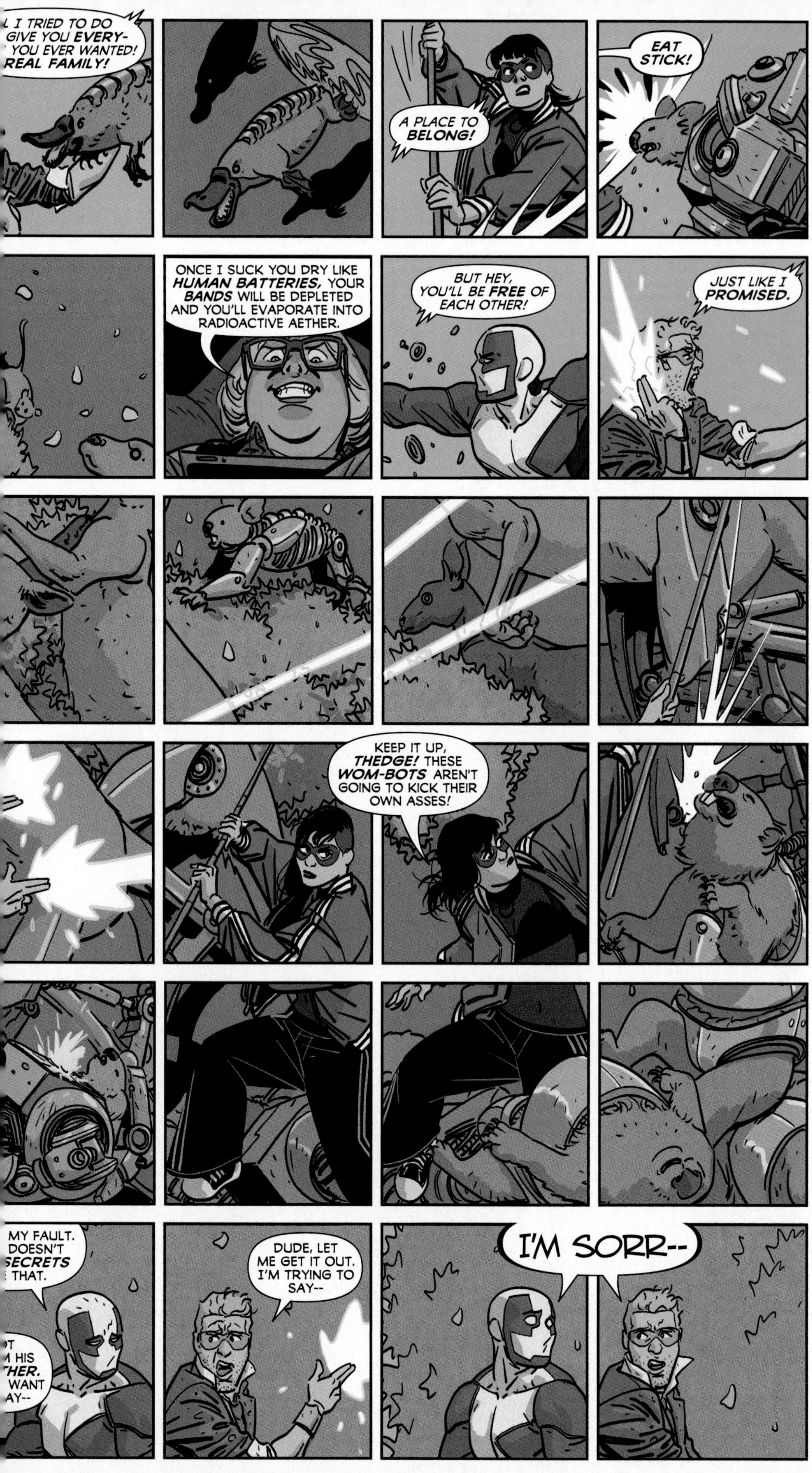
I TRIED TO DO
GIVE YOU EVERY-
YOU EVER WANTED!
REAL FAMILY!
A PLACE TO BELONG!
EAT STICK!
ONCE I SUCK YOU DRY LIKE HUMAN BATTERIES, YOUR BANDS WILL BE DEPLETED AND YOU'LL EVAPORATE INTO RADIOACTIVE AETHER.
BUT HEY, YOU'LL BE FREE OF EACH OTHER!
JUST LIKE I PROMISED.
KEEP IT UP, THEDGE! THESE WOM-BOTS AREN'T GOING TO KICK THEIR OWN ASSES!
MY FAULT.
DOESN'T
SECRETS
THAT.
HIS
THER.
WANT
DUDE, LET ME GET IT OUT. I'M TRYING TO SAY--
I'M SORR--

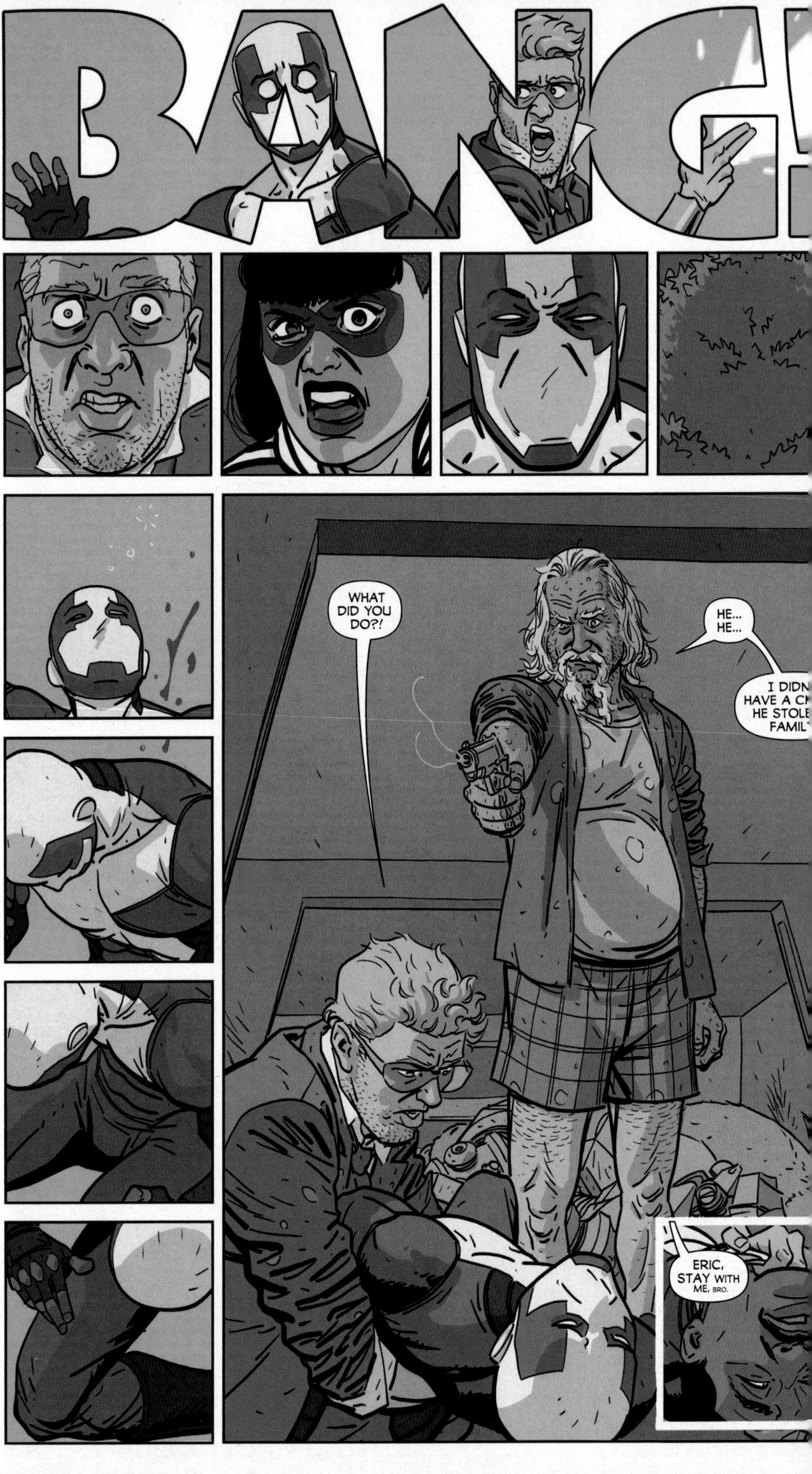
BANG!
WHAT DID YOU DO?!
HE... HE...
ERIC, STAY WITH ME, BRO.

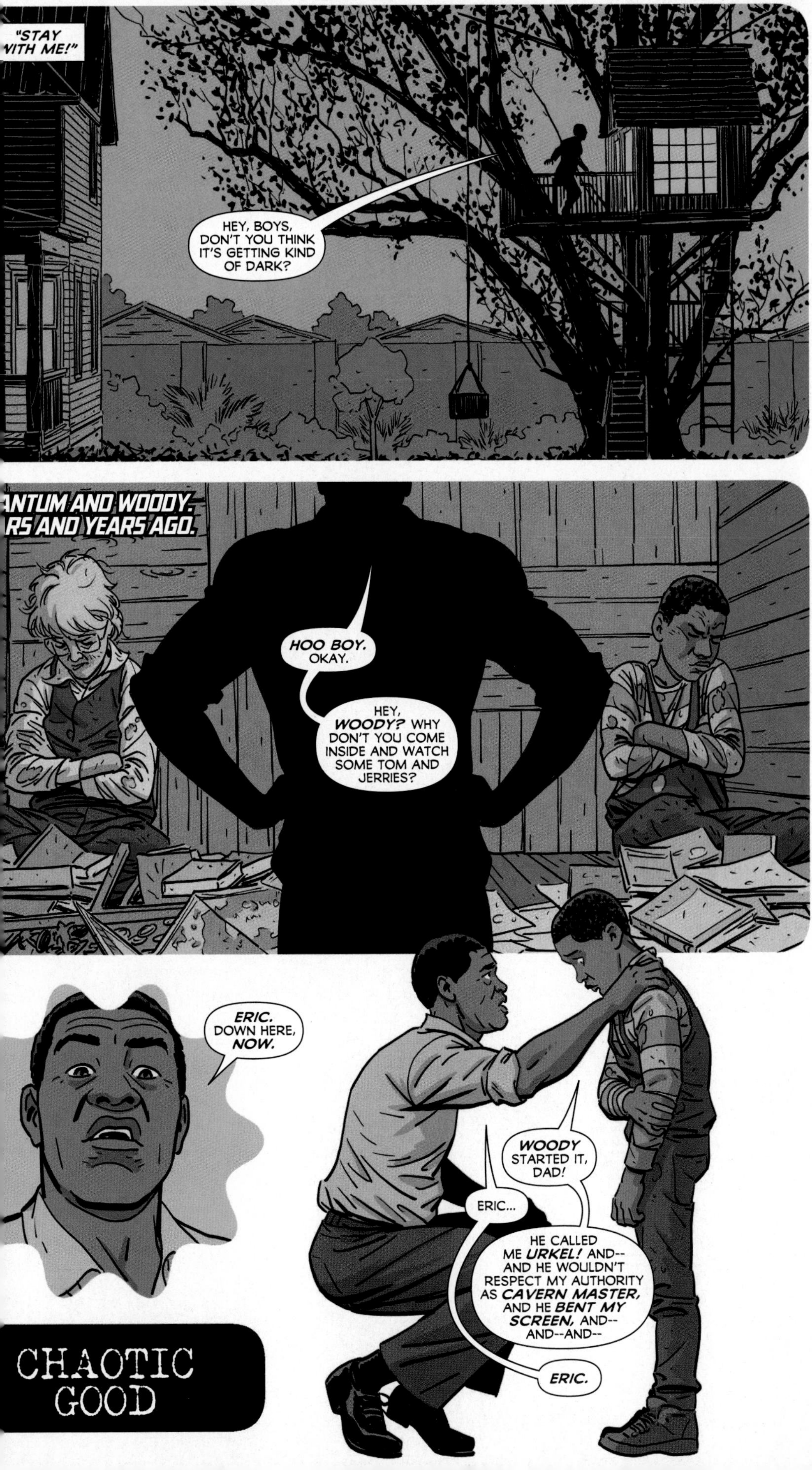
"STAY
VITH ME!"
HEY, BOYS, DON'T YOU THINK IT'S GETTING KIND OF DARK?
ANTUM AND WOODY.
RS AND YEARS AGO.
HOO BOY. OKAY.
HEY, WOODY? WHY DON'T YOU COME INSIDE AND WATCH SOME TOM AND JERRIES?
ERIC. DOWN HERE, NOW.
WOODY STARTED IT, DAD!
ERIC...
HE CALLED ME URKEL! AND-- AND HE WOULDN'T RESPECT MY AUTHORITY AS CAVERN MASTER, AND HE BENT MY SCREEN, AND-- AND--AND--
ERIC.
CHAOTIC
GOOD

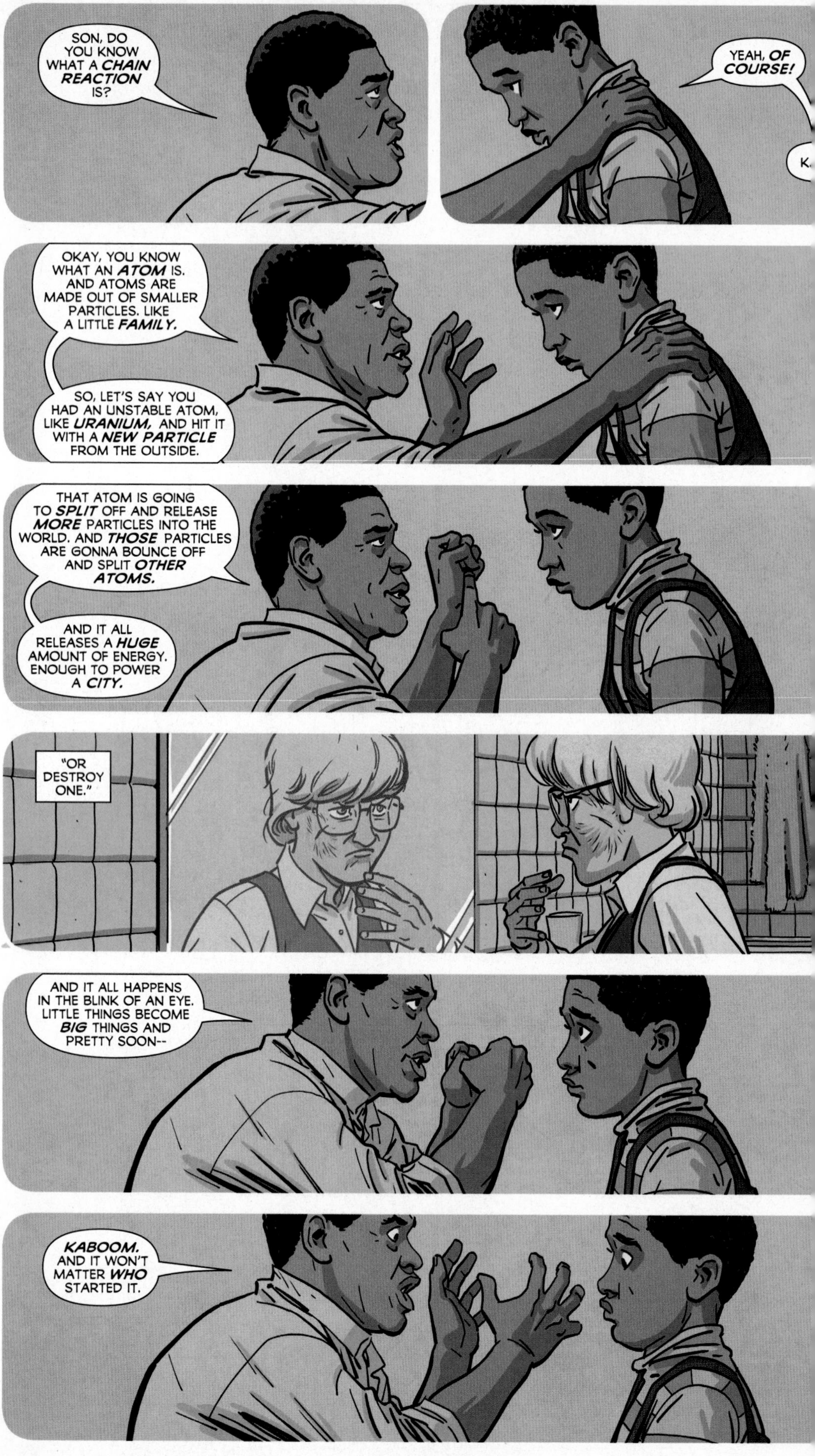

SON, DO YOU KNOW WHAT A *CHAIN REACTION* IS?
YEAH, *OF COURSE!*
OKAY, YOU KNOW WHAT AN *ATOM* IS. AND ATOMS ARE MADE OUT OF SMALLER PARTICLES. LIKE A LITTLE *FAMILY.*
SO, LET'S SAY YOU HAD AN UNSTABLE ATOM, LIKE *URANIUM,* AND HIT IT WITH A *NEW PARTICLE* FROM THE OUTSIDE.
THAT ATOM IS GOING TO *SPLIT* OFF AND RELEASE *MORE* PARTICLES INTO THE WORLD. AND *THOSE* PARTICLES ARE GONNA BOUNCE OFF AND SPLIT *OTHER ATOMS.*
AND IT ALL RELEASES A *HUGE* AMOUNT OF ENERGY. ENOUGH TO POWER A *CITY.*
"OR DESTROY ONE."
AND IT ALL HAPPENS IN THE BLINK OF AN EYE. LITTLE THINGS BECOME *BIG* THINGS AND PRETTY SOON--
KABOOM. AND IT WON'T MATTER *WHO* STARTED IT.

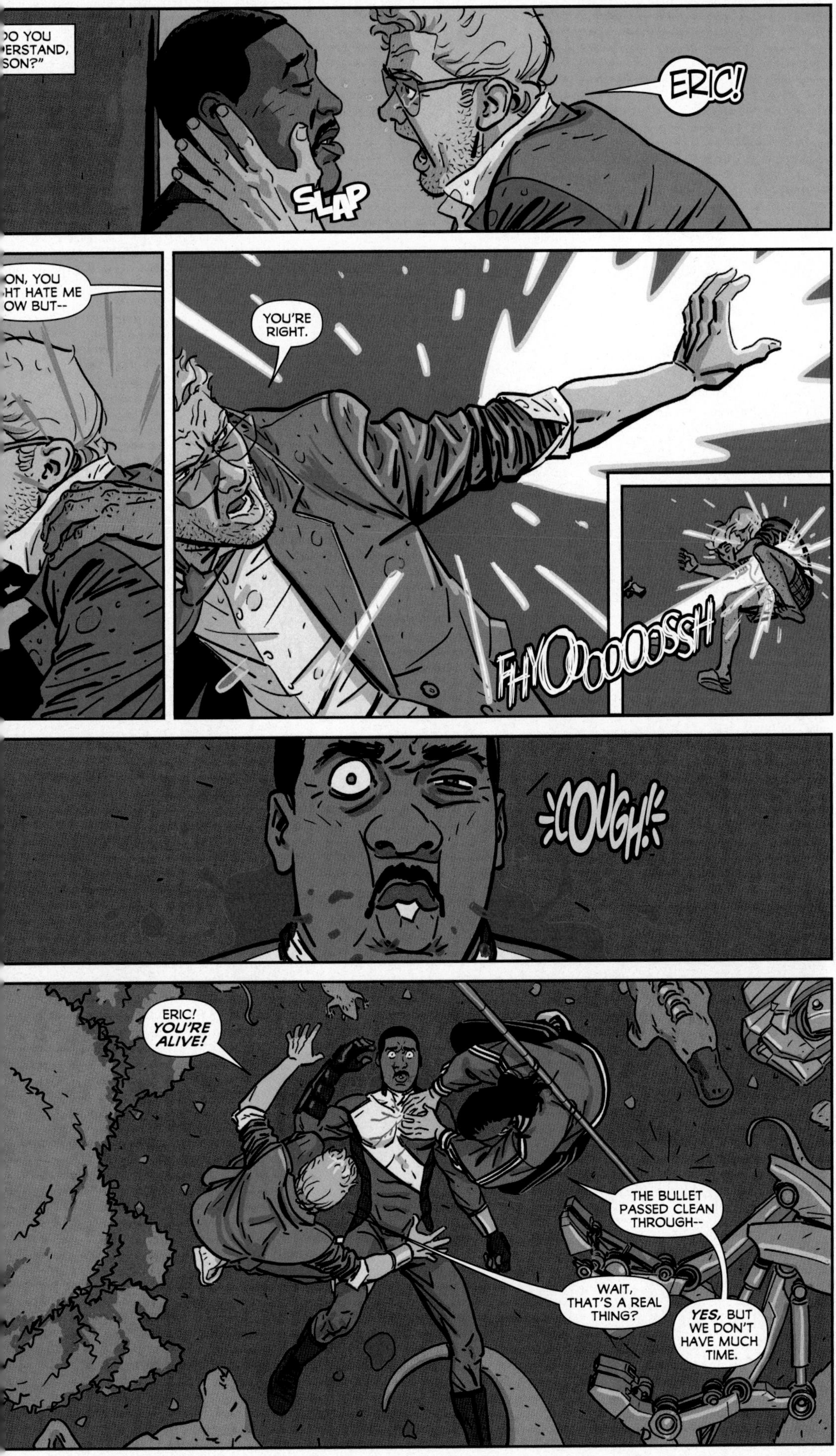

DO YOU
ERSTAND,
SON?"
ERIC!
SLAP
ON, YOU
HT HATE ME
OW BUT--
YOU'RE
RIGHT.
FHYOOOOOOSSH
COUGH!
ERIC!
YOU'RE ALIVE!
THE BULLET PASSED CLEAN THROUGH--
WAIT, THAT'S A REAL THING?
YES, BUT WE DON'T HAVE MUCH TIME.

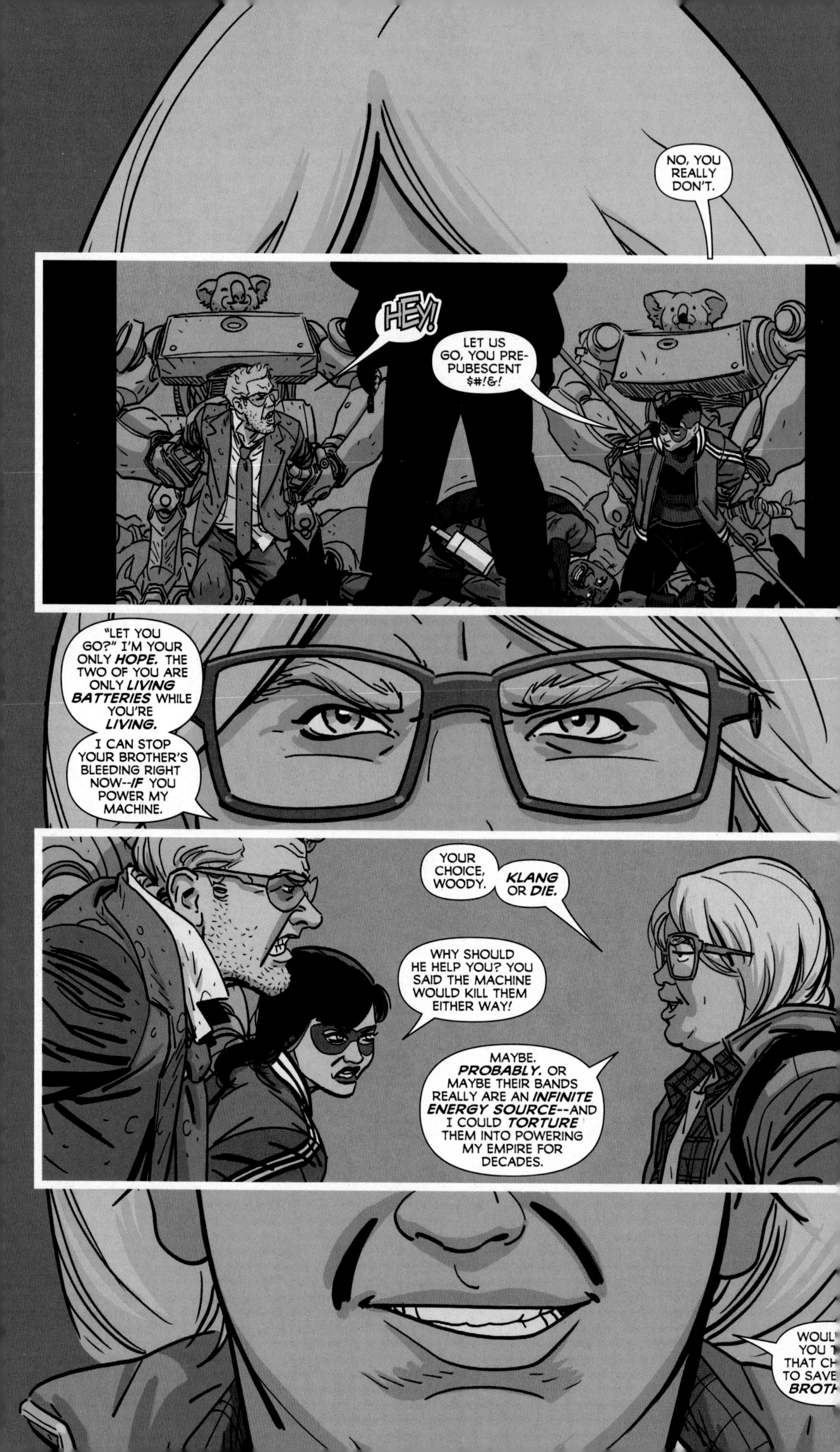

NO, YOU REALLY DON'T.
HEY!
LET US GO, YOU PRE-PUBESCENT $#!&!
"LET YOU GO?" I'M YOUR ONLY HOPE. THE TWO OF YOU ARE ONLY LIVING BATTERIES WHILE YOU'RE LIVING.
I CAN STOP YOUR BROTHER'S BLEEDING RIGHT NOW--IF YOU POWER MY MACHINE.
YOUR CHOICE, WOODY.
KLANG OR DIE.
WHY SHOULD HE HELP YOU? YOU SAID THE MACHINE WOULD KILL THEM EITHER WAY!
MAYBE. PROBABLY. OR MAYBE THEIR BANDS REALLY ARE AN INFINITE ENERGY SOURCE--AND I COULD TORTURE THEM INTO POWERING MY EMPIRE FOR DECADES.

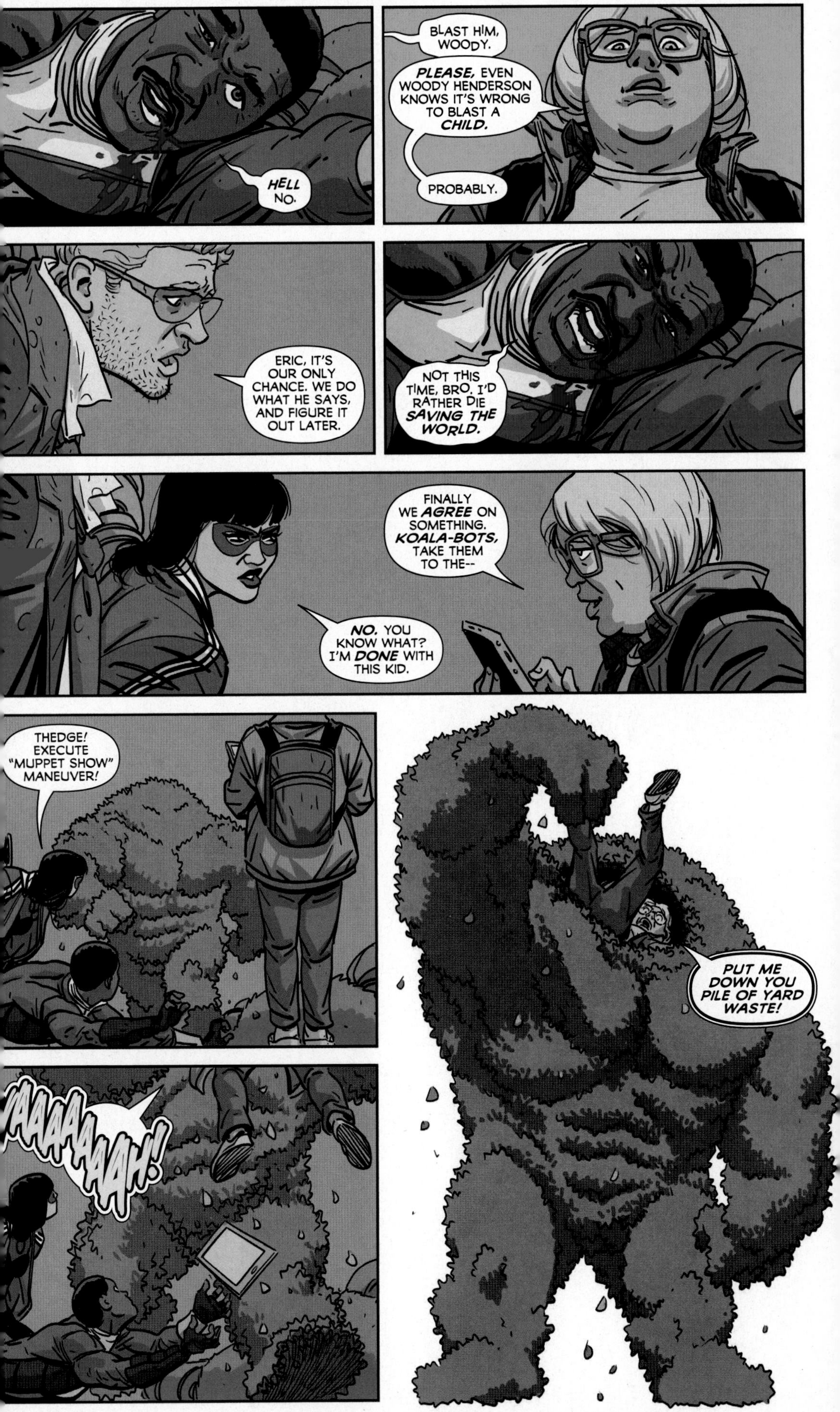
HELL NO.
BLAST HIM, WOODY.
PLEASE, EVEN WOODY HENDERSON KNOWS IT'S WRONG TO BLAST A CHILD.
PROBABLY.
ERIC, IT'S OUR ONLY CHANCE. WE DO WHAT HE SAYS, AND FIGURE IT OUT LATER.
NOT THIS TIME, BRO. I'D RATHER DIE SAVING THE WORLD.
FINALLY WE AGREE ON SOMETHING. KOALA-BOTS, TAKE THEM TO THE--
NO. YOU KNOW WHAT? I'M DONE WITH THIS KID.
THEDGE! EXECUTE "MUPPET SHOW" MANEUVER!
PUT ME DOWN YOU PILE OF YARD WASTE!
AAAAAAAAAH!

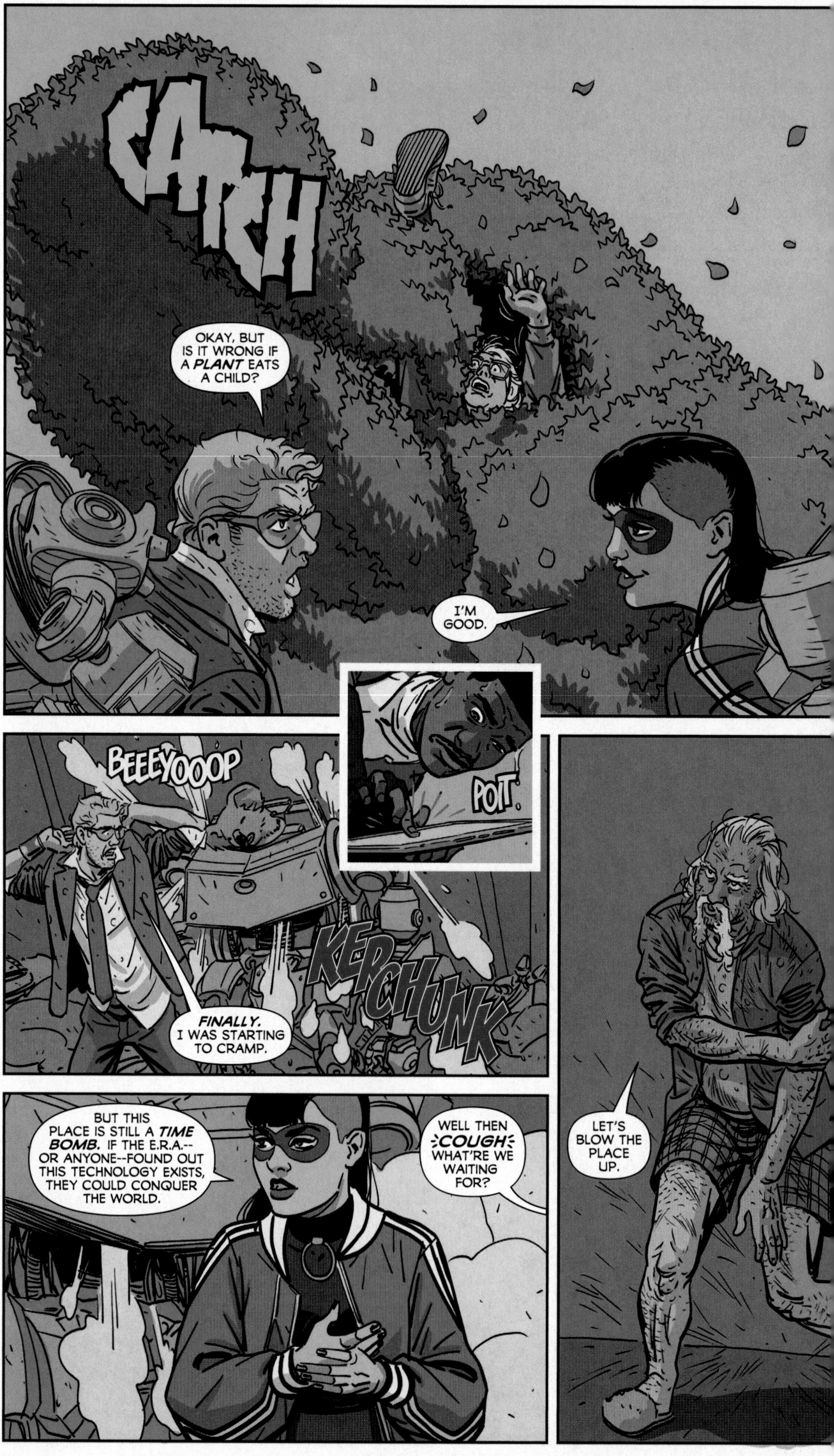
CATCH
OKAY, BUT IS IT WRONG IF A *PLANT* EATS A CHILD?
I'M GOOD.
BEEEYOOOP
POIT
KERCHUNK
FINALLY. I WAS STARTING TO CRAMP.
BUT THIS PLACE IS STILL A *TIME BOMB.* IF THE E.R.A.--OR ANYONE--FOUND OUT THIS TECHNOLOGY EXISTS, THEY COULD CONQUER THE WORLD.
WELL THEN *COUGH* WHAT'RE WE WAITING FOR?
LET'S BLOW THE PLACE UP.

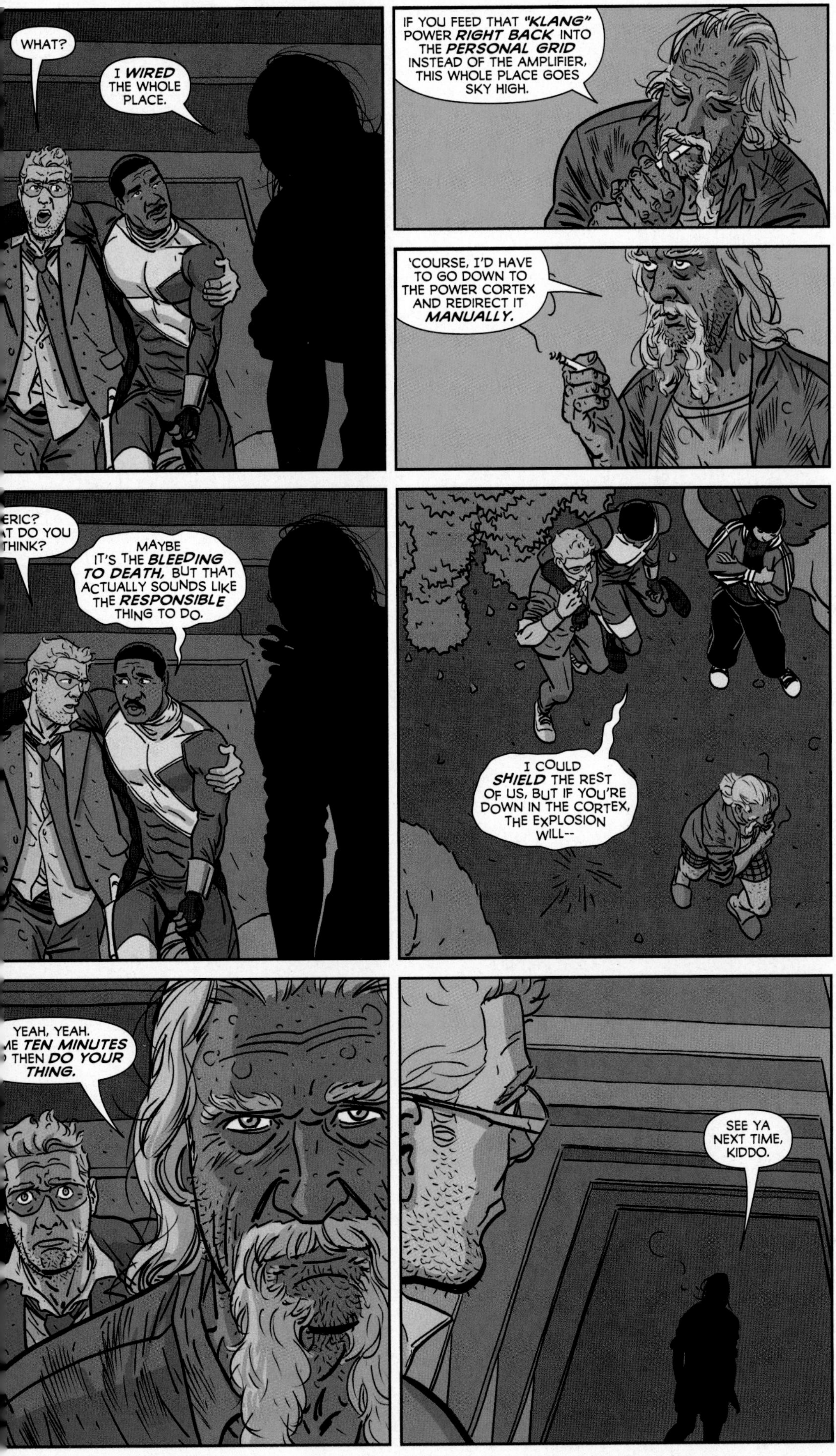
WHAT?
I WIRED THE WHOLE PLACE.
IF YOU FEED THAT "KLANG" POWER RIGHT BACK INTO THE PERSONAL GRID INSTEAD OF THE AMPLIFIER, THIS WHOLE PLACE GOES SKY HIGH.
'COURSE, I'D HAVE TO GO DOWN TO THE POWER CORTEX AND REDIRECT IT MANUALLY.
ERIC? T DO YOU THINK?
MAYBE IT'S THE BLEEDING TO DEATH, BUT THAT ACTUALLY SOUNDS LIKE THE RESPONSIBLE THING TO DO.
I COULD SHIELD THE REST OF US, BUT IF YOU'RE DOWN IN THE CORTEX, THE EXPLOSION WILL--
YEAH, YEAH. ME TEN MINUTES THEN DO YOUR THING.
SEE YA NEXT TIME, KIDDO.

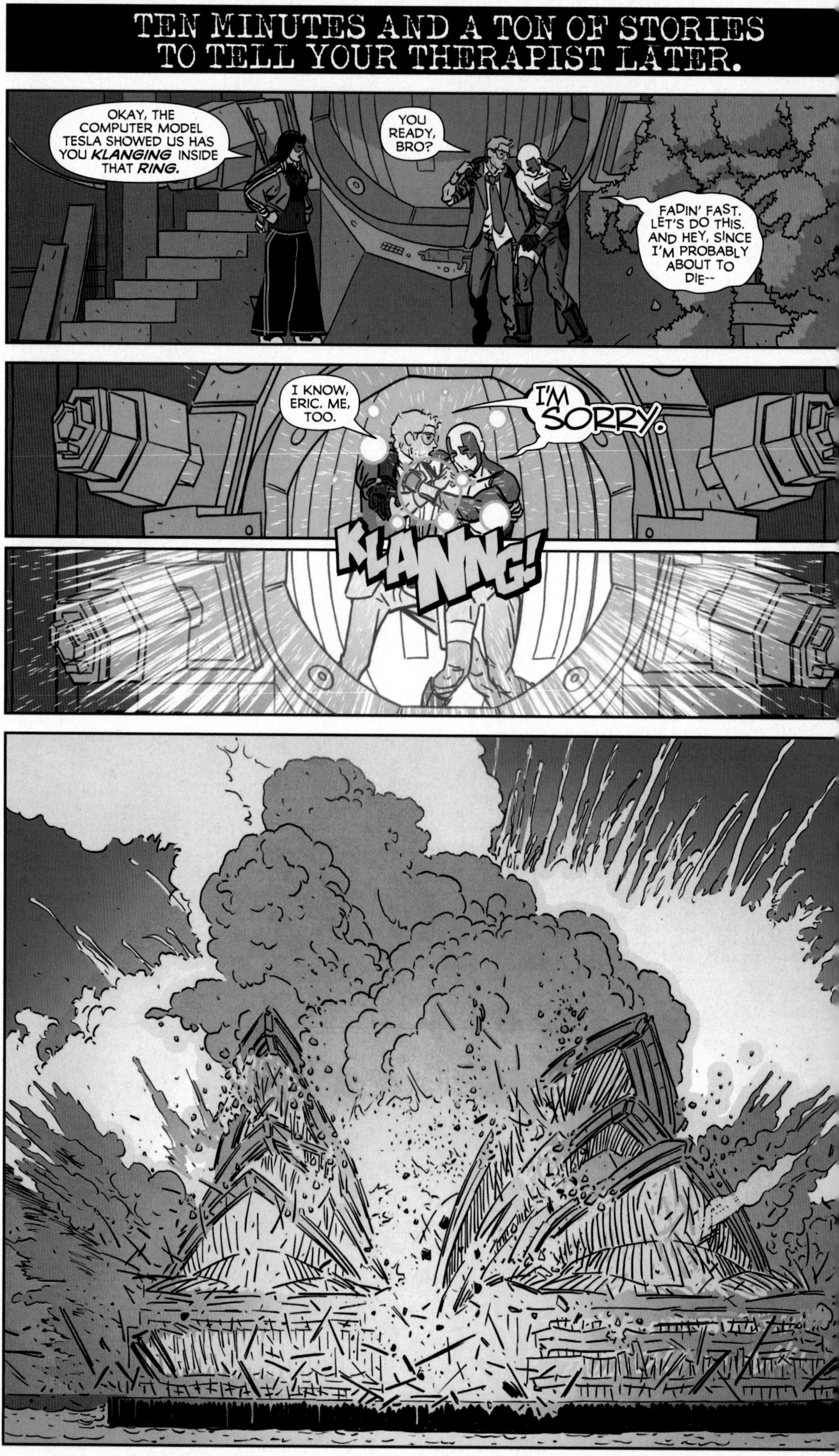
TEN MINUTES AND A TON OF STORIES TO TELL YOUR THERAPIST LATER.
OKAY, THE COMPUTER MODEL TESLA SHOWED US HAS YOU KLANGING INSIDE THAT RING.
YOU READY, BRO?
FADIN' FAST. LET'S DO THIS. AND HEY, SINCE I'M PROBABLY ABOUT TO DIE--
I KNOW, ERIC. ME, TOO.
I'M SORRY.
KLANNNG!

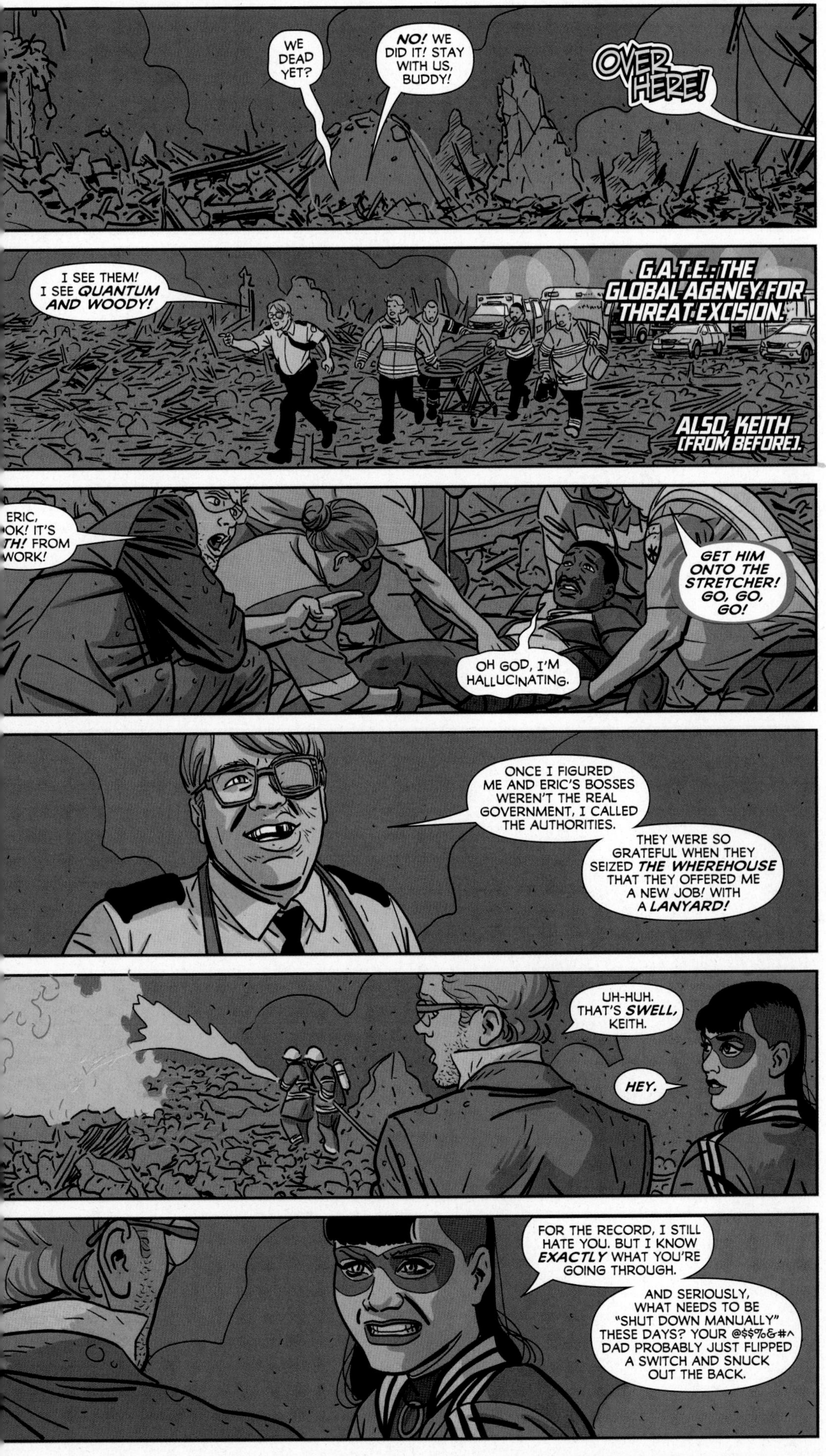
WE DEAD YET?
NO! WE DID IT! STAY WITH US, BUDDY!
OVER HERE!
I SEE THEM! I SEE QUANTUM AND WOODY!
G.A.T.E.: THE GLOBAL AGENCY FOR THREAT EXCISION.
ALSO, KEITH (FROM BEFORE).
ERIC, OK! IT'S TH! FROM WORK!
GET HIM ONTO THE STRETCHER! GO, GO, GO!
OH GOD, I'M HALLUCINATING.
ONCE I FIGURED ME AND ERIC'S BOSSES WEREN'T THE REAL GOVERNMENT, I CALLED THE AUTHORITIES.
THEY WERE SO GRATEFUL WHEN THEY SEIZED THE WHEREHOUSE THAT THEY OFFERED ME A NEW JOB! WITH A LANYARD!
UH-HUH. THAT'S SWELL, KEITH.
HEY.
FOR THE RECORD, I STILL HATE YOU. BUT I KNOW EXACTLY WHAT YOU'RE GOING THROUGH.
AND SERIOUSLY, WHAT NEEDS TO BE "SHUT DOWN MANUALLY" THESE DAYS? YOUR @$$%&#^ DAD PROBABLY JUST FLIPPED A SWITCH AND SNUCK OUT THE BACK.

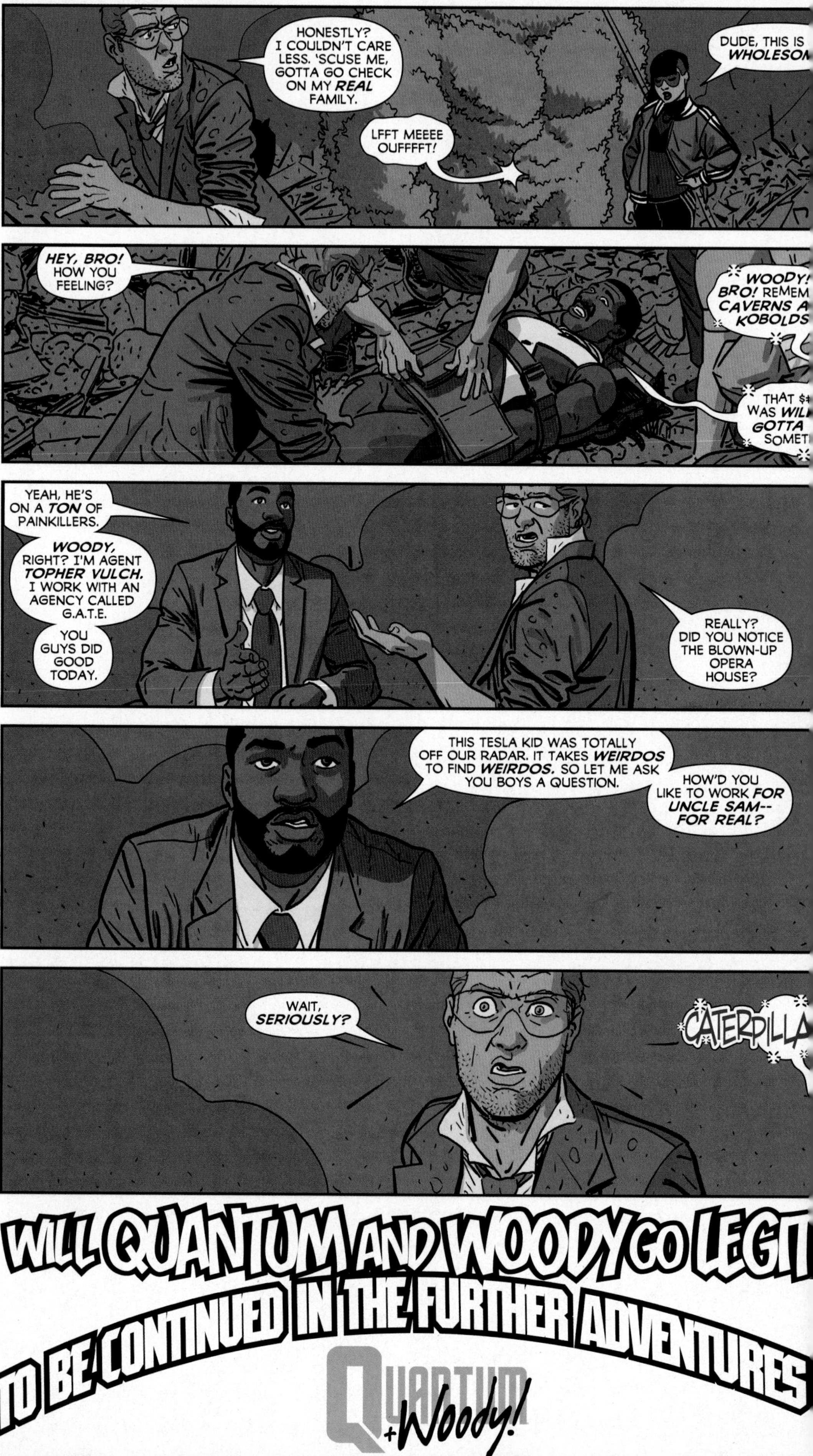
HONESTLY? I COULDN'T CARE LESS. 'SCUSE ME, GOTTA GO CHECK ON MY *REAL* FAMILY.
LFFT MEEEE OUFFFFT!
DUDE, THIS IS *WHOLESOM*
HEY, BRO! HOW YOU FEELING?
WOODY! BRO! REMEM *CAVERNS A KOBOLDS*
THAT $# WAS *WIL GOTTA* SOMET
YEAH, HE'S ON A *TON* OF PAINKILLERS.
WOODY, RIGHT? I'M AGENT *TOPHER VULCH.* I WORK WITH AN AGENCY CALLED G.A.T.E.
YOU GUYS DID GOOD TODAY.
REALLY? DID YOU NOTICE THE BLOWN-UP OPERA HOUSE?
THIS TESLA KID WAS TOTALLY OFF OUR RADAR. IT TAKES *WEIRDOS* TO FIND *WEIRDOS.* SO LET ME ASK YOU BOYS A QUESTION.
HOW'D YOU LIKE TO WORK *FOR UNCLE SAM-- FOR REAL?*
WAIT, *SERIOUSLY?*
CATERPILLA
WILL QUANTUM AND WOODY GO LEGIT
TO BE CONTINUED IN THE FURTHER ADVENTURES
QUANTUM + Woody!

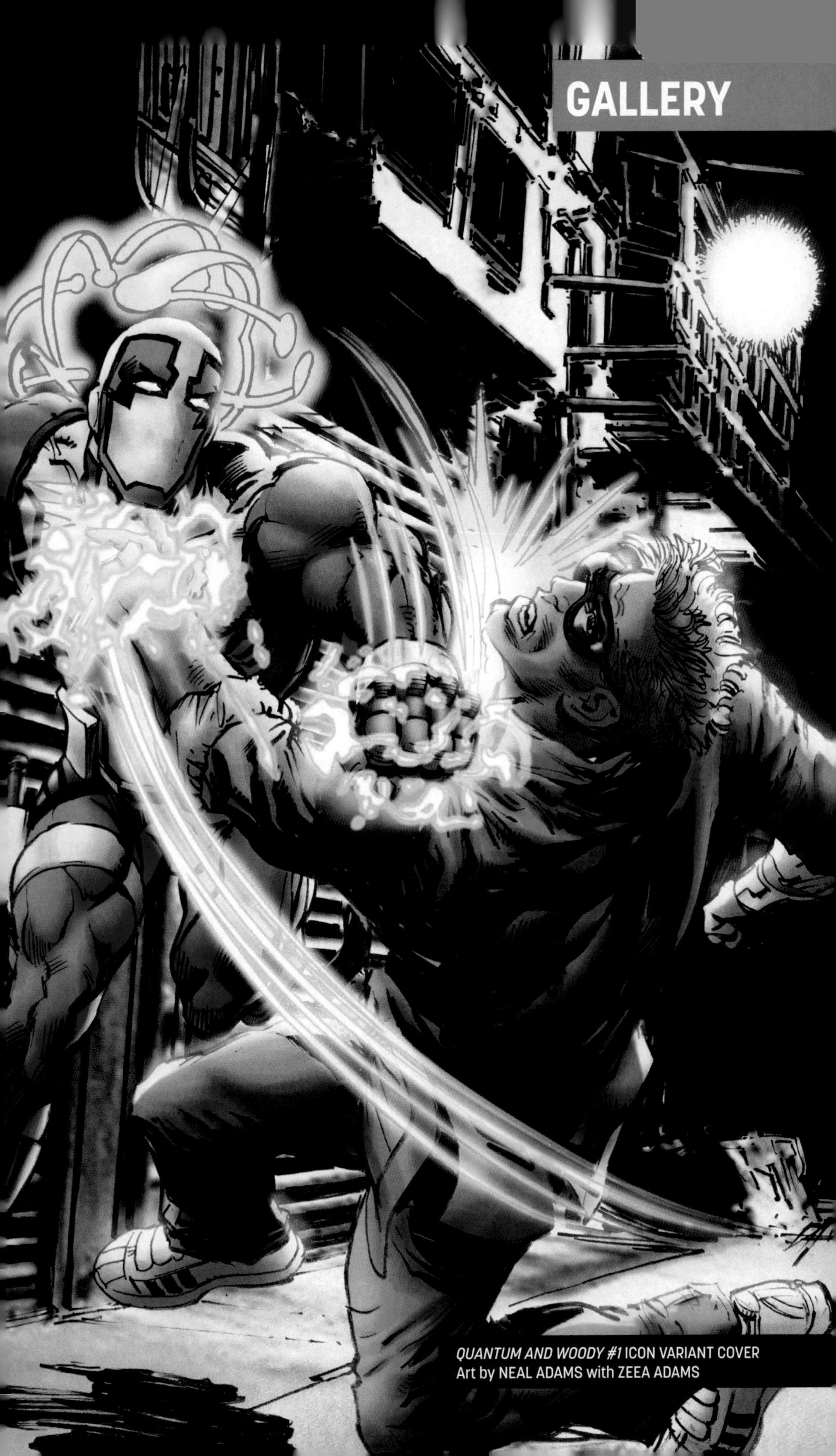

QUANTUM AND WOODY #1 ICON VARIANT COVER
Art by NEAL ADAMS with ZEEA ADAMS

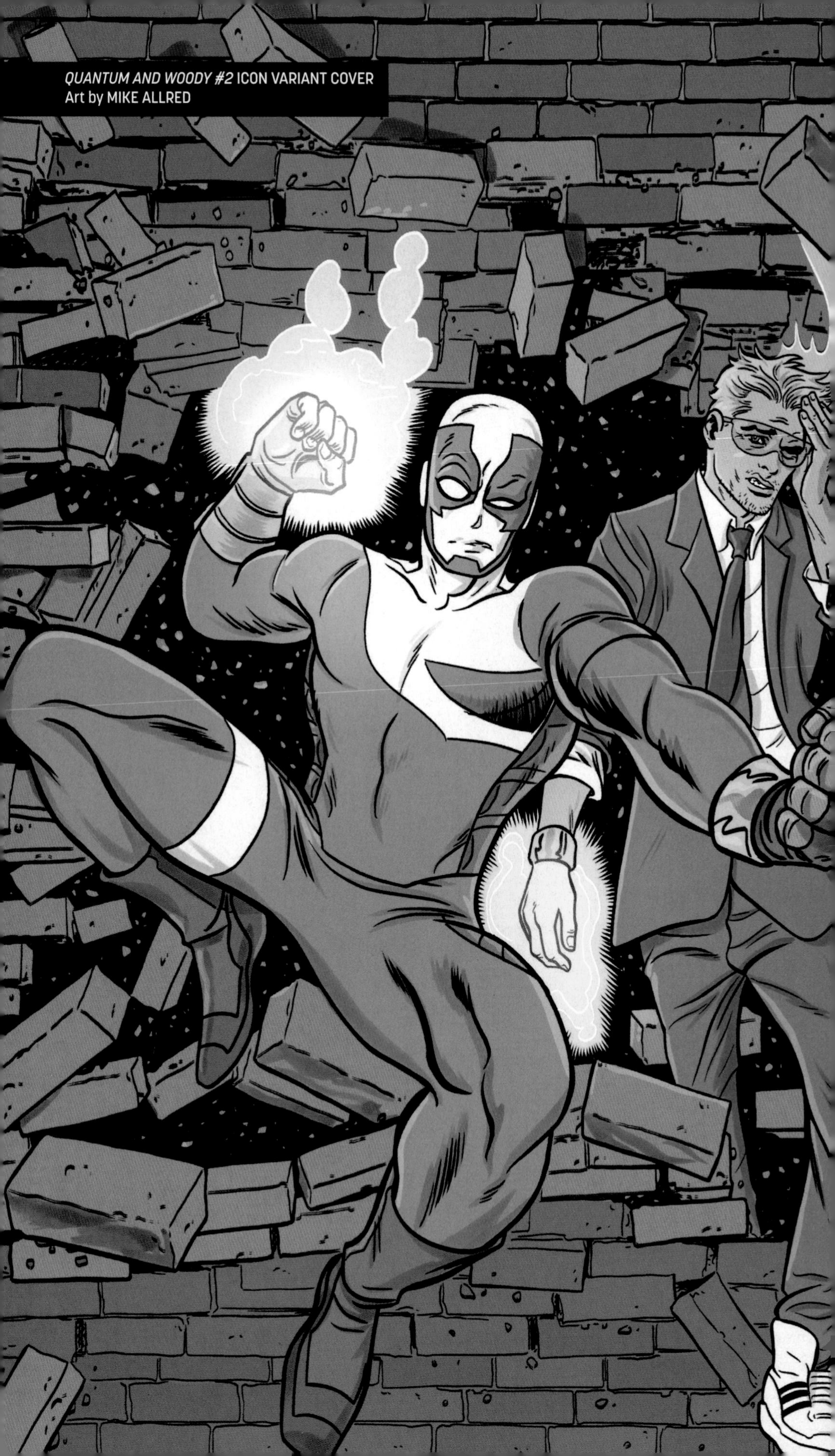

QUANTUM AND WOODY #2 ICON VARIANT COVER
Art by MIKE ALLRED

UANTUM AND WOODY #3 ICON VARIANT COVER
rt by DAVE JOHNSON

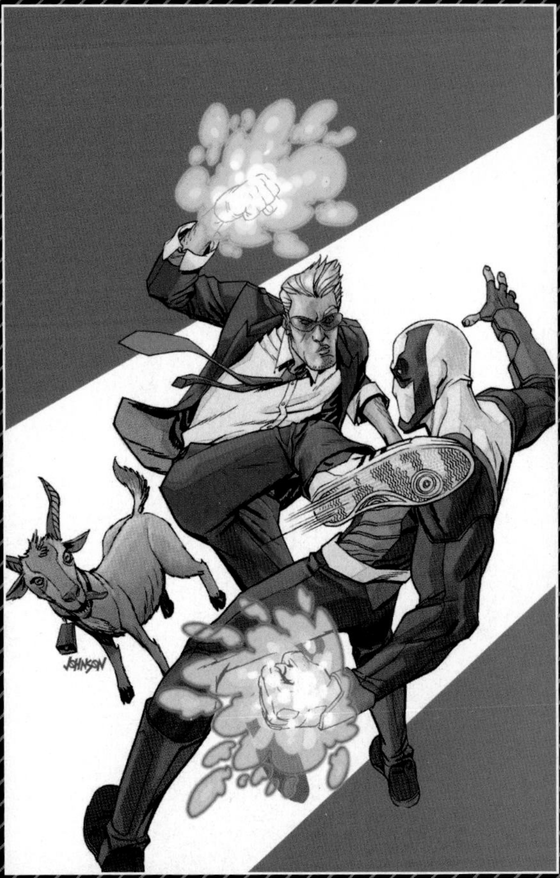
JOHNSON

UANTUM AND WOODY #4 ICON VARIANT COVER
rt by FRED HEMBECK

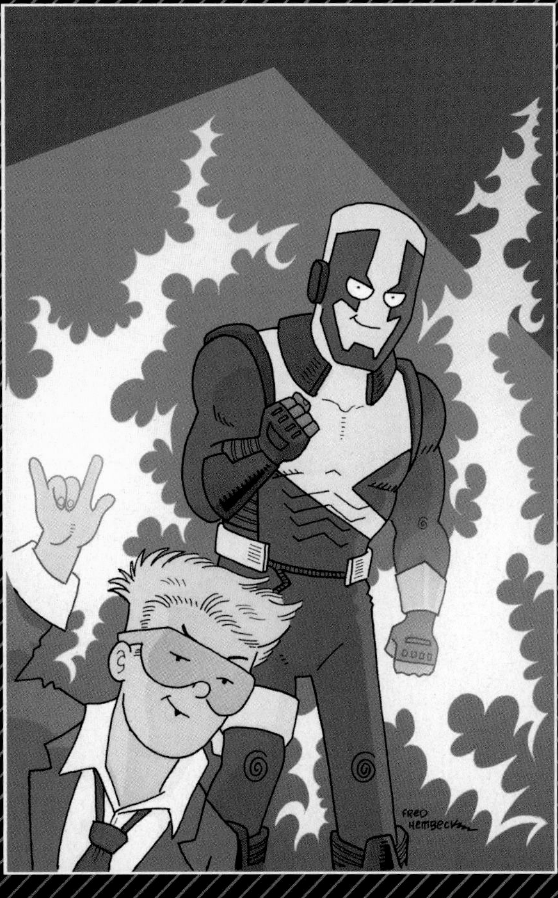
FRED
HEMBECK

QUANTUM AND WOODY #4
EXTREME ULTRA-FOIL VARIANT COVER
Art by GEOFF SHAW with GABE ELTAEB

QUANTUM AND WOODY #5
EXTREME ULTRA-FOIL VARIANT COVER
Art by GEOFF SHAW with GABE ELTAEB

QUANTUM AND WOODY #5 ICON VARIANT COVER
Art by PETER BAGGE

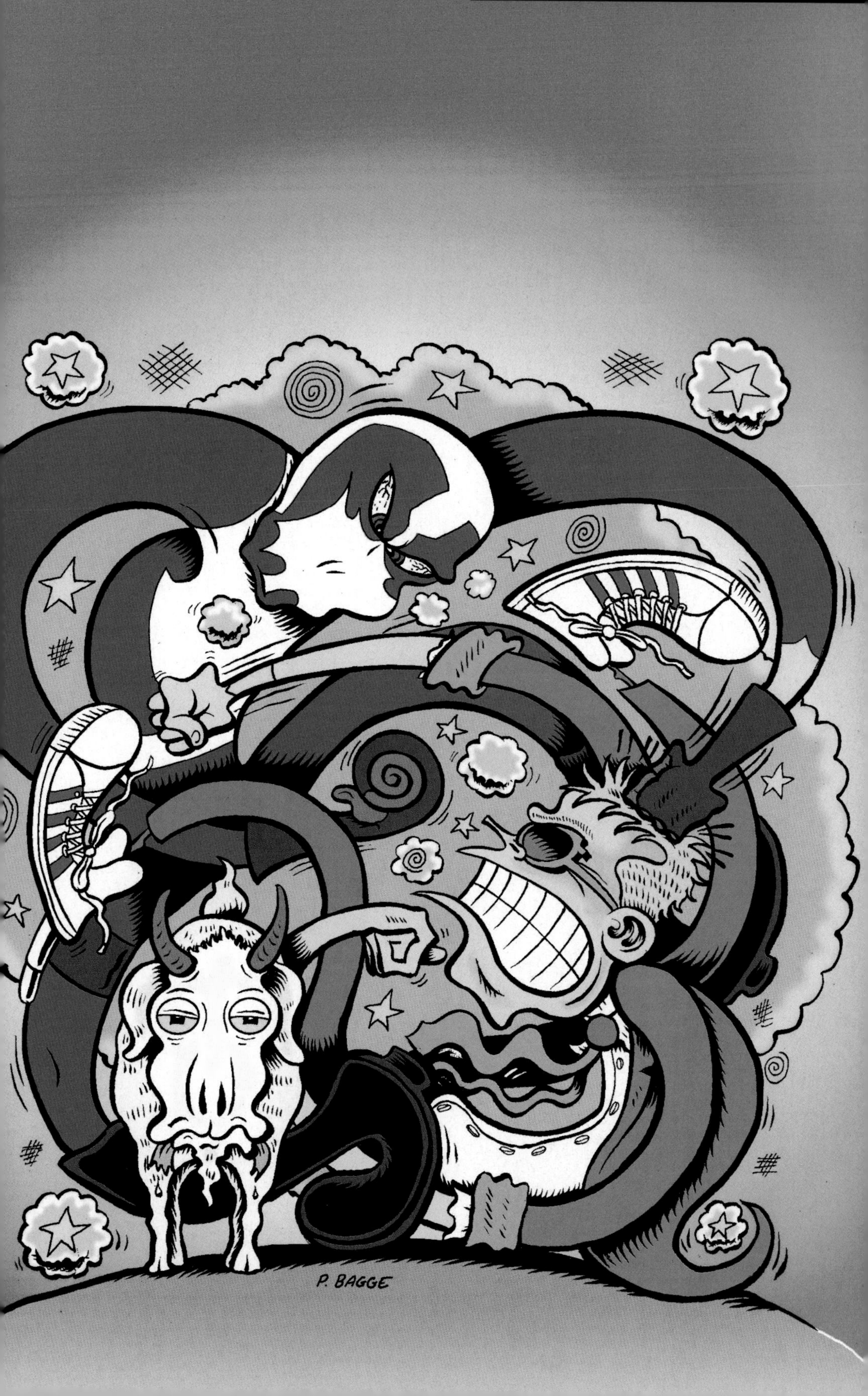
P. BAGGE

QUANTUM AND WOODY #1, pages 1, 2, and 3 (facing)
Art by KANO

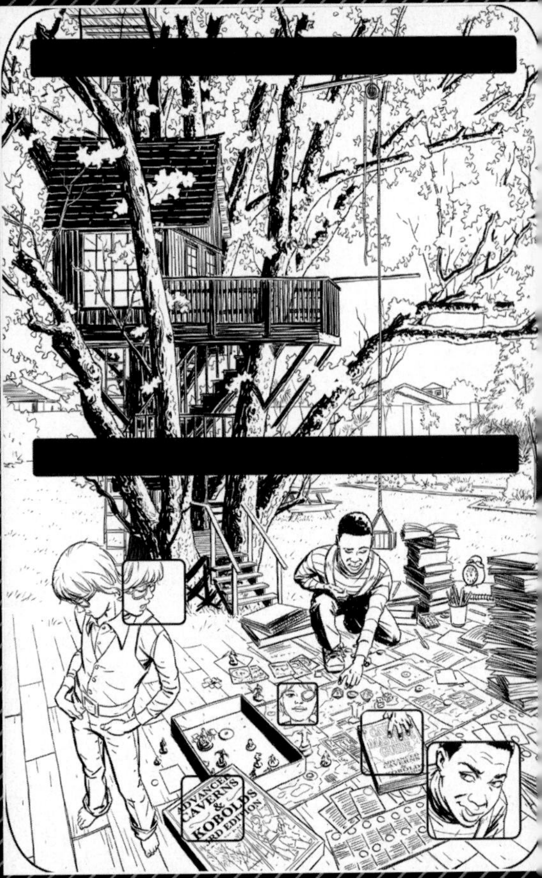
ADVANCED CAVERNS & KOBOLDS

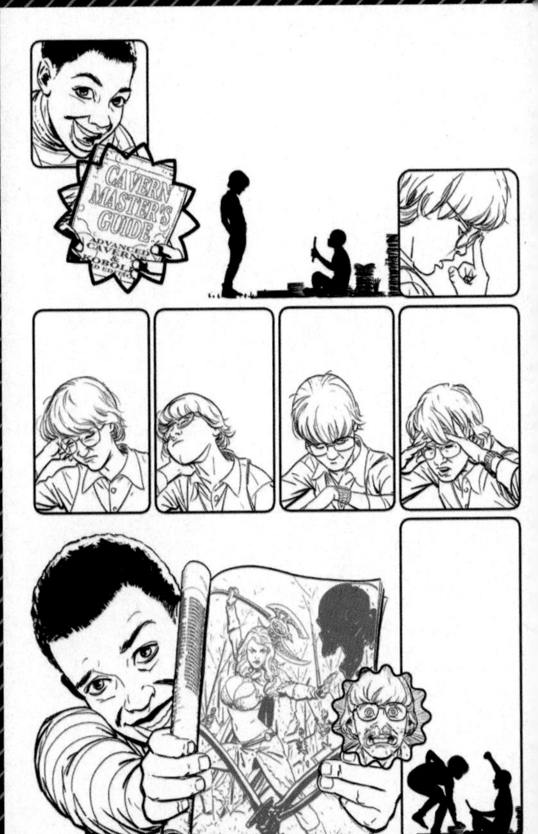
CAVERN MASTER'S GUIDE

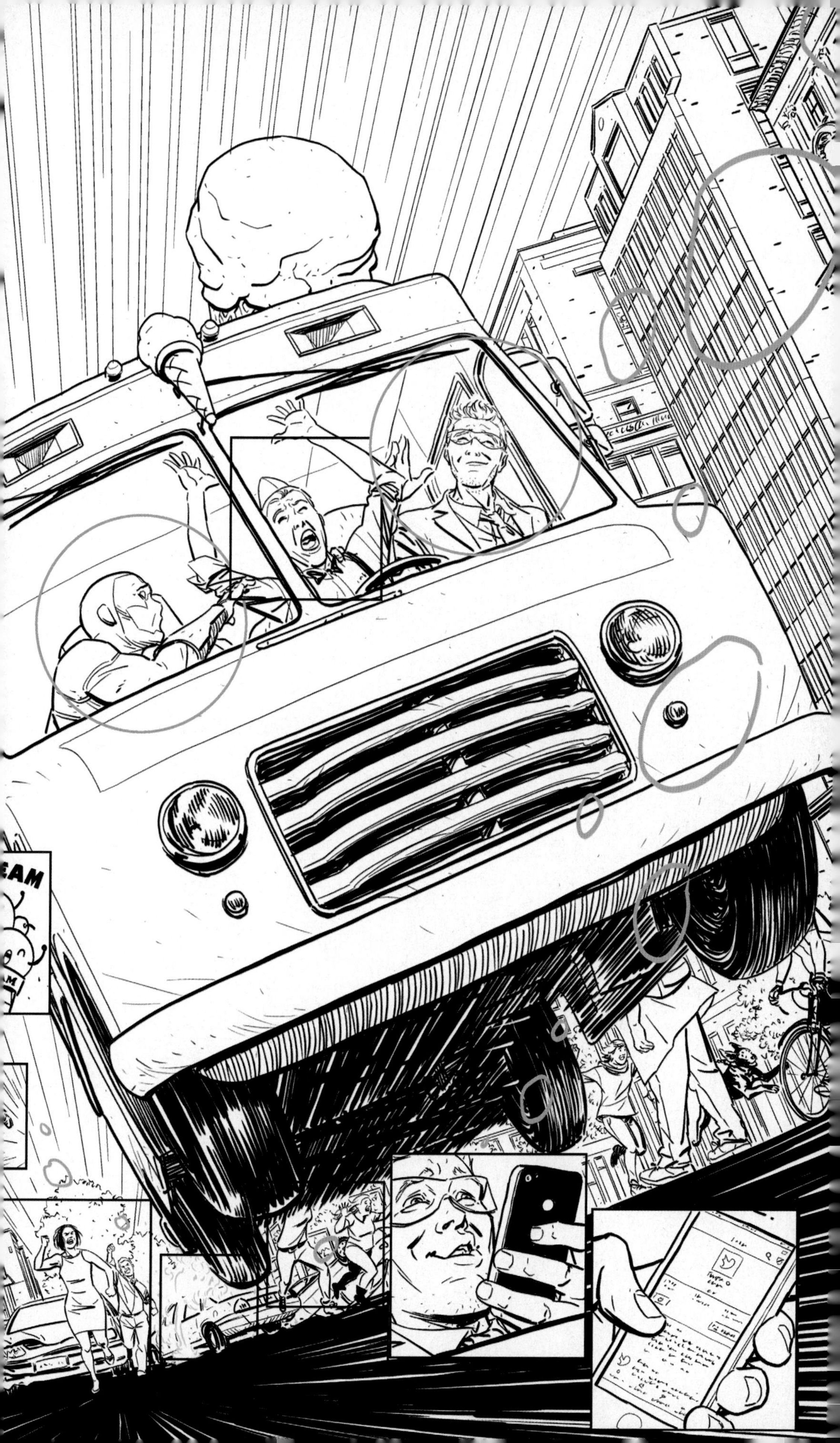
EAM

QUANTUM AND WOODY #2, pages 3, 4, and 5 (facing)
Art by KANO

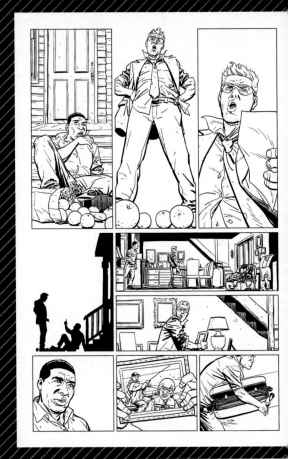

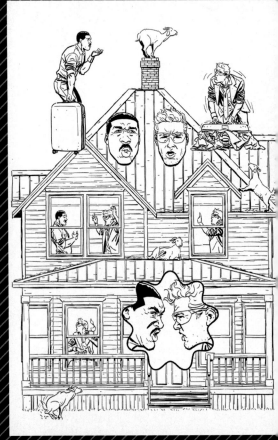

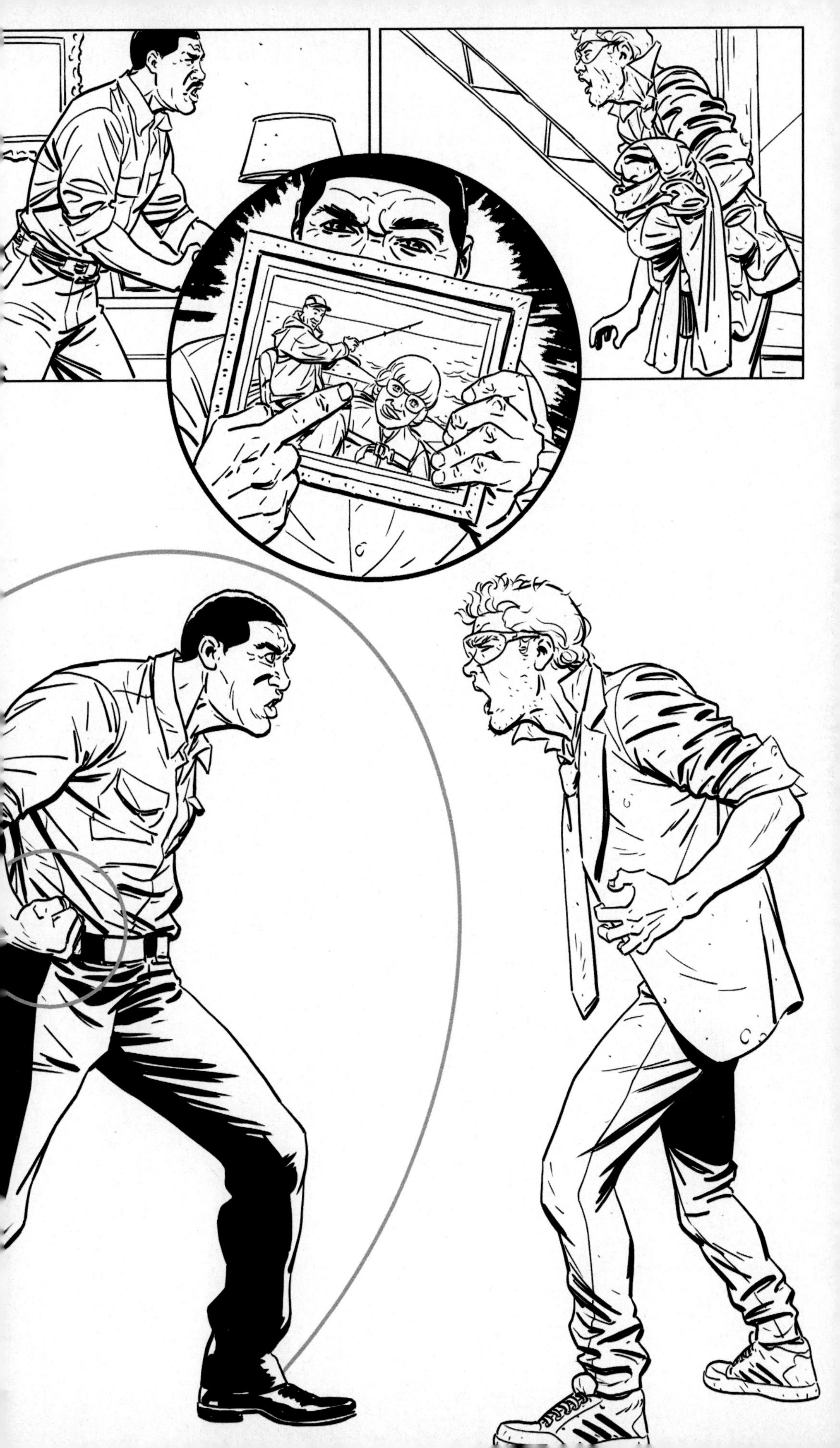

QUANTUM AND WOODY #2, pages 16-17
Art by KANO

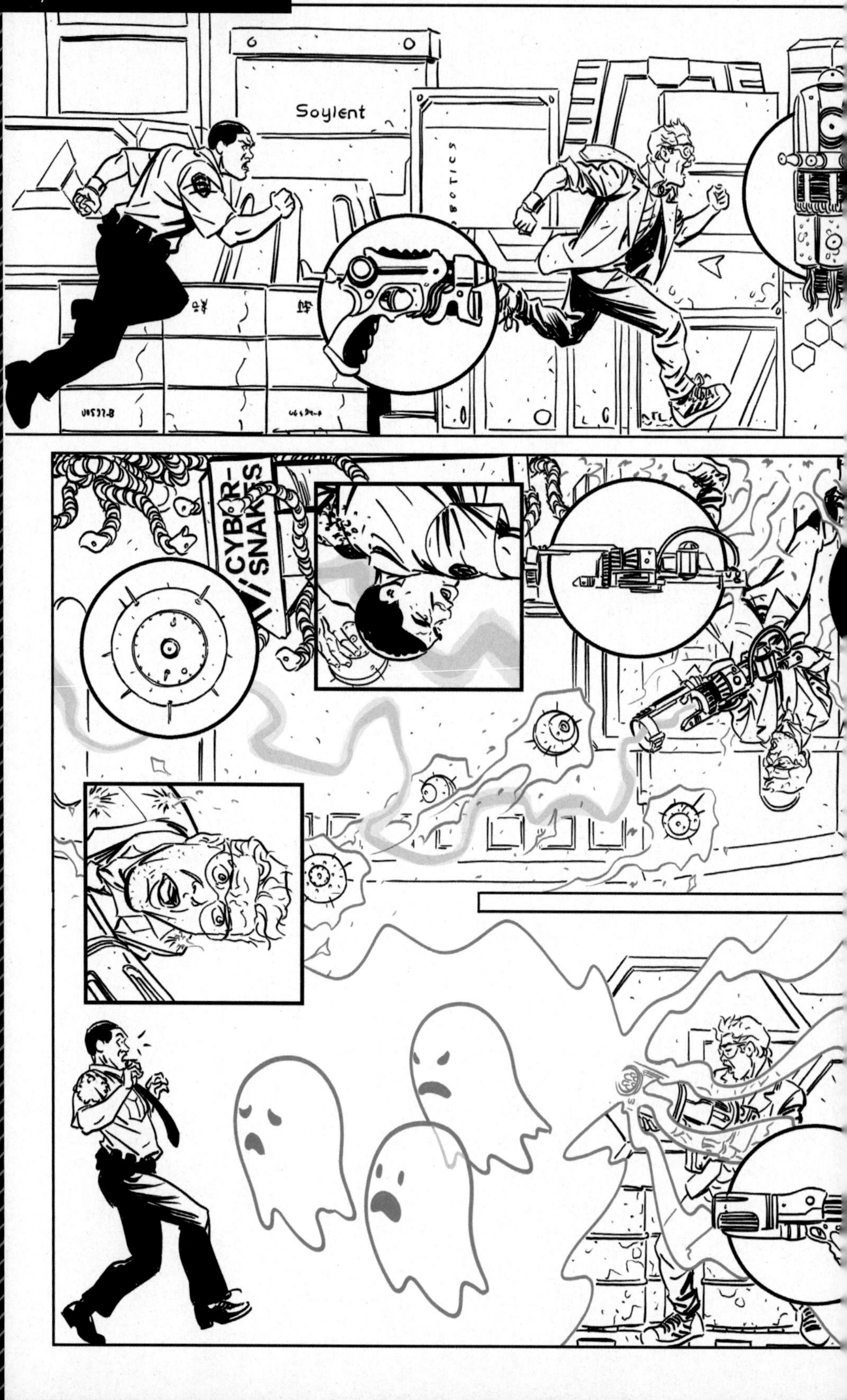

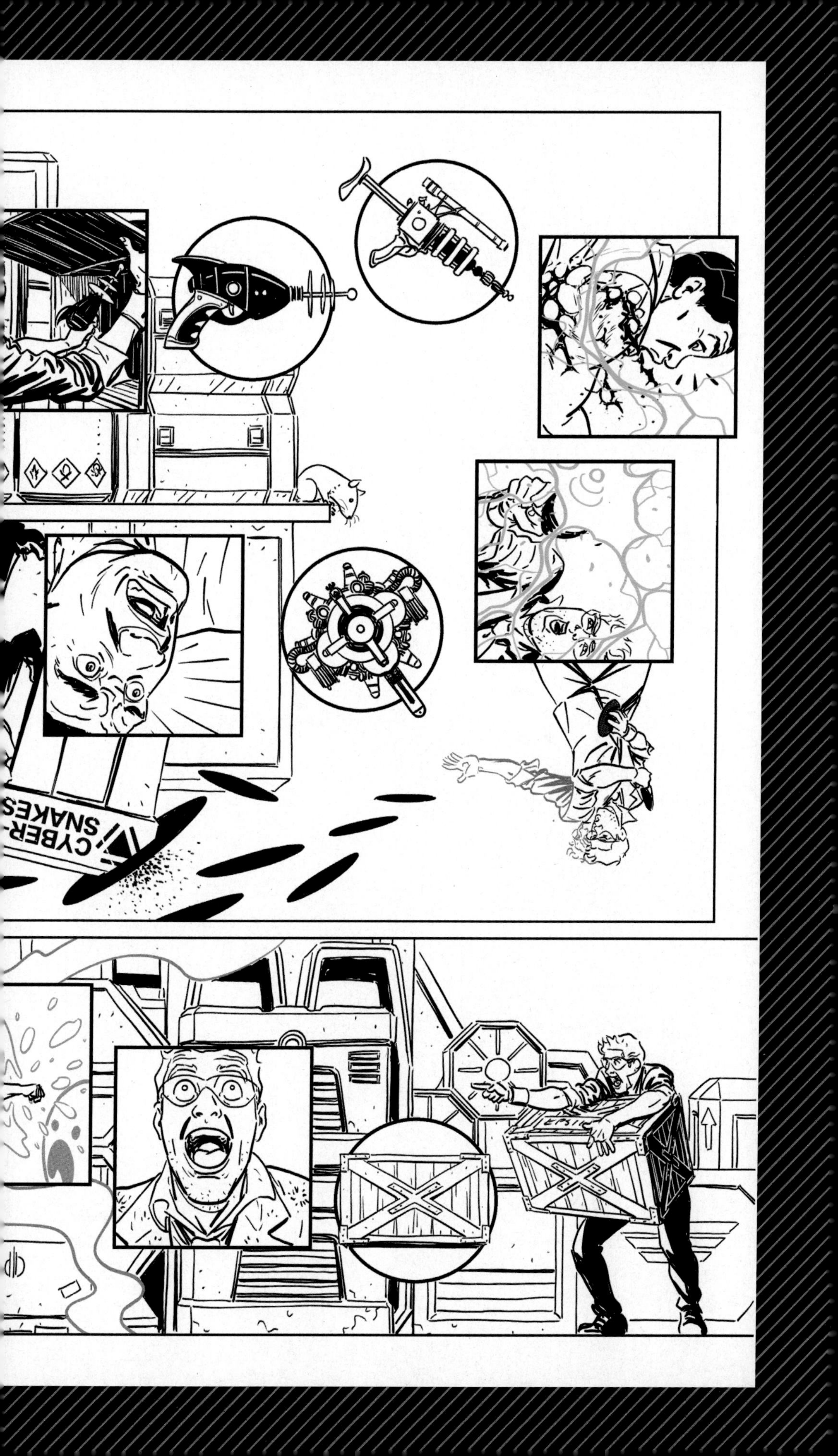
CYBER-SNAKES

QUANTUM AND WOODY #3, pages 1, 2, and 3 (facing)
Art by FRANCIS PORTELA

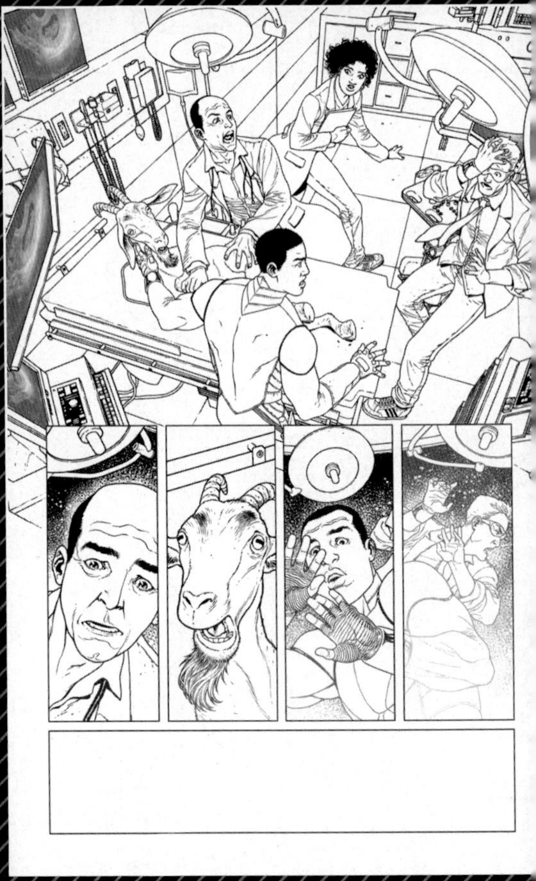

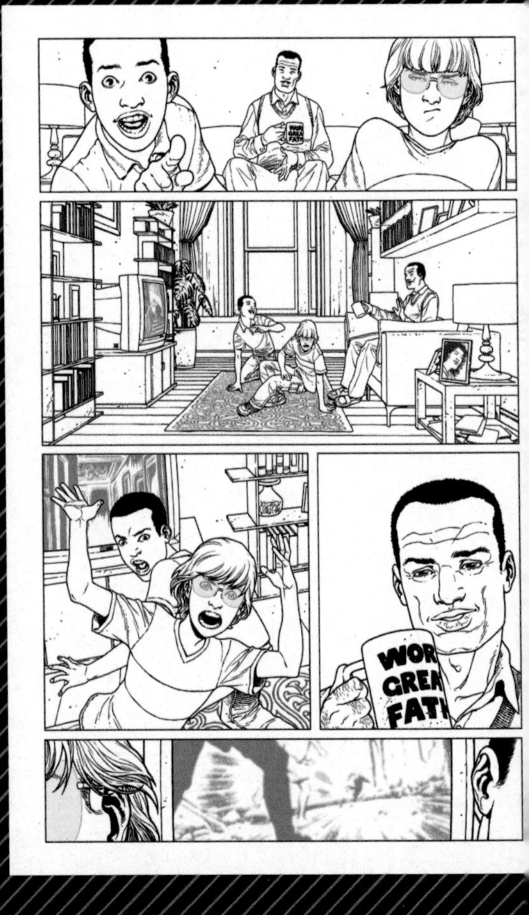
WOR
GREA
FAT

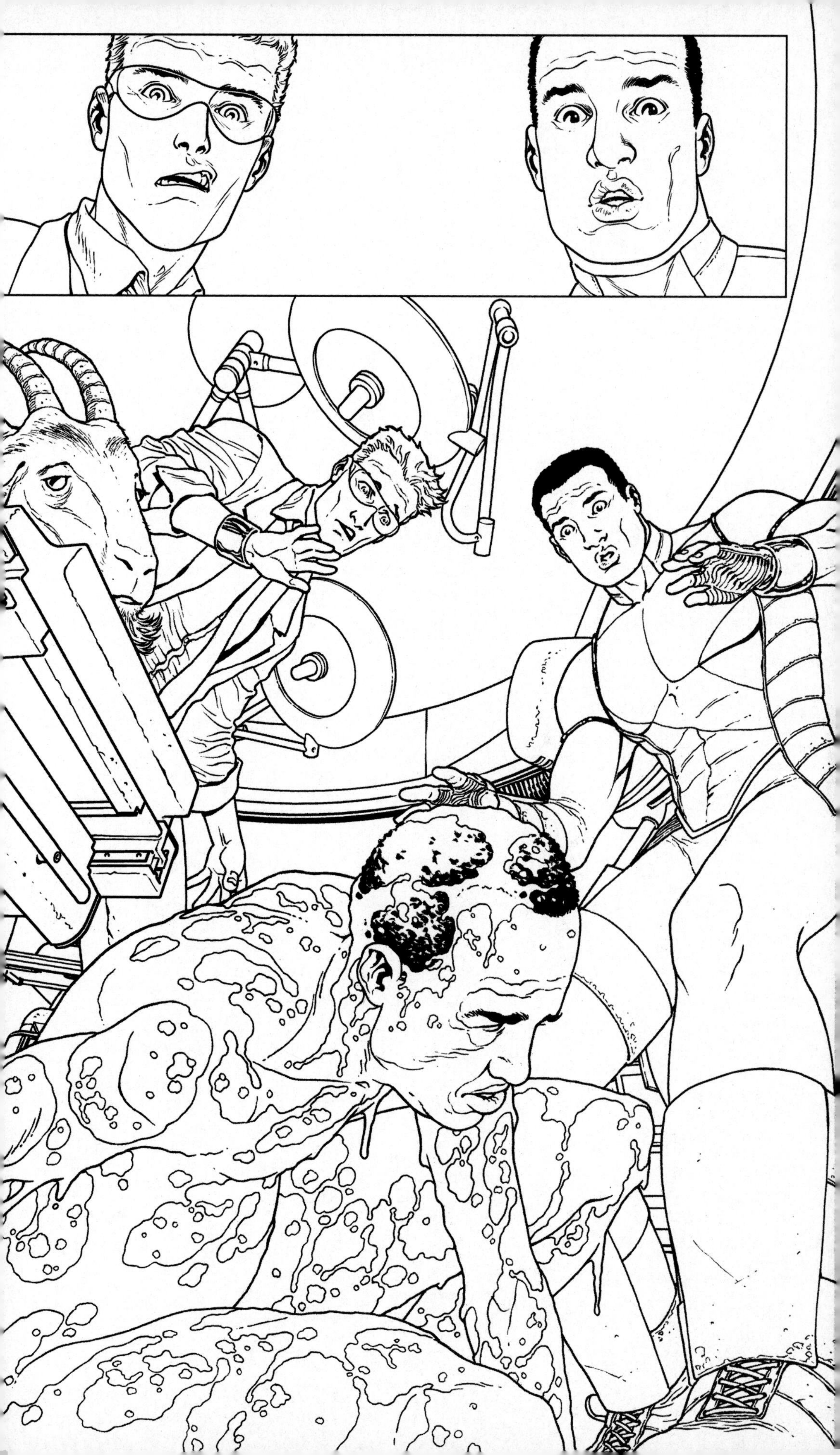

EXPLORE THE VALIANT UNIVERSE

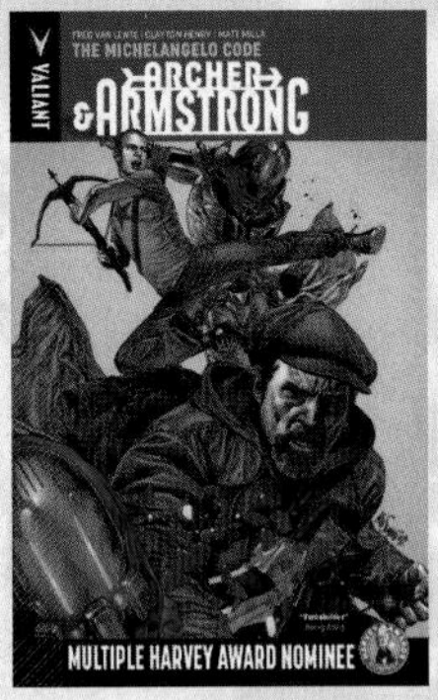
VALIANT
THE MICHELANGELO CODE
ARCHER & ARMSTRONG
MULTIPLE HARVEY AWARD NOMINEE

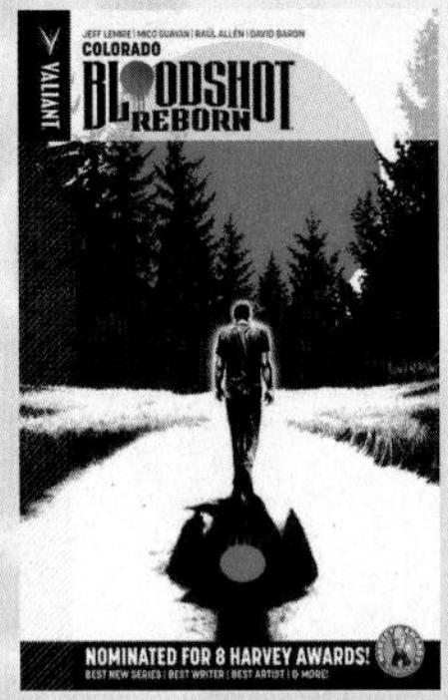
VALIANT
COLORADO
BLOODSHOT REBORN
NOMINATED FOR 8 HARVEY AWARDS!

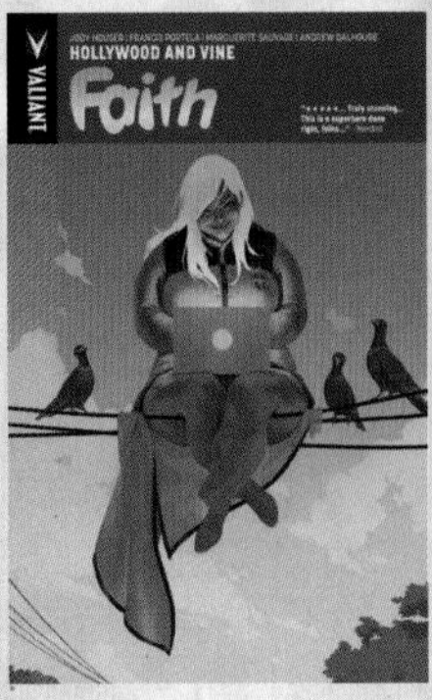
VALIANT
HOLLYWOOD AND VINE
Faith

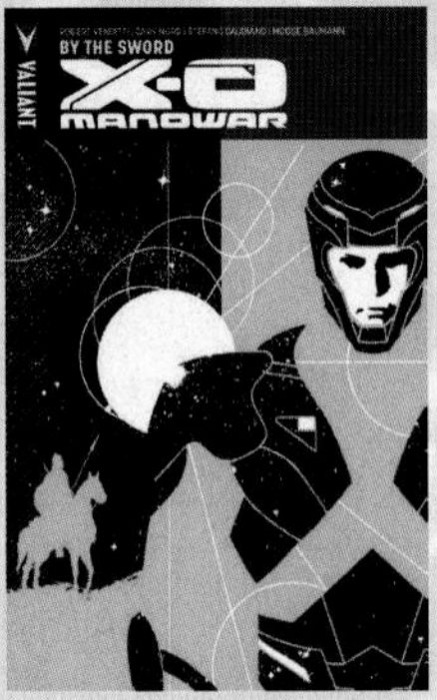
VALIANT
BY THE SWORD
X-O MANOWAR

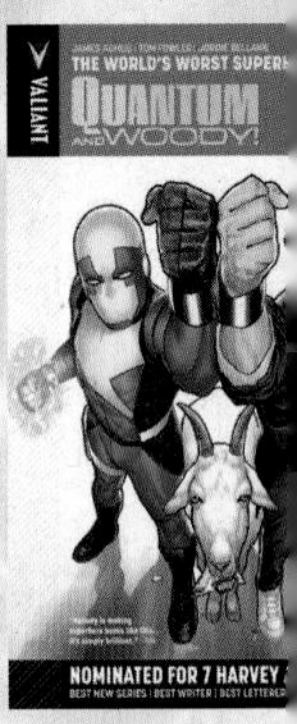
VALIANT
THE WORLD'S WORST SUPER
QUANTUM AND WOODY!
NOMINATED FOR 7 HARVEY

4001 A.D.
4001 A.D.
ISBN: 9781682151433
4001 A.D.: Beyond New Japan
ISBN: 9781682151464
Rai Vol 4: 4001 A.D.
ISBN: 9781682151471

A&A: THE ADVENTURES OF ARCHER AND ARMSTRONG
Volume 1: In the Bag
ISBN: 9781682151495
Volume 2: Romance and Road Trips
ISBN: 9781682151716
Volume 3: Andromeda Estranged
ISBN: 9781682152034

ARCHER & ARMSTRONG
Volume 1: The Michelangelo Code
ISBN: 9780979640988
Volume 2: Wrath of the Eternal Warrior
ISBN: 9781939346049
Volume 3: Far Faraway
ISBN: 9781939346148
Volume 4: Sect Civil War
ISBN: 9781939346254
Volume 5: Mission: Improbable
ISBN: 9781939346353
Volume 6: American Wasteland
ISBN: 9781939346421
Volume 7: The One Percent and Other Tales
ISBN: 9781939346537

ARMOR HUNTERS
Armor Hunters
ISBN: 9781939346452
Armor Hunters: Bloodshot
ISBN: 9781939346469
Armor Hunters: Harbinger
ISBN: 9781939346506
Unity Vol. 3: Armor Hunters
ISBN: 9781939346445
X-O Manowar Vol. 7: Armor Hunters
ISBN: 9781939346476

BLOODSHOT
Volume 1: Setting the World on Fire
ISBN: 9780979640964
Volume 2: The Rise and the Fall
ISBN: 9781939346032
Volume 3: Harbinger Wars
ISBN: 9781939346124
Volume 4: H.A.R.D. Corps
ISBN: 9781939346193
Volume 5: Get Some!
ISBN: 9781939346315
Volume 6: The Glitch and Other Tales
ISBN: 9781939346711

BLOODSHOT REBORN
Volume 1: Colorado
ISBN: 9781939346674
Volume 2: The Hunt
ISBN: 9781939346827
Volume 3: The Analog Man
ISBN: 9781682151334
Volume 4: Bloodshot Island
ISBN: 9781682151952

BLOODSHOT SALVATION
Volume 1: The Book of Revenge
ISBN: 9781682152553

BLOODSHOT U.S.A.
ISBN: 9781682151952

BOOK OF DEATH
Book of Death
ISBN: 9781939346971
Book of Death: The Fall of the Valiant Universe
ISBN: 9781939346988

BRITANNIA
Volume 1
ISBN: 9781682151853
Volume 2: We Who Are About to Die
ISBN: 9781682152133

DEAD DROP
ISBN: 9781939346858

THE DEATH-DEFYING DOCTOR MIRAGE
Volume 1
ISBN: 9781939346490
Volume 2: Second Lives
ISBN: 9781682151297

THE DELINQUENTS
ISBN: 9781939346513

DIVINITY
Divinity I
ISBN: 9781939346766
Divinity II
ISBN: 9781682151518
Divinity III
ISBN: 9781682151914
Divinity III: Glorious Heroes of the Stalinverse
ISBN: 9781682152072

ETERNAL WARRIOR
Volume 1: Sword of the Wild
ISBN: 9781939346209
Volume 2: Eternal Emperor
ISBN: 9781939346292
Volume 3: Days of Steel
ISBN: 9781939346742

WRATH OF THE ETERNAL WA
Volume 1: Risen
ISBN: 9781682151235
Volume 2: Labyrinth
ISBN: 9781682151594
Volume 3: Deal With a Devil
ISBN: 9781682151976

ETERNITY
ISBN: 9781682152652

FAITH
Volume 1: Hollywood and Vine
ISBN: 9781682151402
Volume 2: California Scheming
ISBN: 9781682151631
Volume 3: Superstar
ISBN: 9781682151990
Volume 4: The Faithless
ISBN: 9781682152195
Faith and the Future Force:
ISBN: 9781682152331

GENERATION ZERO
Volume 1: We Are the Future
ISBN: 9781682151754
Volume 2: Heroscape
ISBN: 9781682152096

HARBINGER
Volume 1: Omega Rising
ISBN: 9780979640957
Volume 2: Renegades
ISBN: 9781939346025
Volume 3: Harbinger Wars
ISBN: 9781939346117
Volume 4: Perfect Day
ISBN: 9781939346155
Volume 5: Death of a Renegade
ISBN: 9781939346339
Volume 6: Omegas
ISBN: 9781939346384

HARBINGER RENEGADE
Volume 1: The Judgment of Solomon
ISBN: 9781682151693
Volume 2: Massacre
ISBN: 9781682152232

EXPLORE THE VALIANT UNIVERSE

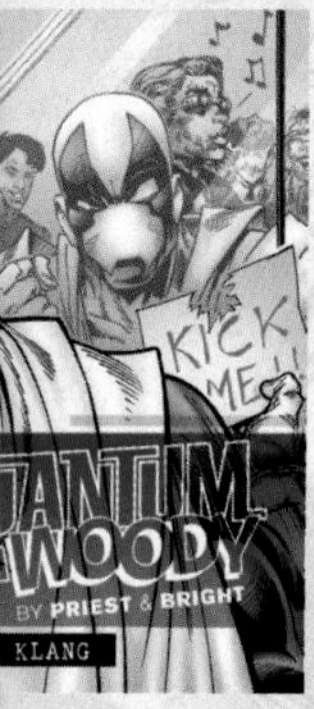
ANTUM
WOODY
BY PRIEST & BRIGHT
KLANG
KICK ME
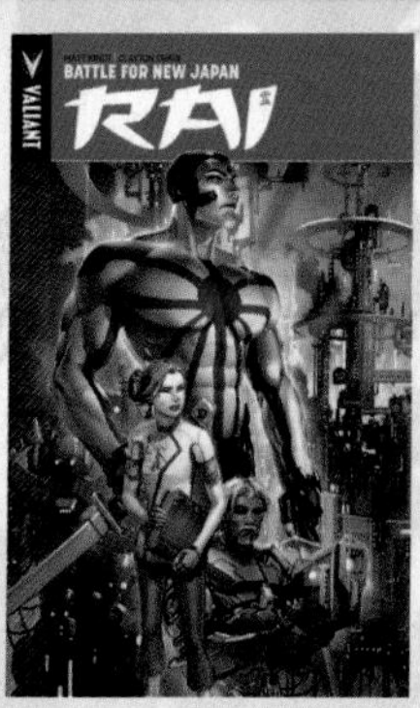
VALIANT
BATTLE FOR NEW JAPAN
RAI
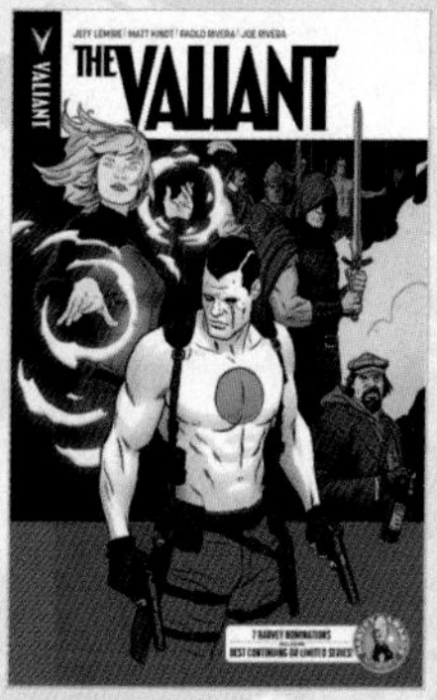
VALIANT
THE VALIANT
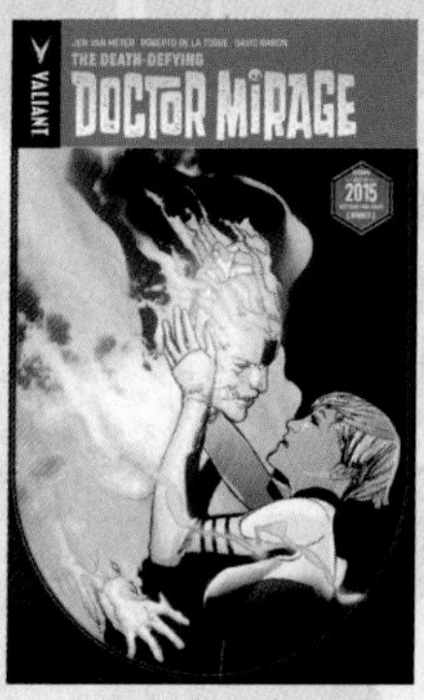
VALIANT
THE DEATH-DEFYING
DOCTOR MIRAGE
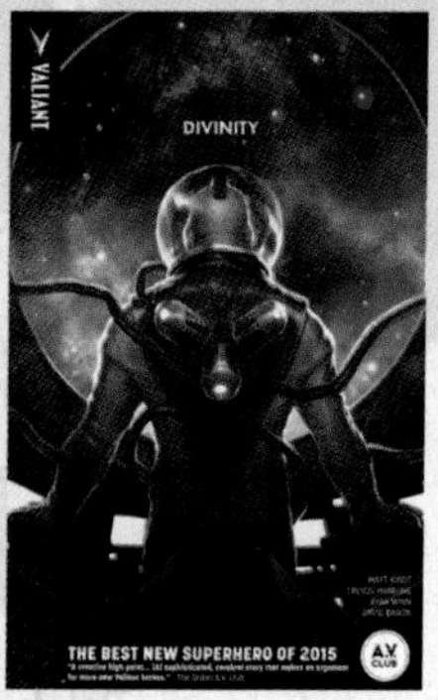
VALIANT
DIVINITY
THE BEST NEW SUPERHERO OF 2015

BINGER RENEGADE
1: The Judgment of Solomon
781682151693
2: Massacre
781682152232

BINGER WARS
er Wars
81939346094
ot Vol. 3: Harbinger Wars
81939346124
er Vol. 3: Harbinger Wars
81939346117

RIUM
1: Collecting Monsters
81939346759
2: Broken Angels
81939346896
3: The Vine Imperative
781682151112
4: Stormbreak
81682151372

AK
: Weaponeer
81939346667
2: The Shadow Wars
81939346940
3: Operation: Deadside
81682151259
: The Siege of King's Castle
81682151617
: The Fist & The Steel
81682151792
: The Seven Blades of Master Darque
81682152119

A-K
: The Ninja Files
81682152591

TUM AND WOODY
: The World's Worst Superhero Team
81939346186
: In Security
81939346230
: Crooked Pasts, Present Tense
1939346391
: Quantum and Woody Must Die!
1939346629

TUM AND WOODY
IEST & BRIGHT
Klang
1939346780

Volume 2: Switch
ISBN: 9781939346803
Volume 3: And So...
ISBN: 9781939346865
Volume 4: Q2 - The Return
ISBN: 9781682151099

RAI
Volume 1: Welcome to New Japan
ISBN: 9781939346414
Volume 2: Battle for New Japan
ISBN: 9781939346612
Volume 3: The Orphan
ISBN: 9781939346841
Volume 4: 4001 A.D.
ISBN: 9781682151471

RAPTURE
ISBN: 9781682151891

SAVAGE
ISBN: 9781682152256

SECRET WEAPONS
ISBN: 9781682152294

SHADOWMAN
Volume 1: Birth Rites
ISBN: 9781939346001
Volume 2: Darque Reckoning
ISBN: 9781939346056
Volume 3: Deadside Blues
ISBN: 9781939346162
Volume 4: Fear, Blood, And Shadows
ISBN: 9781939346278
Volume 5: End Times
ISBN: 9781939346377

SHADOWMAN BY ENNIS & WOOD
ISBN: 9781682151358

IVAR, TIMEWALKER
Volume 1: Making History
ISBN: 9781939346636
Volume 2: Breaking History
ISBN: 9781939346834
Volume 3: Ending History
ISBN: 9781939346995

UNITY
Volume 1: To Kill a King
ISBN: 9781939346261
Volume 2: Trapped by Webnet
ISBN: 9781939346346
Volume 3: Armor Hunters
ISBN: 9781939346445
Volume 4: The United
ISBN: 9781939346544

Volume 5: Homefront
ISBN: 9781939346797
Volume 6: The War-Monger
ISBN: 9781939346902
Volume 7: Revenge of the Armor Hunters
ISBN: 9781682151136

THE VALIANT
ISBN: 9781939346605

VALIANT ZEROES AND ORIGINS
ISBN: 9781939346582

WAR MOTHER
ISBN: 9781682152379

X-O MANOWAR
Volume 1: By the Sword
ISBN: 9780979640940
Volume 2: Enter Ninjak
ISBN: 9780979640995
Volume 3: Planet Death
ISBN: 9781939346087
Volume 4: Homecoming
ISBN: 9781939346179
Volume 5: At War With Unity
ISBN: 9781939346247
Volume 6: Prelude to Armor Hunters
ISBN: 9781939346407
Volume 7: Armor Hunters
ISBN: 9781939346476
Volume 8: Enter: Armorines
ISBN: 9781939346551
Volume 9: Dead Hand
ISBN: 9781939346650
Volume 10: Exodus
ISBN: 9781939346933
Volume 11: The Kill List
ISBN: 9781682151273
Volume 12: Long Live the King
ISBN: 9781682151655
Volume 13: Succession and Other Tales
ISBN: 9781682151754

X-O MANOWAR (2017)
Volume 1: Soldier
ISBN: 9781682152058
Volume 2: General
ISBN: 9781682152171
Volume 3: Emperor
ISBN: 9781682152355
Volume 4: Visigoth
ISBN: 9781682152638

EXPLORE THE VALIANT UNIVERSE

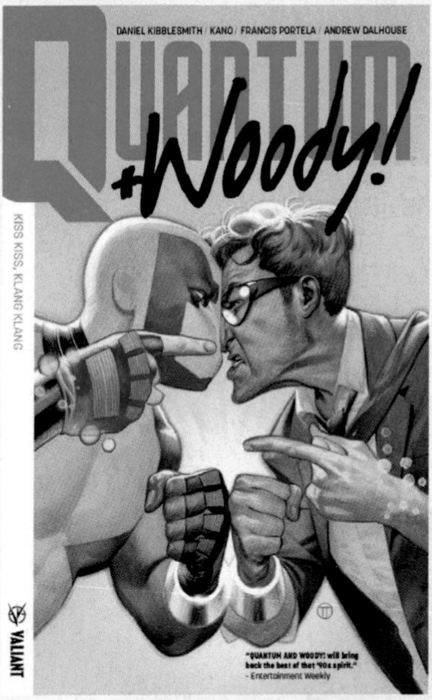
DANIEL KIBBLESMITH / KANO / FRANCIS PORTELA / ANDREW DALHOUSE
QUANTUM
+Woody!
KISS KISS, KLANG KLANG
VALIANT
"QUANTUM AND WOODY! will bring back the best of that '90s spirit."
- Entertainment Weekly

Quantum and Woody! (2017)
Vol. 1: Kiss Kiss, Klang Klang

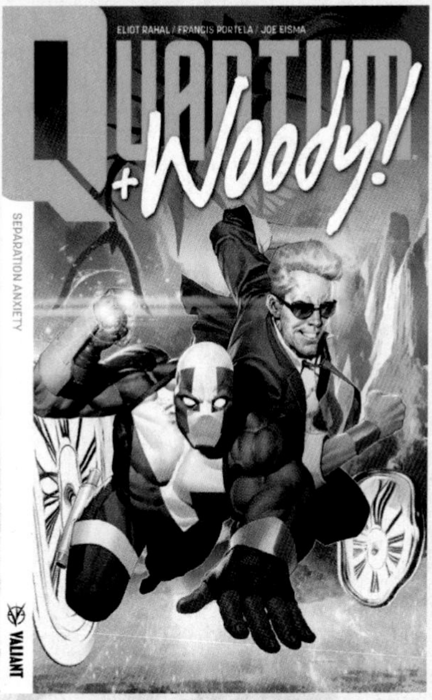
ELIOT RAHAL / FRANCIS PORTELA / JOE EISMA
QUANTUM
+Woody!
SEPARATION ANXIETY
VALIANT

Quantum and Woody! (2017)
Vol. 2: Separation Anxiety

Read the complete critically acclaimed (mis)adventures of the world's worst superhero team!

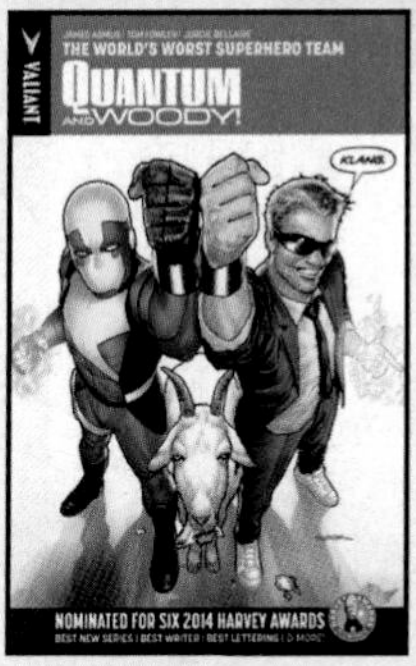
THE WORLD'S WORST SUPERHERO TEAM
QUANTUM AND WOODY!
VALIANT
KLANG
NOMINATED FOR SIX 2014 HARVEY AWARDS

Quantum and Woody Vol. 1:
The World's Worst Superhero Team

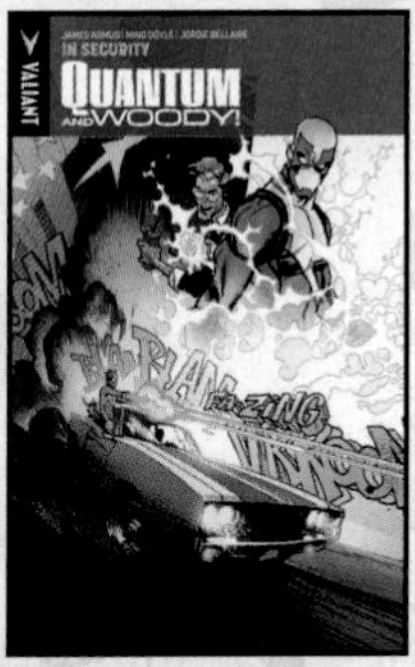
IN SECURITY
QUANTUM AND WOODY!
VALIANT

Quantum and Woody Vol. 2:
In Security

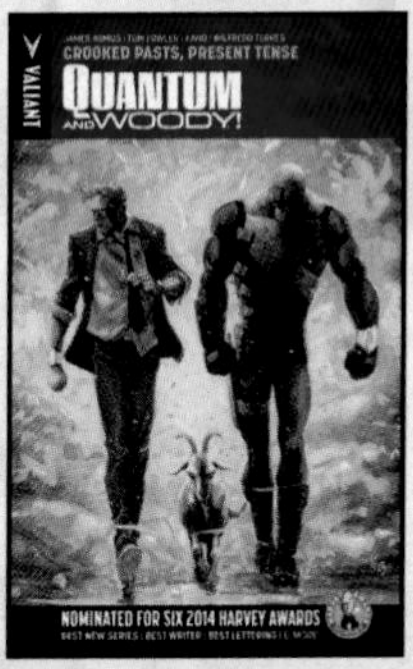
CROOKED PASTS, PRESENT TENSE
QUANTUM AND WOODY!
VALIANT
NOMINATED FOR SIX 2014 HARVEY AWARDS

Quantum and Woody Vol. 3:
Crooked Past, Present Tense

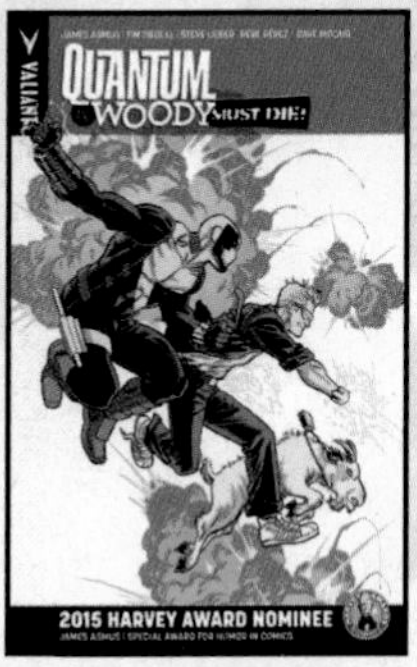
QUANTUM AND WOODY MUST DIE!
VALIANT
2015 HARVEY AWARD NOMINEE

Quantum and Woody Vol. 4:
Quantum and Woody Must Die!

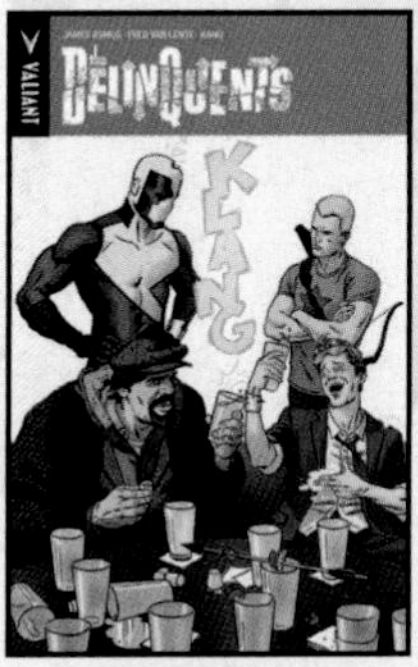
THE DELINQUENTS
VALIANT
KLANG

The Delinquents

VALIANT

QUANTUM + WOODY!

VOLUME TWO: SEPARATION ANXIETY

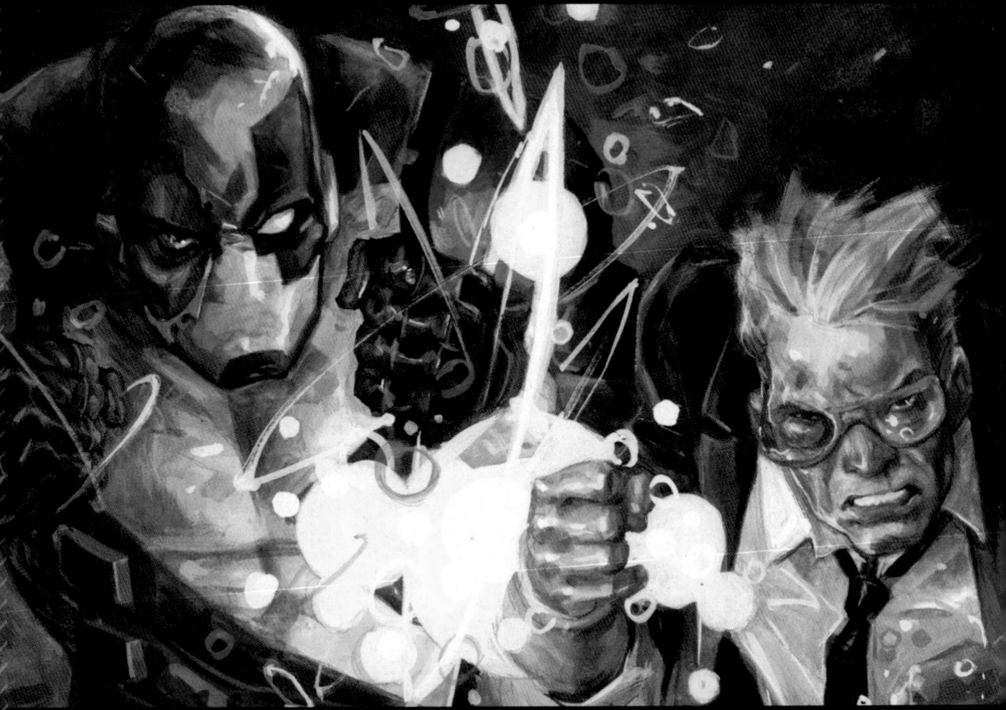

"KLANG, KLANG...KLUNK?"

In the ultimate display of power, Livewire has plunged the United States into darkness. From coast to coast, once-vital technology has now been rendered worthless... No cars... No phones... No quantum bands?!? Without the high-tech gauntlets that bind them together, the world's worst superhero team have 24 hours before they disintegrate into nothingness...Now, stripped of their powers and unable to "klang," can Quantum and Woody become the heroes they've always aspired to be and secure the streets of the nation's capital...before time runs out?

The world's worst superhero team is going to have to go it alone as "SEPARATION ANXIETY" presents a super-powered stress test, courtesy of rising stars Eliot Rahal (*The Paybacks*), Eisner Award-nominated artist Joe Eisma (*Morning Glories*, *Archie*), and acclaimed artist Francis Portela (FAITH)!

Collecting QUANTUM AND WOODY! (2017) #6-12.

TRADE PAPERBACK
ISBN: 978-1-68215-295-9

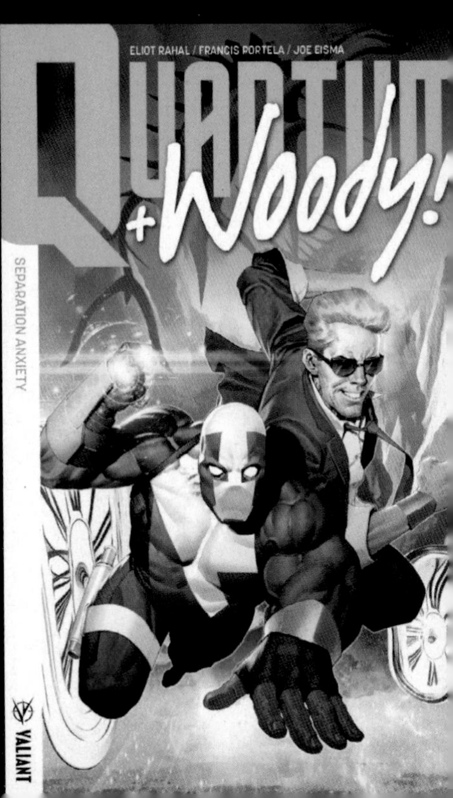
ELIOT RAHAL / FRANCIS PORTELA / JOE EISMA
QUANTUM
+Woody!
SEPARATION ANXIETY
VALIANT